The Manse

£1.00

JEREMIAH
THE MAN AND HIS MESSAGE

BY THE SAME AUTHOR

THE FREE CHURCH OF SCOTLAND

1843–1910 (JOINTLY)

Out of Print

A PROPHET OF GRACE

AN EXPOSITORY AND DEVOTIONAL STUDY OF THE LIFE OF ELISHA

"These discourses are of an admirable quality, written in a style which, by its measure and sobriety, shows the disciplined mind, and deal with experimental religion in a masterly manner."—*The Glasgow Herald.*

ROMAN DOGMA AND SCRIPTURE TRUTH

"Thoroughly reliable on questions of fact, and scrupulously fair in tone, besides being eminently readable. . . . It is a work of real ability, thoroughly up-to-date, and most timely."—*The Expository Times.*

JEREMIAH

THE MAN AND HIS MESSAGE

BY

ALEXANDER STEWART, D.D.

EDINBURGH
W. F. HENDERSON
19 GEORGE IV BRIDGE
1936

TO

E. J. S.

PREFACE

THIS volume has had its origin in an article which I contributed some years ago to *The Princeton Theological Review*, and which—with considerable additions here and there, and especially in its closing section—forms the Introduction to the present work. In the paragraphs which make up this Preface, I trust that the frequent occurrence of the pronoun "I" may not be set down to mere egotism, but that the reader in his charity may regard the direct form of speech as more or less inevitable in the expression of what is a kind of personal testimony.

Before the time when the task referred to was undertaken, I acknowledge frankly that the Book of Jeremiah had made no special appeal to me. I can at least understand the confession of Sir Arthur Quiller-Couch in his work *On the Art of Reading*, when, in the notable passage in which he commends the duty of reading the Bible, he declares that he found Jeremiah 'the contributor least to his mind,' the reason assigned for this distaste being that he was "not constitutionally disposed to lamentation." In my own case the lack of appreciation was certainly the result of insufficient study; it is even possible—although the mere suggestion appears to savour of impertinence—that the unsympathetic attitude of the distinguished Cambridge Professor may have been due to a similar cause: in any case his reference to "lamentation" would seem to indicate an acceptance of the popular misconception of the prophet's character. Following a closer acquaintance with *Jeremiah*, however, came understanding and sympathy, until ere long it became for me, as it now is, one of the most living books in the Bible, none the less Divine because it is so intensely human.

The prophet himself is a singularly fascinating personality. The story of the diffident, sensitive lad who was summoned from the obscurity of his native village to assume, at so critical an hour in the national life, the overwhelming responsibilities of the prophetic office, ranks—although its appeal does not always lie on the surface—among the most moving records of human history. In Jeremiah we find a combination of apparently irreconcilable qualities, each of them active within its own province without in any instance suspending the exercise of the other. At one moment, for example, we hear him delivering his message of doom with a voice which never falters; at the next, he is appealing to the heart of his unfaithful countrymen with a tenderness of compassion which sometimes finds an outlet in abundant tears. Or, again, we hear him, with a holy boldness which exceeds that of Isaiah, remonstrating with God for having "deceived" him into acceptance of his commission, and almost in the next breath giving utterance to some "secret of the Lord" which bears witness to the intimacy of his fellowship with Heaven. And, above all, we find in this amazing man a longing for escape from the almost intolerable burden of his destiny, and at the same time a courage which never flinched in the face of danger or death, but flamed on with ever-increasing splendour, till at last the indomitable figure disappears from our view in the darkness of Egypt. Hard indeed must be the heart that is not profoundly stirred by a tale in which weakness and strength, sorrow and consolation, timidity and heroism, are blended in such vivid, though often unconscious, self-portraiture.

Reference is made in the Introduction to various questions of criticism which have long been associated with *Jeremiah*, and it may be stated at once that the position taken up in this book is definitely conservative. One is under no illusion regarding the reception with which, in many quarters, this attitude is likely to be met. It will be summarily dismissed as an example of the stubborn and repellent obscurantism which, in matters of this kind, is the mark of an unenlightened mind. With becoming deference, however, one may ask leave to enter a caveat against the passing of so sweeping a judgment. Even a humble member of the tribe of Karshish may form some conception of the abundance which is provided at learning's feast, because now and then he is fortunate enough to pick up some of the crumbs which fall from its table. If to be an obscurantist means that a man resolutely closes his eyes to every ray of fresh light which modern learning, with the fuller equipment which lies at its command, is able to cast on the Scriptures, and clings with pathetic tenacity to traditional positions, for no more convincing reason than than they are *old*, then I respectfully decline to own the impeachment. I acknowledge with gratitude the service which a reverent scholarship has rendered in unfolding the treasures which are imbedded in the sacred oracles, and for that service I am conscious of no small personal indebtedness. And with regard even to those critics whose labours are subversive of the traditional views, I may be permitted to say that I covet their vast learning, and marvel at their tireless industry. I feel bound to add, however, that I am utterly opposed to some of their methods, and, for that reason, am compelled to reject their main conclusions.

If, therefore, on the other hand, an obscurantist is one who believes that an approach to the study of *Jeremiah*—to confine our attention meantime to the Book under discussion—which, either in whole or in part, is governed by materialistic presuppositions with respect to the nature of Old Testament prophecy, is opposed to the principles of true historical investigation, then I admit that I belong to that much derided company. Or if to be an obscurantist means that a man refuses to regard the speculations of a purely subjective criticism as invested with unchallengeable authority, then, too, I readily accept the unflattering designation. Or, again, if to be an obscurantist means that one protests against the principle that obscurities in the text are to be ascribed, in nearly every instance, to the hand of a different author—a principle which in practice results in a ruthless dismemberment of the documents—then once more I am content to wear that label of reproach. It may fairly be claimed, however, that the application of such a term to convictions which are not entirely based on ignorance would be a flagrant misuse of language.

The greater part of the book is devoted to an exposition of the main features of Jeremiah's teaching, and to the practical application of his message to the conditions of our own modern life. One has often regretted that so many of the ablest scholars who have written on *Jeremiah* have, to a great extent, devoted their attention to the details of textual criticism and the elucidation of disputed passages, rather than to those great religious truths which constitute its abiding contribution to prophetic literature. They are so occupied with the examination of each particular tree—in order to discover whether their axe should be laid to the root of it—that they often fail to show us the splendour of the far-extending wood. It is of course a needful thing that questions of that kind should receive the most careful study, but the researches of Christian scholarship should always serve the ends of spiritual edification. Browning's "Grammarian" was so intent on mastering "learning's crabbed text" that he neglected the more difficult art of living. And although the poet defends his absorbing passion for knowledge, on the ground that "man has Forever," and that, accordingly, the intellectual attainments reached in this life will be the basis of further progress in the life to come, yet the scholar who "settled *Hoti's* business— . . . properly based *Oun*—gave us the doctrine of the enclitic *De*," is in reality a pathetic figure, for he was "dead from the waist down," while still poring over his grammar and lexicon. It is true that man has Forever, but it is open to serious question whether in that future existence *Hoti's* business will be reckoned of any great account. But man certainly has the Present, and that Present is charged with momentous personal responsibilities, which include his duty to his neighbour and his God. To be really useful, therefore, knowledge must be applied to life. When it is divorced from life and is made an end in itself, its possessor may not perhaps be dead from the waist down, but he is dead, in a very real sense, from the waist up.

All of which brings us back to the message of Jeremiah. That message has abiding lessons for the guidance of human life to its highest issues. It is the aim of the following pages to set forth some of the outstanding elements which the prophet's teaching contains. I am fully conscious of the imperfections which mark the result. But if, with the blessing of God, the effort, such as it is, should bring some renewal of strength or hope or courage to any soul that is wrestling with the difficulties of the Christian pilgrimage, the time devoted to its accomplishment will not have been expended in vain.

A. S.

CONTENTS

JEREMIAH

THE MAN AND HIS MESSAGE

INTRODUCTION

JEREMIAH was a native of Anathoth, a village of Benjamin some three miles north-east of Jerusalem. His father Hilkiah was a priest, belonging in all probability to the family of Abiathar, who, on being deposed from the high-priesthood by Solomon, had been condemned to retirement within his " own fields " in Anathoth.[1] Jeremiah, accordingly, would have inherited the traditions of an illustrious ancestry, and his early life would have been moulded by the distinctive religious influences of the community to which he belonged. God, however, had " provided some better thing " for him than to spend his days in serving at the altars of a proscribed and degenerate priesthood. The young son of Hilkiah had been appointed to the tremendous destiny of being a prophet of the Lord in one of the most testing hours in the history of His chosen people.

I. THE CALL

It was in the thirteenth year of the reign of Josiah,[2] that is, in the year 626 B.C., that Jeremiah received his call to the prophetic office.[3] His ministry extended

[1] 1 Kings, ii. 26. [2] i. 2.

[3] In a suggestive article in *The Expository Times* of September 1933, the Rev. T. Crouther Gordon, B.D., basing his argument on the cuneiform tablet in the British Museum which fixes the date of the Fall of Nineveh, maintains that Jeremiah's Call took place in 616 B.C.. But (*a*) the siege of Nineveh does not determine the year of Jeremiah's Call, and (*b*) in explaining away the precise date assigned for that event in i. 2, Mr Gordon resorts to the desperate expedient of assuming a copyist's error. On the other hand, Oesterley and Robinson in their *Introduction to the Books of the*

through the disastrous years which culminated in the tragedy of the Exile, and after that was continued in Egypt, we know not how long. Altogether it lasted for at least well over forty years. While lacking to some extent in the overwhelming splendour which marks the inaugural vision of Isaiah or of Ezekiel, the circumstances of his call have an impressiveness which strikes an even deeper note. Several of these circumstances are so charged with meaning that a true conception of their significance is essential to a right understanding of the prophet's subsequent history. The wider meanings of the experience will be considered in the chapter which follows this Introduction; for the present it may be enough to indicate the directly personal features of the colloquy which took place in the day when "the word of the Lord came" with such startling illumination to the lad in the quiet village of Anathoth.

That word made known to him, first of all, that he had been chosen by God for the prophetic ministry before he ever saw the light of this world.[1] The word which constituted his ordination to office revealed to him at the same time his *fore*ordination to that high honour. Nor was this all. The Divine disclosure also made mention of a preparation for the tasks which were to engage his strength, a preparation which stretched away into the mysterious past, till, in its starting-point at least, it bore the seal of eternity, and included gifts of natural endowment and spiritual consecration which preceded the discipline of his conscious experience.

Now the significance of this unveiling of the Divine purpose was not so much its manifestation of the gracious favour of God to Jeremiah. It included, of course, that element of lofty personal distinction. But to an even greater extent it pointed to the vastness of the undertaking to which the young priest of Anathoth was being

Old Testament, a work which was published in 1934, and which, therefore, may be regarded as representing, on this point, the judgment of modern scholarship, give the date as 626 B.C., and add that "various attempts have been made to suggest another date, but none has received any serious recognition" (p 288 n.).

[1] i. 5.

called to put his hand. A preparation so extraordinary assumed a correspondingly extraordinary task. And indeed Jeremiah was not left to infer the difficulty of his mission from the mystery of his foreordination. From the very outset he was confronted with the stupendous demands of his calling. His work was to be unusually extensive in its activities, and for the most part intensely painful in its character. He was set "over the nations and over the kingdoms," and his commission was "to root out, and to pull down, and to destroy, and to throw down, to build, and to plant." The two closing terms indicate a generative purpose as the final goal of the prophet's activities; but by far the greater part of his work was to be of a destructive nature. Both these ends were, of course, to be achieved by Jeremiah in a ministerial capacity, as the instrument of the resistless energies of the word of the Lord.

A second outstanding fact in connection with Jeremiah's call is his own shrinking from the task with which he was faced. "Ah, Lord God!" he cried, "Behold I cannot speak, for I am a child."[1] He was, of course, no mere child in the literal sense, for he must have been more than twenty years of age; but he felt himself a child in knowledge and experience, and he was specially apprehensive of unfitness for the prophetic office on the ground of a conscious lack of the gift of utterance. There were also, however, temperamental causes to which Jeremiah's hesitation must be partly ascribed. That indeed is the main significance of this part of the story. If the terms of the Divine communication revealed the character of the work, the response which the communication elicited laid bare the heart of the workman. And it is a striking illustration of the mysterious working of the sovereign will of God that He should have chosen as "a prophet unto the nations" a man so apparently unfitted by temperament and aptitude for that tremendous task. In any case this early disclosure of the prophet's natural qualities is a suggestive foreshadowing, and furnishes at

[1] i. 6.

least a partial explanation, of the inward conflict and the anguish of soul which come to light at various stages of his after history.

A third feature of vital significance in Jeremiah's call is the special equipment which he received for his life work. This equipment was symbolised by the touch of the Divine hand on his mouth, an action which was accompanied by the explanatory assurance, "Behold I have put my words in thy mouth."[1] The communication of the word of the Lord conveyed to the future prophet the gift of insight and of foresight. It lay, of course, behind the authority which breathed through his message and the conviction which rang in his voice. It also explains the keenness of his spiritual discernment and the soundness of his political judgment, as well as the predictive element in his prophecies, the loftiness of his religious teaching, and the destructive energy which sometimes accompanied his word. It was an endowment, in short, which meant nothing less than the gift of inspiration.

Jeremiah's equipment included also a message from the Lord which was particularly adapted to his need. It consisted, first of all, of a word of command in answer to his protestation of unfitness.[2] The twice-repeated, "thou shalt," of this solemn charge—"thou shalt go," and "thou shalt speak"—swept aside the young prophet's objections, and made it plain to him that he must subject himself unreservedly to the authority of his Divine Master with respect alike to the sphere of his labour and to the character of his message. But the word of command was followed by a word of gracious encouragement: "Be not afraid of their faces; for I am with thee, to deliver thee." Hostile faces there certainly would be in plenty—brows lowered in resentment, eyes flashing in hatred, and lips curled in scorn or clamorous in denunciation; but here was a promise of the Lord's own presence throughout all the days, and in that fact there lay for Jeremiah a guarantee of strength and protection amid all the difficulties and dangers of his future ministry.

[1] ii. 9. [2] i. 7.

II. The Time

The prophet certainly needed a full share of courage, for few men have ever been confronted with a more formidable task. The Northern Kingdom had already passed to its doom, and Judah was steadily advancing to a similar catastrophe. It is true that the national decline appeared to have been arrested by the reforming zeal of Josiah. For some time before Jeremiah began his ministry the young king had been applying himself to the work of purging the land from idolatry, and five years after the prophet's call this cleansing work received a mighty impetus through the rediscovery of the Book of the Law in the Temple.

Professor A. C. Welch believes that this Book of the Law was the Book of Deuteronomy. He does not, however, believe—and here, with the courageous independence of judgment which marks all his writings, he breaks a lance with a great array of modern scholars—that this book was written in the reign of Josiah, still less that it was of post-exilic origin. He is indeed somewhat scornful of the post-exilic hypothesis as a receptacle for inconvenient facts—although he himself does not hesitate, when hard pressed, to avail himself of this spacious dumping-ground. Dr Welch holds that the Code of Deuteronomy was the Law Book of the Northern Kingdom, that it was brought to Jerusalem at some period between the reign of Hezekiah and that of Josiah, most probably during the reign of the latter king, and that it was adopted by the reformers of Judah in order to promote the interests of political and religious unity between the two Kingdoms.[1] It is at this point that Professor Welch indulges in a speculation which—although it is not altogether original—he rightly anticipates will appear " startlingly novel " to many of his readers. Not only, he suggests, was Deuteronomy brought to Jerusalem at this time, but also various other books of the Old

[1] *Jeremiah : His Time and his Work,* p. 23 ff.

Testament, which were amalgamated with the religious literature of Judah. It was at this time, according to Dr Welch, that "the accounts of the origins of Israel, the two documents called J and E in Genesis," which "are derived from Judah and Israel or Ephraim respectively," were woven into a unified record, the aim of the incorporation being the furtherance of the great reform of the centralisation of worship in Jerusalem. The Code of Deuteronomy, Dr Welch affirms, was specially used to serve this end. But the Book in its original form contained no warrant for such a course of action. This difficulty was got over by the men who edited the Code in the time of Josiah. They introduced into it a passage [1] which lends its sanction to the Josianic reform. Thus did "the pen of the scribes" deal falsely, not hesitating to resort to forgery in order to serve the ends of ecclesiastical propaganda! But it is difficult to reconcile Dr Welch's view that Deuteronomy was a recent importation into Jerusalem with the fact that its discovery in the Temple manifestly came upon the whole community as an overwhelming surprise. It is not easy to believe that a document of such importance could have been laid aside and completely forgotten within so short a time, especially if we accept the view that meanwhile the hand of the scribe was busily engaged in the task of editing the other sacred books which had come from the Northern Kingdom.[2]

In spite, however, of the solemn covenant by which, under Josiah's direction, the people had pledged themselves to loyalty to their God, it is evident that their repentance was lacking in depth and their new obedience in sincerity. Their reformation was little more, indeed, than a scratching on the surface of the national life. The fallow ground had not been broken up with anything like thoroughness.[3] Certain at least it is that the

[1] xii. 1-7.

[2] In the foregoing paragraph I have drawn upon a review of Dr Welch's volume which I wrote at the time of its publication.

[3] iv. 3.

account which Jeremiah gives of the state of the nation during the earlier years of his ministry forms one of the darkest pictures ever drawn of the religious and moral corruption of a community.

To begin with, there was the disease of idolatry. Josiah's efforts had secured the removal of the local sanctuaries, and had centralised the worship of the Lord in Jerusalem. But the love of idolatry remained in the heart of the people, and the practice of it, in one form or another, had never really been given up; it held sway over them indeed like an insatiable lust.[1] They set up the altars of Baal in every street,[2] burned incense to all the host of heaven on the roofs of their houses,[3] joined together—men, women, and children—in rendering homage to the queen of heaven in the cities of Judah and the thoroughfares of Jerusalem,[4] and introduced their idolatrous abominations into the very Temple of the Lord.[5] And the crowning inquity of all was the sacrifice of their innocent sons and daughters to Baal in the valley of the son of Hinnom.[6] Judah, in short, had changed her God, and in so doing had displayed a greater inconstancy than the surrounding heathen nations, who remained faithful to their own false deities.[7]

Then there was the plague of moral corruption, propagated by idolatry, and flourishing to a great extent under its sanction. Adultery ate like a canker into the entire life of the community,[8] and covetousness held an equally extensive sway,[9] followed by dishonesty, oppression, violence, and even murder.[10] Lying took the place of truth on men's lips,[11] and so complete was the lack of ordinary integrity in the land that a man could not trust his own brother.[12] Jeremiah challenged his hearers to discover, after the most diligent search through all

[1] iii. 2. [2] xi. 13. [3] xix. 13.
[4] vii. 18. [5] vii. 30. [6] ii. 34; vii. 31; xix. 4, 5.
[7] ii. 10, 11. [8] v. 7, 8; vii. 9; ix. 2; xxiii. 14.
[9] vi. 13. [10] v. 27, 28; vii. 9. [11] vii. 28.
[12] ix. 4.

the streets and broad places of Jerusalem, a single man who executed judgment and sought the truth.[1] Set as an assayer over the people, he had tested their quality, and found them to be reprobate silver.[2]

For this appalling condition of things the religious guides of the nation were in no small degree responsible. Prophets, priests, and people, indeed, were banded together in an unholy conspiracy against the Lord.[3] The influence of the prophets was specially pernicious. These unfaithful shepherds were themselves infected with the prevailing moral foulness,[4] and they fed their flock with lying assurances in the name of the Lord.[5] Scorning the idea of approaching calamity,[6] and appealing to the Law and the Temple as guarantees of the Divine protection,[7] they created in the minds of men a fatal sense of security. So the people shared the light-hearted optimism of their teachers, and with tragic blindness placed their confidence in their external privileges and observances. Were they not the Lord's covenant people, and were they not attending with diligence to the ritual prescribed in His law?[8] And if these spiritual defences were not enough, had they not the strength of Assyria or of Egypt to fall back on in times of special need?[9] They accordingly listened to the warnings of Jeremiah with faces that were harder than a rock,[10] refusing to admit their guilt or to accept correction,[11] and devoting themselves to their evil practices with a proud and shameless abandonment.[12] This was the state of Judah when Jeremiah began his ministry.[13]

As he was entering on his appointed task Jeremiah

[1] v. 1. [2] vi. 27-30. [3] v. 31.
[4] xxiii. 14. [5] xiv. 14 [6] xiv. 13.
[7] vii. 4. [8] viii. 8. [9] ii. 18.
[10] v. 3. [11] ii. 23, 35; vii. 28. [12] v. 23; vi. 15.

[13] The Rev. George Douglas, in *The Book of Jeremiah*, contends, with a good deal of force, that the Book begins with the reign of Jehoiakim, and that it contains nothing that belongs to the time of Josiah except the narrative of the prophet's call and the expressly dated passage in iii. (vv. 6-25). But while this view meets certain difficulties, the argument just fails to carry conviction.

received two visions, each of which, with its accompanying interpretation, was a disclosure of the Divine purpose with reference to the nation, and consequently exercised a determining influence on the general character of his message. First of all he saw a rod of an almond tree,[1] and was told that this was a sign that the Lord would hasten His word to perform it. The appropriateness of the sign is not at once apparent, but it comes to light when we learn, on the one hand, that the name of the almond-tree—or " wake-tree," as the word has been rendered—points to the fact that it is the first of the trees to wake from the sleep of winter, and on the other, that the word translated " hasten," in the Lord's message, bears the meaning of being " wakeful." The strengthening effect of this communication on the prophet's mind can well be understood. In its general sense it was an assurance that the Lord stood committed to the fulfilment of the Word which He put in His servant's mouth, in its element of judgment as well as in its aspect of grace. Sometimes He might seem to be asleep, so far as giving effect either to His threatenings or to His promises was concerned, but not one jot or tittle of His message would fall to the ground.

The second vision, that of the seething cauldron,[2] with its face toward, or rather from, the north, was explained to the prophet as a sign of the trouble which was brewing in the north for Judah, and would ere long break forth. As instruments of Divine judgment on the apostate nation, the kingdoms of the north were to overrun the land and encamp before the very gates of Jerusalem. Following this vision there is a final message from the Lord to the young prophet, containing a renewed exhortation to courage, and a fresh assurance of help in his work—help so mighty as to transform the timid waverer into a man of rock-like strength, who would stand before his enemies as a " defenced city and an iron pillar and brazen walls."

[1] i. 11, 12. [2] i. 13.

III. The Ministry

In the earlier years of his ministry Jeremiah's message, for the most part, took the form of denunciation and warning. With unsparing vigour he exposed the wickedness of the people, summoned them to repentance, and threatened them with the judgments of the Lord if they refused to return. Especially did he dwell on the peril from the north represented by the vision of the seething cauldron. With a remarkable wealth of imagery he described the terrible mission of those nameless avengers. Like the hot sirocco from the wilderness,[1] or a raging lion breaking forth from his thicket;[2] with chariots like the whirlwind and with horses swifter than eagles,[3] they were to sweep over the land, spreading terror before them and leaving ruin in their train.[4]

[1] iv. 11. [2] iv. 7. [3] iv. 13.

[4] Most modern scholars maintain that it was the Scythians that Jeremiah had in view in those early premonitions of danger, and that, since his fears from that quarter were proved by the event to be groundless, he was compelled at a later stage to change his mind. Sir George Adam Smith, for example, bluntly affirms (*Jeremiah*, pp. 111, 117, 259) that the prophet was mistaken in his first identification of the invaders, and suggests that he made alterations in the text of his original prophecies when it became clear to him that the Chaldeans were the real enemy. But, to say nothing about the question of the prophet's inspiration, this is surely doing less than justice to his honesty. Professor A. C. Welch, who devotes a whole chapter to the question of "the foe from the North" (*Jeremiah*, pp. 97 ff.), deals faithfully with those critics who sponsor this view, and claims that modern research has cleared the air of so "unhappy" a suggestion. But Professor Welch himself does not admit that Jeremiah is referring either to the Scythians or to the Chaldeans in these early oracles. He denies, in fact, that the prophet had any particular enemy before his mind at all, and explains the references to the northern peril in terms of general apocalyptic. As regards "the North," the term, he maintains, is not to be understood of geographical direction: it merely represents the idea of mysterious terror. "It has become no longer a point of the compass, but the expression of an idea" (p. 124). Nor was the destroyer of the nations a historical figure, he also was an idea. An obvious objection to this refinement of interpretation is that the "idea" is invested with attributes so detailed and specific that it is scarcely possible to believe that the prophet's mind was occupied with nothing more than a vague impression of impending judgment. It is indeed the case that the northern enemy of

It is probable that for some time after his call Jeremiah continued to reside in Anathoth, but ere long he was compelled to leave the home of his birth and take up his abode in Jerusalem. The reason was that the men of Anathoth entered into a conspiracy to put him to death.[1] The cause of their hostility we are not told; but it may be that the priestly community from which Jeremiah was sprung resented his assumption of the prophetic office as a betrayal of his own order. The treachery of his neighbours, and especially of his own kinsfolk, came as a painful shock to the unsuspecting prophet, and gave rise to inward perplexities which he poured forth before the Lord in a kind of wondering expostulation.[2] The answer he received was in effect an intimation that this experience was only the beginning of his troubles, and that it was designed to be a preparation for still more exacting trials in the days to come.[3]

Of Jeremiah's work during the later years of Josiah's reign we have little record. There is no warrant for believing that he was out of sympathy with the reforming activities of the young king, and that "his insight into the nature of religion makes it inconceivable that he could ever have had any sympathy with an attempt to convert the nation by a forcible change in its forms of worship."[4] We find, on the contrary, that in a later day he paid a high tribute to the character and work of Josiah,[5] and that instead of being opposed, as is sometimes alleged, to the teaching of the newly discovered Book of the Law, he puts his cordial Amen to the demands of "this covenant," and declares that he was called by the Lord to proclaim its message throughout the land.[6] He realised indeed, as

the earlier oracles are to a large extent an undefined and mysterious terror, and that it is only in the fourth year of the reign of Jehoiakim that they are given a local habitation and a name; but although Jeremiah's knowledge may have grown in clearness with the development of events, there is not a particle of evidence that it was ever open to correction on any question of fact. Nor is there any evidence that the Scythians ever actually invaded the land of Judah.

[1] xi. 18-23. [2] xii. 1-4. [3] xii. 5.

[4] Dr John Skinner, *Prophecy and Religion*, p. 105.

[5] xx. 15, 16. [6] xi. 1-6.

we have seen, that Josiah's reformation did not go deep enough, but, so far as it went, it was a work of God, and so could not but receive his support.[1]

Through the death of Josiah at Megiddo, in a gallant attempt to withstand an Egyptian army advancing against Assyria under Pharaoh Necho, Judah was stricken with a calamity from which it never recovered. Josiah was succeeded by his younger son Jehoahaz, whom "the people of the land" placed on the throne in preference to his older brother Eliakim. But Jehoahaz was allowed to reign for only three months, being deposed by Necho, and carried off in chains to Egypt, where he died. As his successor on the throne, Necho—now virtually over-lord of Judah—appointed Eliakim, whose name he changed to Jehoiakim. This took place in the year 608 or 609 B.C.

The accession of Jehoiakim was a bad day for the nation, as well as for its one faithful prophet. Jehoiakim was "the ideal of a bad ruler"[2]—proud, vindictive, selfish, and covetous. He laid the land under heavy taxation to meet the demands of his Egyptian conqueror,[3] and

[1] Professor Welch (*Jeremiah*, pp. 86 f.) argues strongly that Jeremiah was opposed to Josiah's reform on the ground that it was false in principle, leading the nation to trust in the Temple with its ceremonial observances rather than in the living God; that it was hurtful in its results, since its effect was to make Judah "worse and less capable of repentance than Israel"; and that it had been introduced by a bad method, namely, the falsification of Deuteronomy, already referred to, by "the pen of the scribes." He himself can find little or nothing in the movement that is worthy of approval; and one cannot help feeling that in his interpretation of the passages on which the foregoing conclusions have been based, the prejudices of the Professor have been unconsciously transferred to the Prophet. In any case the present writer feels that the construction which he puts on ch. iii. 6-13, and ch. viii. 8, does not rest on a convincing exegesis. To ask us, for example, to believe that the words of ch. viii. 8—"the pen of the scribes hath wrought falsely" (R.V.)—are a specific reference to the insertion into the original text of Deuteronomy of the section xii. 1-7, is to impose too great a strain on our confidence in Professor Welch's exegetical insight. There is no reliable evidence that Jeremiah regarded the reform as essentially false in principle, however unsatisfactory he may have discovered it to be in its results. Professor Welch dismisses too readily the evidence supplied by ch. xi. 1-6 in support of this fact.

[2] Professor A. B. Davidson, in *Hastings' D. B.*, vol. ii., p. 571.

[3] 2 Kings xxiii. 35.

with callous indifference to the consequent sufferings of his people, devoted most of his attention to the task of enlarging and adorning his palace, ceiling its chambers with cedar and painting them with vermilion. With incredible meanness, too, he carried out those costly schemes with labour for which he never paid. Jeremiah did not hesitate to denounce such shameless wrong-doing. In a memorable indictment of the royal iniquities,[1] he places Jehoiakim in the pillory, and scourges him with the lash of a righteous scorn, predicting that he would die without being lamented, and would be buried with the burial of an ass.[2] Under Jehoiakim's rule the reforming policy of Josiah was abandoned, and the nation relapsed into open idolatry. Jeremiah accordingly comes into greater prominence, and from this time forward we have a fuller account of his personal history.

An incident which took place at the beginning of Jehoiakim's reign is of special significance.[3] Standing in the courts of the Lord's House, probably on one of the national feast days, Jeremiah declared in the name of the Lord that unless the people hearkened to the Divine appeal and turned from their evil ways, the Temple in which they trusted would share the fate of Shiloh, and Jerusalem itself would become a desolation. The scene which followed stands out from the sacred page with arresting distinct-

[1] xxii. 13-19.

[2] Sir George Adam Smith's assertion (*Jeremiah*, p. 259) that this prediction was not fulfilled is surely unwarranted. The assertion is based on 2 Kings xxiv. 6, where it is stated that Jehoiakim "slept with his fathers." But there is no contradiction between the prophecy and the recorded fact; for the one refers to the king's burial and the other to his death. In proof of this it will be enough to recall that the phrase "to sleep with one's fathers," with its various equivalents, is used in cases like those of Abraham, Jacob, Aaron, Moses, and David, where the place of burial was far removed from the ancestral graves. Cf. Salmond's *Christian Doctrine of Immortality*, 3rd Ed., p. 201.

[3] xxvi. 1 ff. A number of critics—*e.g.*, Davidson, Driver, Peake, Skinner, and Welch—maintain that this chapter is a different version of ch. vii., supplied by the hand of some later "editor." On this point I agree with the comment of Sir G. A. Smith: "Why may Jeremiah not have spoken more than once on the same theme to the same or a similar effect?" (*Jeremiah*, p. 147).

ness. Jeremiah's hearers were horrified at words which appeared to them to be nothing less than blasphemy, and the priests and the prophets, aided at first by the people, laid hold of him and threatened him with death. The prophet alone remained calm in the midst of the general commotion, standing like "an iron pillar" before the whole array of menacing faces. Attracted by the tumult the princes appeared on the scene, and to them Jeremiah's accusers appealed to support their demand. With quiet dignity the prophet replied that the message he had delivered was the word of the Lord, and that accordingly if his opponents put him to death they would be guilty of shedding innocent blood. This defence made a profound impression, not only winning the princes, but turning round the people to the prophet's side. Some of the elders also were able to quote a precedent for leniency from the history of Micah in the days of King Hezekiah. Finally, through the intervention of Ahikam, Jeremiah was delivered from the hand of his enemies.

The fourth year [1] of Jehoiakim's reign was a year that marked an epoch in the history of the adjoining nations, as well as in the fortunes of Judah and in the experience of Jeremiah. Several years before, the Medes and the Chaldeans had joined their forces in a successful attack on Nineveh, and following the overthrow of the Assyrian dominion Mesopotamia and the provinces south of the Euphrates passed into the hands of the Chaldeans. This region, however, had already been conquered by Egypt, and a conflict between the two rival claimants could not be long delayed. A battle was fought at Carchemish in the year 604 B.C., resulting in the defeat of Pharaoh Necho by Nebuchadnezzar. In the same year Nebuchadnezzar invaded Judah, and it was then that Daniel and his companions were carried away to Babylon.[2] Jehoiakim him-

[1] To the earlier years of this reign probably belong the mysterious incident of the linen girdle (xiii. 1-7), and Jeremiah's discourses in connection with the drought (xiv.) and with Sabbath observance (xvii. 19-27).

[2] 2 Kings xxiv. 1; 2 Chron. xxxvi. 6, 7; Daniel i. 1 ff. The date given in Daniel is calculated according to the Babylonian method of reckoning, and is the fourth year of Jehoiakim according to the Jewish method.

self was also put in chains, with a similar end in view, but in his case, for some unexplained reason, Nebuchadnezzar did not carry his purpose into effect. Jehoiakim, however, became his vassal, and for three years paid him tribute. As a result of the battle of Carchemish, accordingly, the sovereignty of Egypt over Judah gave place to that of Babylon.

An interesting confirmation of a Chaldean invasion at this time is furnished by the fact that the Rechabites, who, according to the laws imposed upon them by Jonathan their ancestor, had for two centuries been living a nomadic life, were constrained by fear of Nebuchadnezzar to leave their desert home and take refuge in Jerusalem.[1] Their loyalty to the commandment of Jonathan in the matter of abstaining from wine was put to the proof by Jeremiah, and the contrast which it presented to the conduct of Judah in refusing to obey the laws of their God was emphasised by him in an address to the people. It was about this time that Jeremiah paid a visit to the potter's house, and saw in the methods of the potter a kind of parable of God's sovereign dealings with nations and individuals.[2] Not long afterwards he was commanded to take a potter's earthen bottle and proceed to the valley of the son of Hinnom, accompanied by a number of the elders of the people and of the priests.[3] There he prophesied that evil from the Lord would come upon that place because of the idolatrous abominations with which it was associated, and, having broken the bottle as a sign of the destruction of people and city by the hand of the Lord, he returned to the Temple and there repeated his message of doom. This incident had an unhappy sequel for the prophet.[4] His words were reported to Pashur, who appears to have been chief of the Temple police, and this official considered it his duty to beat Jeremiah and place him in the stocks, where he remained the whole night. On being released in the morning he addressed Pashur in terms of stern remonstrance and warning, prophesying that he would become a terror to himself and to all his

[1] xxxv. 11. [2] xviii. 1-10. [3] xix. 1 ff. [4] xx. 1-6.

friends, and that he and they would die in captivity in Babylon. The humiliation involved in this experience filled the prophet's soul with mingled indignation and pain, and caused him deep searchings of heart. The passage in which he pours out his complaint unto the Lord [1]—one of those passages of intimate self-disclosure which are characteristic of the Book of Jeremiah, and give it a unique place among the prophetic writings—shows how intense were the writhings of his spirit under persecution, and how earnestly he sometimes longed to be released from his task.

The reference to Babylon in the sentence pronounced on Pashur is significant as marking a change which from this time forward appears in Jeremiah's allusions to the enemy from the North. The political upheavals among the nations cast light for him on the Divine purpose, and the instruments of judgment are now definitely named as the Chaldeans. Not only so, but in one striking oracle [2] which bears the date of the fourth year of Jehoiakim, Nebuchadnezzar is described as a servant of the Lord, the captivity in Babylon is clearly predicted, and its duration is fixed at seventy years. At the close of the seventy years the Chaldeans in turn were to be punished for their iniquity, and all the nations indeed were to drink the wine cup of the wrath of God. This is one of the most remarkable of Jeremiah's prophecies.

The fourth year of Jehoiakim is also memorable as the year in which Jeremiah's previous prophecies were first committed to writing and formed into a roll, the immediate aim being that they should be read to the people in their completeness as a final call from God to repentance.[3] As his amanuensis in this undertaking Jeremiah employed Baruch the son of Neriah, who became his intimate friend, and whose sympathy and companionship would seem to have been almost his only earthly solace during the trials of his remaining years. On the completion of his task Baruch read the roll in the hearing of the people on a fast-day in Jerusalem towards the close of the following year,

[1] xx. 7-10. [2] xxv. 1 ff. [3] xxxvi. 1 ff.

Jeremiah himself being for some reason prevented from entering the Temple. One of his audience, Micaiah, was so impressed with the message that he proceeded to the royal palace and gave the princes an account of what he had heard. The princes immediately sent for Baruch, and requested him to read the roll a second time. And so great was the cumulative effect of the prophetic warnings and appeals that the princes turned in fear one toward another, and decided that the roll must be brought before the notice of the king. Knowing full well the character of Jehoiakim, however, they wisely advised Jeremiah and Baruch to go into hiding before the roll was read in the royal presence. On being informed of the nature of Jeremiah's words, the king sent a messenger to fetch the roll. But as Jehudi proceeded to read the manuscript, Jehoiakim was unable to restrain his wrath. When the reading of every three or four pages was completed, he cut them with his pen-knife, and cast them into the fire, until the whole roll was burned. The witnesses of this impious act looked on with apparent indifference, although two or three of the princes made a futile appeal to the king to desist from his purpose. Having made an end of the roll, Jehoiakim was ready to deal after a similar fashion with Jeremiah and Baruch, and gave orders to have them arrested. Their hiding-place, however, could not be discovered. Nor had the king, for all his fury, succeeded in destroying the word of the Lord. Jeremiah was commanded to secure another roll, and in it Baruch wrote down all the prophecies which Jehoiakim had committed to the flames, with "many like words" added to the original collection. This enlarged roll forms, no doubt, the nucleus of our present book.

Jehoiakim acknowledged the supremacy of Babylon for three years, and then threw off the yoke. Nebuchadnezzar did not immediately come against him in person, but he sent bands of his own forces, together with Moabite, Syrian, and Ammonite auxiliaries, to lay waste the land. Before more effective measures for the reconquest of Judah could be initiated, however, Jehoiakim died.

He was succeeded by his son Jehoiachin, a youth of eighteen years of age, who, during his brief reign of three months and ten days, appears to have maintained his father's policy both in religious and in political affairs. In any case the Chaldean army soon appeared before the gates of Jerusalem, and after a three months' siege the city was captured. Jehoiachin and the queen-mother, together with the princes and the flower of the Jewish people, were carried into Babylon; none were left "save the poorest sort of the people of the land."[1]

On the throne of the stricken kingdom Nebuchadnezzar set Zedekiah, who was a half-brother to Jehoiakim. Zedekiah was personally disposed to be friendly to Jeremiah; but he was a weak man, without courage or independence of judgment, and he was as clay in the hands of the upstart princes who surrounded his throne. These dignitaries were ill qualified for the task of government, but they were filled with the usual arrogance of men of their class, and looked upon themselves as the true nobility of the nation, in contrast with those who had been carried into captivity. Jeremiah was not long in discerning their real character, and in the parable of the baskets of figs[2] he exposed their worthlessness and announced their doom, while at the same time he affirmed the superior quality of the exiles and predicted their ultimate return to their own land. This parable of the figs is significant as marking a definite stage in the enlightenment of the prophet's mind with regard to the future of the Kingdom of God. From this time forward his hopes are centred in the captives in Babylon.

Jeremiah incurred the displeasure of the prophets who were in Babylon because, in a letter to the exiles, he directly opposed their prediction of an early return from captivity;[3] and for the same reason, as well as because of his repeated counsels of submission to Nebuchadnezzar, he came into conflict with the prophets who remained in Judah. A dramatic encounter took place one day between Jeremiah and Hananiah in the Temple, Jeremiah appear-

[1] 2 Kings xxiv. 14. [2] xxiv. [3] xxix.

ing with a yoke on his neck as a sign of the necessity for subjection to the king of Babylon, and Hananiah, who was a leading representative of the false prophets, declaring with equal emphasis that the yoke of Nebuchadnezzar would be broken within two years, and, in token of the truth of his prediction, removing the yoke from Jeremiah's neck and breaking it. A sequel to the interview was a message from Jeremiah to the optimistic prophet, announcing that he would die that year for teaching "rebellion against the Lord." Within two months this sentence of doom was fulfilled.[1]

Zedekiah's advisers as a whole were in favour of throwing off the Chaldean yoke, and were looking to Egypt for help to achieve this end. Their counsels at length prevailed, and Zedekiah broke his covenant with the king of Babylon.[2] Nebuchadnezzar swiftly marched against Jerusalem, and the final siege of the city began. After some time the Chaldeans withdrew before the advance of an Egyptian army, and during this interval in the siege Zedekiah sent a deputation to the prophet, requesting his prayers on behalf of the land, and at the same time seeking enlightenment on the future development of events. Jeremiah's reply was an emphatic assurance that the relief afforded by the Egyptian intervention was only temporary, and that the Chaldeans would certainly return and capture the city.[3]

It was during this lull in the storm also that Jeremiah was first cast into prison.[4] He was proceeding to Anathoth, on some business relating to his property there, when he was arrested by Irijah, the captain of the guard, on the charge of being a deserter, and after being beaten was placed in confinement in a dungeon attached to the house of Jonathan the scribe. He never regained his liberty until the city was captured.

During his imprisonment in Jonathan's house the king sent for him secretly, and enquired once more if there was "any word from the Lord" regarding the future of

[1] xxviii.
[2] Ezek. xvii. 15-18.
[3] xxxvii. 3-10.
[4] xxxvii. 11-15.

the nation. And once more Jeremiah gave the uncompromising reply that Zedekiah would be delivered into the hand of the king of Babylon. At the same time he appealed to the king not to send him back to the dungeon in the house of Jonathan. Zedekiah granted this request and the prophet was accordingly removed to the court of the prison where he was allowed a certain measure of freedom and could be visited by his friends.

His confinement indeed was not all gloom and hopeless dejection; it was sweetened and to a great extent transfigured by the strong consolations of God. Like John in Patmos or Paul in Rome, Jeremiah was favoured in his prison in Jerusalem with the brightest visions of his prophetic career—visions of a restored and regenerated nation, a re-established sanctuary, a purified priesthood, and a happy and prosperous people serving the Lord under a new and better Covenant.[1] These revelations of the future Jeremiah was commanded to write in a book.[2]

It was during this period of comparative liberty that an incident took place which has a special significance in its bearing on the quality of the prophet's faith. The Egyptian army had meantime been compelled to retire and the Chaldeans had resumed the siege of Jerusalem. One day Jeremiah was visited in his prison by his cousin Hanameel from Anathoth.[3] A piece of ground in the prophet's native place had fallen vacant, and Hanameel had come to give Jeremiah an opportunity of buying it for himself as the next of kin. The prophet promptly closed with the offer and bought the land at the price of seventeen shekels. The transaction was carried out with a strict regard to legal formalities. A deed of purchase was drawn up and was duly signed, witnessed, and sealed. Then Jeremiah handed the deed to Baruch, and charged him to deposit it in a safe place, where it might be preserved for many days. What was the meaning of this strange transaction? It was at once a test and an evidence of the prophet's faith in his own predictions. He was asked to buy a piece of land which for all practical

[1] xxx.-xxxiii. [2] xxx. 2. [3] xxxii. 6 ff.

purposes was worthless, because it was in the hands of the enemy. Was he so convinced that houses and lands would yet be bought and sold in Judah in a new era of prosperity as to be prepared, in simple reliance on God's promise, to make this apparently hopeless investment? In other words, was his assurance of the future hope strong enough to carry the day against all the opposing evidence of the present fact? And Jeremiah's faith survived this searching test. His purchase of the land provided those who witnessed the transaction with a practical evidence of the prophet's confidence in the ultimate restoration of Judah, while the rediscovered deed would furnish future generations with a striking testimony to the faithfulness of God to His own promises. It is significant that no sooner was the transaction completed than Jeremiah betook himself to prayer, for his faith, even in the hour of its victory, needed fresh confirmations and reinforcements from God.

As the siege proceeded, the hostility of Jeremiah's enemies became more intense. Charging him with counselling desertion to the Chaldeans, and thus with weakening the hands of the men of war within the city, they petitioned the king to have him put to death.[1] With characteristic weakness Zedekiah yielded to the clamour of his princes, and delivered Jeremiah into their hands. Then followed the most terrible ordeal of the prophet's career. For some reason or other the princes shrank from killing him out of hand; but they chose for him a more dreadful end. Lowering him with cords into a miry dungeon, they left him there to die of starvation and exposure. From an unexpected quarter, however, the Lord sent deliverance to His servant in his extremity. An Ethiopian eunuch, named Ebed-melech, who was attached to the royal palace, heard of Jeremiah's plight, and immediately made his way to the king and interceded on the prophet's behalf. Zedekiah at once gave instructions for his release, and Ebed-melech, accompanied by a number of assistants, proceeded without delay to carry

[1] xxxviii. 4.

out his merciful task. Lowering into the dungeon a quantity of "old cast clouts and old rotten rags" for the prophet to place under his arm-pits beneath the cords—Jeremiah was "sunk in the mire," and the work of extrication would have involved an immense strain—they raised him from his "horrible pit," and removed him to his former place of confinement in the court of the prison. Ebed-melech's action revealed not only his sympathy but his understanding. "Many a man"—it is Dr F. B. Meyer who makes the whimsical but appropriate comment—"might have hurried to the pit's mouth with ropes; only one of God's own gentlemen would have thought of the rags and the clouts." For this courageous action, which was prompted not merely by natural compassion but by religious faith, the Ethiopian received "a prophet's reward." Jeremiah afterwards conveyed to him an assurance from the Lord that in the day of Jerusalem's desolation his life would be given him for a prey.[1]

After Jeremiah's rescue from the dungeon Zedekiah sent for him again with the ostensible aim of obtaining guidance on the course he should follow.[2] This final interview between the two men presents an interesting psychological study. On the one hand, we see the king, struggling in the toils of a now desperate situation, wavering between conflicting views of duty, and perhaps secretly hoping that now at length, as a result of his recent experiences, Jeremiah might find it possible to deliver a more accommodating message to his royal benefactor. And before him stands the prophet, newly saved from a terrible death, and weak and shaken, no doubt, by the privations and horrors of that experience. For him the interview meant a fresh trial of courage and fidelity. But the brave heart never faltered. Whatever the condition of his body, he stood "as an iron pillar" in the steadfastness of his soul. Stipulating only that he should not be put to death for telling the truth, he assured Zedekiah once more that surrender to the king of Babylon would mean deliverance for himself and the city, while

[1] xxxix. 15-18. [2] xxxviii. 14.

continued resistance would involve irretrievable disaster. Zedekiah expressed his fear that if he surrendered to the Chaldeans he would be delivered to the mocking of those Jews who had already gone over to the enemy, and Jeremiah met this objection with a warning that if he refused to yield he would incur, as a prisoner, the more bitter mocking of his own women. Zedekiah's only answer to this scathing message was a request that the nature of his interview with the prophet might not be divulged to his princes, and to this request Jeremiah acceded.

After a siege of eighteen months Jerusalem was taken. Zedekiah and some of his men tried to escape by night, but they were overtaken in the plains of Jericho and brought to Nebuchadnezzar at Riblah. Zedekiah's sons were put to death in his own presence, and then he himself was blinded and afterwards carried in fetters to Babylon.[1] Jeremiah was brought out of prison by the Chaldean officers, and handed over to the care of Gedaliah, who was appointed governor of Judah.[2] Afterwards he was brought to Ramah by Nebuzaradan—who had been charged by the king of Babylon to treat the prophet with every respect—and was given the choice of going to Babylon, where freedom and honour awaited him, or of remaining behind in Judah. With rare courage and self-denial Jeremiah elected to cast in his lot with the remnant who were left in the land.[3]

The rest of the sad story need not detain us long. Under the wise rule of Gedaliah there was some hope that Judah might regain a measure of prosperity. But Gedaliah was murdered by Ishmael,[4] and Ishmael in turn was put to flight by Johanan.[5] Fearing the vengeance of Nebuchadnezzar, Johanan and his companions, in spite of the warnings of Jeremiah, resolved to flee to Egypt, and the prophet and Baruch were compelled to accompany them.[6] On arriving at Tahpanhes, Jeremiah—making characteristic use of symbolical action to reinforce his message—buried great stones in front of the royal palace,

[1] xxxix. 1-7. [2] xxxix. 11-14. [3] xl. 1-6.
[4] xli. 2. [5] xli. 11-15. [6] xlii.

and predicted that over these the throne of Nebuchadnezzar would yet be set up when he came to conquer the land.[1]

Even in Egypt we find the prophet carrying out his commission to root out and to pull down. The Jews who dwelt in the Nile valley were practising idolatry, and Jeremiah sternly denounced this wickedness. And when they refused to listen to his remonstrances, boldly challenging the truth of his assertions, and justifying themselves in their worship of other gods, Jeremiah declared that the stroke of Divine judgment would fall on them as surely and as terribly as it had fallen on Judah, and that as a sign of the fulfilment of this prophecy Pharaoh-Hophra himself would be delivered into the hand of his enemies.[2]

This is the last that we hear of Jeremiah. How long he lived in Egypt afterwards, and in what circumstances he came to his end, we do not know.

IV. The Man

Jeremiah has sometimes been called the greatest of the prophets, and beyond question there are elements in his character and in his message which go far to justify this lofty claim. It is certainly true, as has been already

[1] xliii. 8-13. In his *Ten Years' Digging in Egypt* Dr Flinders Petrie tells of a remarkable confirmation of Jeremiah's narrative at this point which he discovered when exploring in the marshy desert about Tanis. Excavations which he conducted at a certain point there soon made it plain that the place had been a Greek camp, " an old fort on the Syrian frontier guarding the road out of Egypt." A remarkable connection with the account given by Jeremiah was found on clearing around the fort. " The entrance was in the side of a block of building projecting from the fort; and in front of it, on the opposite side of its roadway, similarly projecting from the fort, was a large platform, or pavement, of brick-work, suitable for out-door business, such as loading goods, pitching tents, etc.—just what is now called a *mastaba*. Now, Jeremiah writes of " The pavement (or brick-work) which is at the entry of Pharaoh's house in Tahpanhes "; this passage, which has been an unexplained stumbling-block to translators hitherto, is the exact description of the *mastaba* which I found; and this would be the most likely place for Nebuchadnezzar to pitch his royal tent, as stated by Jeremiah " (pp. 50-54).

[2] xliv.

indicated, that the task committed to his hands was one of the most difficult ever assigned to mortal man. For, apart altogether from the fact that Jeremiah was constitutionally disinclined to be a prophet of judgment, his mission brought him into conflict with a tremendous combination of forces. There are men who drink delight from battling with their peers, and on whom the dust of controversy has the effect of a tonic. But Jeremiah was not of that pugnacious tribe. He instinctively recoiled from strife. But we have already seen that he was engaged in strife throughout his whole career. The priests and prophets were, of course, his bitterest enemies, for by the purity of his life, as well as by the faithfulness of his message, he rebuked their corruptions and condemned their shallow optimism. The princes were at first his protectors, but in the later years of his ministry they became his most violent persecutors. The kings for the most part resented his plainness of speech, and even Zedekiah never once acted on his advice although he frequently asked for it. The people too, with characteristic fickleness, at one time befriended him, but latterly joined with the princes in clamouring for his life. His enemies plotted against him secretly, and cursed him openly. He had to endure at their hands repeated public humiliations, the restraints of a long imprisonment, and the horror of being left to die in a miry pit. And sometimes the anguish of his spirit under these experiences could not be restrained. "Woe is me, my mother," we hear him crying, "that thou hast borne me a man of strife, and a man of contention to the whole earth . . . everyone of them doth curse me."[1] Was there ever a man, indeed, whose fidelity to his commission exposed him to more cruel misrepresentation? He was a true patriot, but he was hated and reproached as a traitor. He toiled and prayed above everything else for the religious well-being of his country, but he was condemned as a betrayer of its most sacred heritage.

In Jeremiah's heart too there flamed a passion of love

[1] xv. 10.

for his own people; but he had not only to endure the hatred with which they repaid his devotion, but had also to be a helpless spectator of their wickedness and a stern herald of their destruction. He pleaded with them to return unto the Lord, but he knew that his task was hopeless. This was indeed one of the most distressing features of his ministry. So far as direct and visible results were concerned, his work appeared to be a complete failure. Other prophets had at least occasional successes to cheer their hearts in the midst of their difficulties; but Jeremiah seemed to be fighting a losing battle to the very end. His warnings were unheeded; his counsels were set aside. Even after the fall of Jerusalem we see him dragged into Egypt by a fleeing rabble, who had at first consulted him as to what they should do, and then angrily refused to follow his guidance. And in the last scene of all, before the curtain falls in Tahpanhes, we see a company of Jewish women boldly giving him the lie and pouring contempt on his message. Who can estimate the pain which such experiences as these occasioned to a spirit so sensitive as Jeremiah's? But his love burned on in a quenchless flame. Like Paul in a later day he had "great heaviness and continual sorrow" in his heart for his kinsmen according to the flesh. "Oh," he exclaims, "that my head were waters and mine eyes a fountain of tears, that I might weep day and night for the slain of the daughter of my people."[1] These are words which, like the still profounder exclamations of Moses and Paul in the same connection, were "sparks from the fire of Christ's substitutionary love."

It was Jeremiah's lot also to live a lonely life throughout all his days. To some extent, of course, this was the inevitable result of the unpopularity of his mission. But solitariness was also imposed upon him by the direct command of God. He was forbidden, for example, to marry,[2] and so was denied the domestic encouragements and sympathies which have often helped men to endure the sorest public trials. He was even charged to remain

[1] ix. 1. [2] xvi. 2.

apart from the social life of the community. Alike from the house of mourning and from the house of feasting he must hold aloof.[1] For Jeremiah was appointed to be a sign to the nation, and his mode of life was intended to reinforce his message. But these restrictions must have been a real trial to him. Jeremiah was no ascetic, who would have practised such austerities from personal choice. He was a man of warm human sympathies, and from various references in his prophecies we may gather that he would have rejoiced in having friendly intercourse with his fellowmen. But from all those alleviations and solaces which sorrow finds in human fellowship Jeremiah was shut out. With the single exception of Baruch, he had not even one friend during his whole lifetime into whose ear he could pour forth the tale of his griefs and his wrongs.

This loneliness, however, was not without its compensations, for it threw him back upon God. If Jeremiah was denied the comfort of earthly friendships, he was favoured in a remarkable degree with the fellowship of the Lord. There is perhaps nothing in the records of the religious life anywhere, in the Bible or out of it, that is quite like the account which Jeremiah gives us of his intercourse with his God. He spoke to God "as a man speaketh unto his friend," not indeed with irreverent familiarity, but with the courage which is inspired by profound emotion. And he weaves the story of these colloquies with Heaven into his prophetic messages with a frankness of self-revelation that lays bare to us the inner workings of his spirit. The struggles of his soul, the tumult of his emotions, the chafing, and sometimes the fainting, of his heart under the burden of his destiny, the tides of anguish that surged through his breast—all these are mirrored for us in brief but vivid sketches of his secret history. We hear him, for example, now giving utterance to his perplexities regarding the Divine government of the world,[2] now expostulating with the Lord for having "beguiled" him into entering the prophetic office.[3] At one time we

[1] xvi. 5-9. [2] xii. 1, 2. [3] xx. 7.

find him longing to escape from the field of battle altogether, and to retire into " a lodging-place of way-faring men " in the wilderness,[1] and again he tells us how on other occasions he actually refrained from delivering his message, until the word of the Lord became as a burning fire in his bones, and he was compelled to seek relief in speech.[2] And finally, in a mood which bordered on despair, we find this tormented man cursing the day on which he was born.[3]

But if Jeremiah had to tread a lonely and sorrowful path, he never wavered in his fidelity. There is nothing indeed that stands out more clearly from his history than the courage of his soul. It was courage, too, of the highest quality. There are men who know no fear, because they are lacking in fineness of sensibility ; they are without imagination, and do not know the meaning of " nerves." The real hero is the man who is conscious of fear, but overcomes the impulse to run away, and triumphs over himself before he grapples with his enemy. Of this more excellent kind was the courage of Jeremiah. If he sometimes felt inclined to quit his post, he refused to yield to such unworthy promptings. If he was naturally timid in disposition, he never failed to play the man in the hour of danger. Again and again he faced his enemies with fearless eyes, and delivered his message with unfaltering voice. What magnificent courage, for example, shines through his final interview with Zedekiah, when the intrepidity of his spirit made light of the feebleness of his bodily strength. And what rare devotion to duty he revealed after the capture of Jerusalem, when, instead of choosing the easier path, he decided to remain behind with the broken remnant whom Nebuchadnezzar did not think it worth while to carry into captivity—the man who a little while before had been cast into prison as a deserter to the enemy !

It is indeed a mistake to think of Jeremiah as a soft and effeminate personality who was often dissolved in tears. That is the traditional conception of his character,

[1] ix. 2. [2] xx. 9. [3] xx. 14-18.

but it receives but scanty support from the recorded facts. The truth is that in the prophet's constitution there was a combination of diffidence and resolution, of gentleness and severity; or shall we rather put it that his natural qualities were reinforced through the inward strengthening of God? In any case his face was often set in righteous anger; he was master of a biting irony; and he could thunder forth the judgments of the Lord with terrific vehemence. Again and again we find him invoking the judgment of Heaven on his enemies,[1] not, we may believe, in a spirit of personal vindictiveness, but because they were the enemies of the Lord as well as of His servant. This at least was the crowning quality of his prophetic ministry; he could not but declare the message which God had given him to deliver.

V. The Message

Jeremiah's message was pre-eminently a message of judgment, and we have seen how loyally he carried out his stern commission, even at the cost of much pain to himself. But we must not lose sight of other elements in his teaching about God.

(1) *The Love of God.*—Few indeed of the prophets excel Jeremiah in their account of the riches of God's grace and the tenderness and patience of God's love. It is a deeply significant fact that it is this aspect of the Divine character that is emphasised in the words which form the introduction to his recorded prophecies.[2] From the position which it occupies, that moving passage is no doubt meant to be regarded as setting forth the conception of God which should be fundamental in all our thinking about Him, and which should be kept steadily in view even when the sterner attributes of His nature appear to receive greater prominence. And how persistent was His pleading with His people throughout the years, and how amazing His assurances of grace and

[1] x. 25; xi. 20; xii. 3; xvii. 18; xviii. 21-23; xx. 12. [2] ii. 1-9.

mercy. Again and again He represents Himself as "rising up early," through the ministry of the prophets, in His eagerness to present His appeals to the heart of the nation, and again and again, notwithstanding the failure of those efforts, He still addresses to them the call to return. Only let them acknowledge their iniquity, and He will receive them back in pardoning and restoring mercy.[1] The God whose word Jeremiah proclaims is assuredly a God of boundless grace and compassion. To a people so laden with iniquity, so defiled in life, and so rebellious in heart, He cries, "Return, O backsliding children . . . for I am married unto you." "Return . . . for I am merciful and will not keep anger for ever."[2]

It is suggestive also that Jeremiah's vision of the almond tree[3]—his first vision before entering on his official work—agrees with those first recorded words of his, in the emphasis which it lays on the graciousness of God's character. The nature of the symbol used determines for us the special aspect of the Divine "wakefulness" which was presented to the prophet's mind. It was the unslumbering vigilance of the love of God "keeping watch above His own" with a view to their final deliverance. The almond tree awaking from its long winter sleep in the beginning of the year was the harbinger of spring, and it spoke to Jeremiah of the brighter days which lay beyond the dark and stormy winter of the nation's present state. In the experience of Judah also, the sleep of spiritual death would be followed by a glorious resurrection. And to secure that end her Divine Keeper, who "shall neither slumber nor sleep," was watching over her life even amid the storms of judgment through which she must first pass. So the vision of the almond tree comes before the vision of the seething cauldron; the promise of grace precedes the threatening of judgment.

(2) *The Wrath of God.*—But the God of Jeremiah was certainly a God of Judgment. He was holy and righteous, as well as long-suffering and kind. His wrath was as real

[1] iii. 13. [2] iii. 12, 14. [3] i. 11, 12.

as His love; and of that fact Jeremiah himself was a standing witness, for his own life reflected both the goodness and severity of the Divine character. If his broken-hearted lamentations over the impending doom of the people were sparks from the fire of the sacrificial love of the Redeemer, the imprecations which were wrung from his heart by their ungodliness may be said—and this too is surely the solving word with regard to the imprecatory Psalms—to have been sparks from the fire of the holy wrath of God; for the servant was "full of the fury" of his Master.[1] Both the insincerities and the impurities of the nation were an abomination unto the Lord. He had long warned them of the punishment which would follow their iniquities; and at last He was "weary with repenting,"[2] and the stroke of judgment fell. It was a terrible stroke when it came, and it was inflicted by the hand of God. The destroyers who swept over the land of Judah were prepared by Him.[3] Nebuchadnezzar was His servant, in the sense of being the instrument of His righteous vengeance. The sword, the famine, and the pestilence were the scourge of His chastisements.[4] And when He rose to do His strange work of judgment, His hand did not spare, as the agonies of "the Babylonian woe" abundantly testified. Let us remember that in so punishing His disloyal children there was no unrighteousness with God. The disease of the people had proved incurable[5] by medicinal treatment, and it became necessary to resort to surgery. It was a terrible operation, but it was the only way to save the life of the nation.

(3) *The Sovereignty of God.*—With equal clearness Jeremiah bore witness to the sovereignty of God. The dominion of Jehovah extended over all the nations, for He was indeed the God of all flesh. The gods of the heathen were but "vanity"[6]—a worthless and empty delusion; and Jehovah was the one living and true God. Nowhere is Jeremiah's irony more effective than in his description of the idols to which the Gentiles bowed down

[1] vi. 11. [2] xv. 6. [3] xxii. 7.
[4] xxiv. 10. [5] xxx. 12. [6] x. 15.

in worship. "They are like a scarecrow in a cucumber-garden, and speak not; they must needs be borne, because they cannot go . . . they cannot do evil, neither also is it in them to do good."[1] In contrast with the helplessness of these dumb images is the majesty of the God of Israel. "Jehovah is the true God, He is the living God, and an everlasting King."[2] And this living and true God has power to make His sovereignty effective. Such is the ease with which He is able to accomplish His purposes, that the sand which He has placed for a bound to the sea is sufficient to hold in check the turbulence of its waters.[3]

Jeremiah's doctrine of the sovereignty of God is indeed particularly full of instruction. As a result of his visit to the potter's house he has much to say on this august theme.[4] Three distinct aspects of the truth come to light in his teaching. First of all, there is the reality of the sovereignty of God in human life. We *are* as clay in the hand of the potter. He controls our destiny and fashions our life according to His own will. In the work of salvation it is He who takes the initiative, "preventing" us in the quickening and liberating operations of His grace. Of that fact Jeremiah's own experience was an outstanding illustration.

But the sovereignty which Jeremiah was taught to claim for his God was not the working out in human life of the arbitrary decrees of an almighty despot. Not, in every sense, as the potter deals with the lifeless clay, does the Lord deal with men. He deals with them as moral beings who are endowed by Himself with certain rights of personality, men who possess the tremendous gift of freedom, and consequently lie under a heavy burden of responsibility. So in the message which accompanied the incident in the potter's house, we find that the Lord associates His sovereignty with freedom—not merely freedom of choice on the part of men, but freedom of change on His own part. As the potter can change into another vessel the article he is making, so the Lord claims

[1] x. 5. [2] x. 10. [3] v. 22. [4] xviii. 1-11.

and exercises the right to modify His attitude to His people in accordance with the changes which may take place in their relation to Him. When they repent of their wickedness He withdraws His threats; when they turn to evil, He recalls His promises.[1]

But, finally, in Jeremiah's teaching the actings of Divine sovereignty are represented as inclining to the side of grace. Surely this is an unmistakable lesson of the incident which the prophet witnessed in the potter's house. As the workman was fashioning a certain vessel on the wheel, it was marred in his hand. It was a vessel of common clay, with little claim to intrinsic value. But instead of throwing it on the scrap-heap as a worthless thing, the potter took the broken pieces into his hand again, and with patient skill, now using the delicate pressure of his fingers, now applying a gentle touch of the revolving wheel, he refashioned it into another vessel as seemed good to him. And with the same unwearying patience God deals with His people. Many a time the human vessel of clay is sadly marred. There are falls that impair its strength, and flaws that disfigure its beauty, but the Divine Potter will not cast off the work which He has once begun. He restores the soul that has been marred through disloyalty, and enables it to make a fresh beginning in the spiritual life. In the whole of Jeremiah's teaching there is scarcely anything that is more encouraging than this.

(4) *Human Sin.*—Jeremiah was a prophet of judgment to the nation because of the sins of the people. There is nothing that he is more careful to make clear than that the calamities which he is threatening are the direct outcome of the guilt of the community. It is indeed part of his mission to "justify the ways of God to men." They had forsaken God, the Fountain of living waters, and had endeavoured to find a substitute for Him in the broken cisterns of idolatrous worship and political diplomacy.[2] This apostasy was the root cause of all their corruptions and miseries. They had lost the true know-

[1] xviii. 7-10. [2] ii. 13.

ledge of God, and had become sottish children, wise to do evil, but understanding not how to do good.[1] We have already considered the prophet's account of the corruption of the national life. He does not, however, merely frame a general indictment against the nation. It is distinctive of his message that he deals with the fact of individual guilt, and takes account mainly of specific moral offences. It is also a feature of his teaching that he traces the evil which appears in men's lives to its source in their corrupt hearts. "The heart," he declares, "is deceitful above all things, and desperately wicked: who can know it?"[2] The wickedness of the heart was abundantly reflected in the iniquities of the people. Its deceitfulness was revealed in the fact that they were resting in a religion which was divorced from morality, imagining that they were pleasing God by the observance of ritual while their life was foul with sin.

(5) *The Ethical Emphasis.*—Jeremiah attaches first importance to the ethical element in human conduct. No adherence to religious ceremonial is acceptable to God which is not accompanied by moral uprightness. The man who trusts in the arm of flesh is lying under the curse of spiritual barrenness and insensibility, while true blessedness is to be found in trusting in the Lord.[3] To know God, indeed—the Lord who exercises "loving-kindness, judgment, and righteousness in the earth"—is the supreme attainment in which men should glory, the final secret of wisdom, and strength, and spiritual riches.[4]

Jeremiah's emphasis on moral and spiritual values, however, has sometimes been invested with an unwarranted significance. It is the fashion in some quarters to-day, for example, to describe him as the discoverer of ethical monotheism. This, however, is a claim which rests on a poor conception of the earlier stages of the religion of Israel. The truth is that the unity of God, as well as the moral perfections of His character, had been made known to Israel long ago by revelation, and while it was given to Jeremiah through the illumination of God's Spirit to

[1] iv. 22. [2] xvii. 9. [3] xvii. 5-8. [4] ix. 23, 24.

unfold those truths with special fulness and clearness, yet he taught nothing that was absolutely new regarding the two great departments of religious knowledge—"what man is to believe concerning God, and what duty God requires of man."

(6) *The Sacrificial System.*—Jeremiah's insistence on ethical standards is also misrepresented in another direction. It is understood to involve a disparagement of the whole ceremonial system which occupied so central a place in the religion of Israel. Not only so, but the prophet is actually represented as teaching that the Levitical sacrifices had no religious value because they had no Divine authority. The famous passage on which this view is based is as follows: "For I spake not unto your fathers, nor commanded them in the day that I brought them out of the land of Egypt, concerning burnt-offerings or sacrifices: But this thing commanded I them, saying, Obey my voice, and I will be your God, and ye shall be my people; and walk ye in all the ways that I have commanded you, that it may be well unto you."[1] These are words on which a certain school of Criticism builds one of its chief arguments for the post-Exilic date of the "Priestly Code." It is plain, however, that Jeremiah's words cannot be understood in an absolute sense; because, for one thing, as a matter of historical fact, sacrifices were commanded to Israel by the Lord;[2] and, for another, Jeremiah himself speaks of sacrifice as an institution which, in a restored and purified commonwealth, is to enjoy the favour of God.[3] We cannot

[1] vii. 22, 23. [2] Exod. xx. 24; xxiii. 14-19; Deut. xii. 6.

[3] xvii. 2-6; xxvii. 17-22; xxxi. 14; xxxiii. 10, 11, 18. Professor A. C. Welch believes with the majority of modern scholars that the prophet's words are to be understood as a definite denial that the sacrificial system had any Divine authority whatever. But, unlike a good many of his fellow-critics, he recognises that there are certain facts with regard to the place which sacrifice occupied in the religious life of Israel that cannot be easily set aside. Jeremiah, he admits, on this view of his words, "contradicted the fundamental position of the Jewish law on sacrifice." How, then, does he get over the difficulty? By assuming that the prophet, in the vehemence of his polemical zeal against the Temple and its ritual, committed the common fault of controversialists by exaggerating the facts!

suppose that he is contradicting either history or himself. It is only an exegetical judgment which is perverted by a critical theory that will fail to recognise that the prophet is speaking in a relative sense—the sense in which Hosea, for example, declares that the Lord will have "mercy and not sacrifice."[1] He is in fact "using the rhetorical negation frequently employed for emphatic antithesis;"[2] and the unreasonableness of pressing for a literal understanding of his words will at once appear if we apply the same principle of interpretation to other passages where this figure of speech is used.[3] Even at the time when sacrifices were originally commanded, it was made clear to Israel that moral loyalty was the thing to which God attached most value[4] and to which, as Driver observes,[5] the promises are generally annexed—the sacrificial system being, in point of fact, the means, and conformity to the will of God, the end. Jeremiah is simply reaffirming this principle with arresting emphasis. He is not depreciating the value of sacrifice in its own place; he is combating the view and denouncing the practice,

(pp. 145, 239). In plain language, he said what was not true. This is surely to place Jeremiah's message in the category of "chaff," which is the description that he himself applies to the declarations of the false prophets. Still more easily does Professor Welch dispose of another fact which runs counter to his view of this much discussed passage. That is the fact that Jeremiah himself speaks of sacrifice as an institution which in a cleansed and rededicated nation is to enjoy the favour of God (cf. particularly xxxiii. 10, 11, 18). Professor Welch in this case simply cuts the knot by denying the authenticity of the passage. And he denies it on the very ground that it speaks with approval of the sacrificial system. "I find it impossible to believe," he affirms, "that a prophet who had declared that the sacrificial system formed no integral part of its religion should have stultified himself by erecting this and the whole Davidic line into the leading factors of the community's restored life" (p. 231). Surely, in this instance, Professor Welch has given us a glaring instance of the fallacy of arguing in a circle.

[1] Hos. vi. 6. [2] J. D. Davis, *Dict. Bib.* s.v. *Jeremiah.*

[3] *E.g.* (*a*) John vi. 27, where, on this view, Christ's teaching lends support to the economic theory of those who like better to live on the dole than to earn their bread by the sweat of their brow. (*b*) 1 Cor. i. 17, where, according to the same principle, Paul denies that he had any authority from Christ to administer the rite of Baptism.

[4] Deut. x. 12.

[5] *The Book of the Prophet Jeremiah,* p. 44, note b.

of his countrymen who were exalting ceremonial into an end in itself, and making it indeed the whole of religion, thereby perverting, with disastrous results for themselves, a Divine institution.

(7) *The New Covenant.*—Jeremiah draws a dark picture of human sin as manifested in the life of his countrymen. The sin of Judah was written with the point of a diamond,[1] so ineffaceably did its dark characters appear to be graven on the tablet of their heart. Their case indeed was beyond the skill of man. No efforts at self-cleansing, however assiduous, could wash away their pollution.[2] As well might the Ethiopian hope to change his skin or the leopard his spots, as that they who were "accustomed to do evil," whose hearts had been hardened through the deceitfulness of sin, and whose lives had been enslaved through the tyranny of habit, should of themselves attain to purity and goodness.[3] Jeremiah, beyond question, despairs of fallen human nature. He proclaims its moral and spiritual bankruptcy. So far as the healing resources of men are concerned, there is "no remedy."

But Jeremiah does not leave us in this dungeon of despair. He is, above all, a messenger of hope to men. For he is the prophet of the New Covenant,[4] and the doctrine of the new covenant represents the high-water mark of Old Testament teaching on the way of life, and is indeed a remarkable foreshadowing of the grace of the Gospel. It is a striking, though perhaps not a surprising fact, that of all the prophets it is Jeremiah—the man whose mission was so largely associated with judgment—who was led into the clearest conception of the grace of God in the salvation of men. But it is just because his consciousness of human need was so profound that his vision of the Divine provision to meet that need was so lofty. His knowledge of the abounding guilt and spiritual impotence of men forced him—speaking from the human point of view—to look for a way of deliverance in which grace would much more abound. So his doctrine of the new covenant is the correlative of his doctrine of human sin.

[1] xvii. 1. [2] ii. 22. [3] xiii. 23. [4] xxxi. 31-34.

The new covenant is first of all contrasted with the old covenant made with Israel at Sinai. That old covenant had proved ineffective. It was "weak through the flesh," for its authority was external, and it could not secure obedience to its own demands. Its precepts discharged their imperatives in vain against the corruption and rebellion of the unregenerate heart. Of this insufficiency the life of Judah in Jeremiah's own day furnished a tragic illustration.

But Jeremiah had a vision of a new covenant whose provisions were completely adequate to human need, alike in its guilt and in its corruption. It is a covenant which is established on better promises. The key-note of the old covenant was "thou shalt"; the key-note of the new covenant is "I will." In other words, the new covenant proclaims as its central fact the gracious activity of God in the sphere of redemption. To begin with, it deals with men's guilty past; for in the forefront of its message is the promise of a complete and final forgiveness. But forgiveness is not of itself complete salvation. The evil record of the past may be blotted out; but there remains the question of the future adjustment of a man's life to the will of God. It is here that the distinctive element in the new covenant comes to light. It speaks of a spiritual illumination, and of a consequent knowledge of God, which mean nothing less than life from the dead. The new covenant involves the gift of a new heart, and on that heart God writes His law. It is, in short, the miracle of regeneration that Jeremiah proclaims as the Divine remedy for the spiritual impotence of men. As the outcome of a new life men are enabled to render a new obedience. They not only stand in a new relation to God because they are forgiven; they manifest a new disposition toward Him because they have been quickened. And this new disposition is loving and submissive and loyal. The fact that the law of God is written on the heart involves that the impulse to obedience comes from within. The demands of the covenant are no longer met in the spirit of forced submission to an external authority;

they receive the glad and spontaneous obedience of loving hearts. Nor does it detract from the grace of this new relationship that it should still be described as a covenant. For the covenant that is intended is of the nature of a marriage bond, and the central fact which it enshrines is set forth in the words, "I will be their God, and they shall be my people."

(8) *The Predictive Element.*—One other outstanding fact in Jeremiah's teaching remains to be noticed. The predictive element is so clearly present in his message that it can be denied only by men who approach the question under the influence of a theory of inspiration which allows to the vision of a prophet no element of the *pre*vision of a seer. His prophecies regarding the future course of Providence in relation to the history of Judah—his intimation, for example, of the conquest of the land by Nebuchadnezzar, of the subsequent Exile, and of the Return from Babylon after a captivity of seventy years, are so definite and so well authenticated as to present rationalistic criticism with one of its most baffling problems. And it would be strange indeed if the prophet who had so clear an understanding of the new covenant should be altogether silent regarding the Redeemer, through Whom its blessings were to be mediated. And Jeremiah speaks of the Messiah with no uncertain voice.[1] In the new age of prosperity for the Church of God which he foresaw, and whose blessings he described under such glowing figures, Israel will own the sway of a new King. He is the "Branch" of the House of David under whose just and gracious rule they will dwell safely, and from whom they will receive the blessing of righteousness. It is through this righteousness that the grace of the new covenant reigns.[2]

VI. The Book

The Book of Jeremiah has suffered severely at the hands of modern critics. There is scarcely any part of the Bible,

[1] xxiii. 5-8; xxx. 4-11; xxxiii. 14-26.

[2] Cf. T. K. Cheyne, *Jeremiah*, in the Pulpit Commentary, p. xiii.

indeed, that has been subjected to more drastic treatment. The fact that the Septuagint version of the Book differs to a considerable extent from the Hebrew text, together with the lack of chronological order which sometimes marks the arrangement of the prophecies, has apparently been regarded by many scholars as a warrant for a specially "free" application of the methods of modern textual criticism. In any case there is scarcely a passage in the Book the authenticity of which has been allowed to pass without some form of challenge; nor is it without significance that it is on some of the richest and loftiest portions of Jeremiah's message that this process of dissection has been put into most active operation. Whole chapters are deleted as later additions, while a large number of other passages are represented as containing only a Jeremianic nucleus which has been expanded in various ways by subsequent writers.[1] In many cases the process of rejection has been carried out under the influence of a certain view of prophetic inspiration; in other cases it is a theory of the literary medium used by the prophet that is made the criterion of genuineness, everything that does not fit into this particular mould being cut off with procrustean thoroughness. Sometimes the deletion of a verse or passage is based on linguistic grounds, the use of a single word or phrase being regarded as sufficient evidence of post-Exilic origin. At other times the objection to a passage is founded on moral considerations: the imprecatory character of some of Jeremiah's utterances, for example, is represented as decisive against their authenticity, the critic's argument apparently being that the prophet ought not to have said such things, and it is charitable therefore to believe that he never did say them. Or again, if a passage for any reason presents

[1] For example, chaps. xxx. and xxxi. The critics admit, says Sir George Adam Smith (*Jeremiah*, p. 374), "post-Exilic elements and consequently a late age for the whole collection, but reserve for Jeremiah various passages." An examination of the passages so "reserved" by different writers reveals a striking lack of agreement among the critics themselves, and, for that reason, shows how little value is to be attached to the judgments of a purely subjective criticism.

some difficulty of interpretation, it is found convenient to throw it out as forming no part of the original text.[1] And sometimes the excision appears to be supported by nothing more substantial than the *ipse dixit* of the critic.[2]

Among the longer passages which, in the view of the great majority of critics, have no claim to be regarded as the work of Jeremiah are the Fiftieth and Fifty-first Chapters. Some observations may therefore be made at this point with regard to the evidence on which these chapters are usually rejected. It may perhaps suffice to indicate the position taken up by two such representative critics as Professor S. R. Driver and Professor A. S. Peake.

Professor Driver affirms quite definitely that "the prophecy cannot be Jeremiah's."[3] He supports this view by three main arguments. The first is that the *historical situation* is not of the year 593 B.C., in which the prophecy purports to have been written, but "much later." The Temple is alluded to as having suffered violence; the Jews are in exile; and the end of Babylon is approaching rapidly. These three facts are certainly true; but it is interesting to note that Professor Driver does not hold that the passage was written *after* the overthrow of Babylon. His view is that "the prophecy must have been the work of a prophet familiar with Jeremiah's writings, and accustomed to the use of similar phraseology, who wrote shortly before the fall of Babylon."[4] This

[1] *E.g.* Sir G. A. Smith's treatment of xxxi. 22. "This couplet," he says, "has been the despair of commentators. Its exilic terms *created* and *female* relieve us of it" (*Jeremiah*, p. 305). Other scholars, however, including Driver, have not been conscious of this despair. They have given an interpretation of the passage which at least yields a reasonable meaning.

[2] A single instance of this arbitrariness of critical judgment may be mentioned. In referring to "utterances which may all belong to the earlier part of the prophet's work, either before or during the Deuteronomic reform," Oesterley and Robinson include within this category ii. 2-3, 5-8, and then add, "verse 4 is clearly a collector's note" (*op. cit.*, p. 293). The collector, it would almost seem, was careless enough to leave his name and address on his note, so "clearly" are those scholars able to recognise his handiwork. Not a scrap of evidence is furnished, however, to enable the reader to share in their illumination.

[3] *The Book of the Prophet Jeremiah*, p. 302.

[4] *Op. cit.*, p. 302.

eminent scholar therefore concedes to the passage, first, the fact of linguistic congruity with the accepted work of Jeremiah, and secondly, the presence in it of a predictive element. But once this latter fact is admitted, the argument based on the historical situation loses its force. Dr Driver allows to some nameless seer a view of the future extending over a period of several years, but he denies to Jeremiah a similar foresight, on the ground that the stretch of time between the fourth year of Zedekiah and the fall of Babylon—about fifty-five years—was too long for the range of his prophetic vision. And yet, with strange inconsistency, Professor Driver admits the authenticity and accepts the Messianic interpretation, of the passage in the Twenty-third Chapter, in which Jeremiah sees, across more than six centuries, the glory of the day of Christ.[1]

Professor Driver's second argument is that "the *point of view* is not that of Jeremiah in or about 593 B.C." At the latter date, he declares, Jeremiah "was earnestly opposing the prophets who promised that the yoke of Babylon would speedily be broken, and was exhorting the exiles to settle contentedly down in their new home." In the chapters now under discussion, however, "he declares confidently that the fall of Babylon is close at hand, and does his utmost to inspire the exiles with the hope of a speedy release." Here again the facts stated by Dr Driver are substantially true, but it does not follow that we are necessarily closed in to the inference which he draws from these facts. The argument indeed appears to rest on the assumption that Jeremiah's utterances in each case were based entirely on his own political sagacity. If we are prepared to admit, however, that in both instances he was delivering messages that were directly communicated to him by God, and that therefore transcended the scope of his natural discernment, we shall not be unduly perturbed by the apparent contradiction between the two points of view. There was good cause, as has already been pointed out, why the exiles should be advised

[1] *Op. cit.*, p. 133.

to settle down in their new home : the hopes inspired by the prophets who predicted a speedy return, unwarranted as they were by the word of the Lord to Jeremiah, and attended as they were likely to be by political repercussions at home, had to be dispelled. On the other hand it was desirable that the captives should receive an emphatic assurance that " the set time " in which God would restore them to their own land was not far distant. Till that appointed hour arrived, it was surely expedient that they should reconcile themselves as best they could to the conditions which were imposed upon them through their own unfaithfulness to God. Even if the two messages were delivered at precisely the same time, the difference in their point of view only meant a slight alteration of focus in the prophetic vision.

Dr Driver's third argument is that " the prophecy is animated by a *temper* which is not Jeremiah's." This contention is based on the fact that the prophecy in question is pervaded by a strong vein of feeling against the Chaldeans, and by a sense of satisfaction at the prospect of their approaching fate, whereas previously the prophet had repeatedly avowed his conviction that the Chaldeans were the appointed agents of Providence for the punishment of Israel's sin. But this objection is so unconvincing that it scarcely calls for refutation. To begin with, it would surely be a bold thing for any man who had studied Jeremiah's history, with its varying moods and its tumult of conflicting emotions—his voice at one moment full of tenderness as he presents the appeal of Divine mercy, at the next, terrible in denunciation as he is " full of the fury of the Lord "—to say what his " temper " might be at any given time, under the pressure of rapidly changing experiences. But, apart from this, there is nothing incompatible between the contrasted attitudes to which Dr Driver refers. Jeremiah certainly recognised that the Chaldeans were the appointed agents of God's judgment on His disloyal people, but he was also conscious of another fact, which is amply demonstrated in the history of Providence throughout the ages, and that is, that God often uses as the instruments of His chastisement evil men and ungodly communities, who are not on that account absolved from responsibility for their own iniquities. In rejecting and crucifying Jesus Christ, for example, the Jews were unconsciously fulfilling the Divine purpose, but nevertheless they were not counted guiltless for their share in that greatest crime in human history. Jeremiah had good reason to rejoice in the overthrow of Babylon, for that event was a definite step towards the fulfilment of God's promise with regard to the restoration of His people to their own land, through the decree of Cyrus, the conquering king of Persia. The vehement exultation which he manifested in the prospect of that development is a "temper" which is neither at variance with his counsel to the exiles to wait with patience for that glad consummation, nor in itself unworthy of a prophet of God. It may indeed be said to be a reflection of the Divine mind.

Professor Peake rejects the historicity of the oracle with no less emphasis. "It is an almost universally accepted result of criticism," he says, "that l. 1–li. 58 cannot be the work of Jeremiah."[1] This denial of Jeremianic authorship, however, is not based on grounds of language or style, for Peake admits, along with many other critics, that "characteristic expressions of the Book of Jeremiah are present in large proportions." The main reasons adduced in support of his view are precisely those advanced by Driver, which have already been examined. Several minor points—such as "its immense length" in comparison with "the oracle on the foreign nations published in the reign of Jehoiakim," and "its frequent repetitions"—are negligible as arguments against the authenticity of the oracle. Jeremiah was more directly interested in the land of the Captivity than in Moab or Elam, and what more natural than that he should deal with it in fuller detail? And if the repetitions are elsewhere "quite unexampled in Jeremiah's prophecies," is that any valid reason why they should not be used in

[1] *The Century Bible*, vol. ii., p. 254.

this oracle, which is charged with unusual intensity of feeling? In Peake's rejection of these chapters we can trace at least an approximation to the view of prophetic inspiration which excludes the likelihood, or even the possibility, of supernatural prediction, and which therefore is inclined to relegate those utterances which claim to foretell future events to a period when these events have become facts of history. Such a naturalistic approach to the documents, however, *creates* difficulties for which it is unable to provide an adequate solution. "The authorship of chaps. l., li. (with the exception of li. 59-64)," says Dr Marcus Dods, "is much disputed; but the reasons assigned are not convincing to those who believe in the reality of Divine predictions."[1] This sentence was written more than forty years ago, but Criticism has achieved nothing since that day which invalidates its closing affirmation.

There is one thing, however, which these scholars and those who share their view should have said, but have refrained from mentioning, and that is that these chapters specifically claim, both at their beginning and at their close, that they are the work of Jeremiah. On the assumption of the critics they are therefore a deliberate forgery, and a forgery which for long centuries escaped detection on the part of those to whom "were committed the oracles of God."

It is the phenomenal skill of the critics in discovering the hand of various late editors interfering with the original *Jeremiah*—sometimes with a deliberately fraudulent purpose, sometimes with a blundering honesty, but always with the effect of corrupting the original text—that causes the ordinary reader to gasp with astonishment. It is scarcely too much to say that the ease with which, after long ages, they are able to recognise the finger-prints of these literary marauders as they "worked over" a sentence, and the confidence with which they reconstruct a "mutilated" passage on the basis of a single word, reduce to a commonplace level the deduc-

[1] *An Introduction to the Old Testament*, p. 184.

tive achievements of the most brilliant detectives of modern fiction.[1]

Now, if the present writer may dare to express an opinion on this subject, the trouble with many of these scholars is that they are altogether too clever. They are too ingenious to be safe. Their cleverness is so nimble that it sometimes breaks away from the restraints of their common sense. When scholarship in this region of investigation is modest enough to recognise its inevitable limitations, its tentative endeavours to arrive at certainty may always be assured of a respectful hearing. When it becomes dogmatic, and invests its conjectures with the authority of truth, it is merely showing that an intensely specialised knowledge, as surely as a little learning, may be " a dangerous thing." The claim of literary criticism that it is able to discover evidences of different authorship in two or three consecutive verses, and even within the compass of a single verse, is a claim that no vigour or frequency of assertion can substantiate. Those who make it are often affirming that the Bible is not an infallible Book, but they come perilously near to arrogating infallibility of discernment to themselves. The efforts of the man who searches " in a dark room for a black cat which is not there " are presumably doomed to failure.

[1] The following passage from Oesterley and Robinson will perhaps show that this is no exaggeration: " iii. 19–vi. 30. The separate pieces included here seem to have been: iii. 19-20, 21-22, 23-25; iv. 1-2, 3-4 (modified by addition at the end, unless it be mutilated), 5-8, 9-12 (worked over and recast as prose, though clear signs of the original poetic form are to be seen, especially in vv. 11 f.), 13-17, 18 (possibly a fragment), 19-21 (to which 22 has been appended), 23-26, 27-28, 29-31; v. 1-6, 7, 8-9, 10-13 (this has probably been expanded towards the end), 15-17 (with a prose introduction in 14 and conclusion in 18-19, the style of which suggests the age of Malachi), 20-25 (much worked over near the beginning), 26, 27, 28-29, 30-31; vi. 1-5, 6-8, 9-12, 13-15 (mutilated at the beginning; the complete form appears in viii. 10-12), 16-19, 20, 21, 22-26, 27-30. . . . While there is nothing which we cannot ultimately ascribe to Jeremiah, several of the pieces have been worked over and recast, and there appear to be traces of the style of the age of Malachi. It is possible that we must date the final form of this collection as late as the end of the fifth century B.C." (*op. cit.*, 293-4). The rest of the Book is subjected to the same microscopic examination.

But the critics to whom I am referring triumph over difficulties of that kind. They explore every inch of the dark room, and ultimately produce the non-existent cat.

It is only fair, however, that they should be asked to exercise this gift of discernment in the field of contemporary literature, where their conclusions can be tested, in order that we may have an opportunity of seeing what measure of success will attend their efforts. There are various books in English literature, for example, which are the product of dual authorship, but it is a well-known fact that Criticism has been unable to say with definiteness where the work of one writer ends, and that of the other begins.[1] And how immeasurably harder is the task of the European critic who attempts to subject to a disintegrating analysis of this kind an Oriental literature which is thousands of years old. No modern scholar—I say it with the utmost respect but with profound conviction—*No modern scholar knows enough to be able, with any degree of certainty, to dissect the Old Testament documents after this fashion.* The best that any critic can do, however profound his learning, is to make conjectural reconstructions of the text.[2] And when it comes to guesswork in this

[1] In this Introduction there have been a number of references to a volume—one of several—in which two distinguished scholars, Dr W. O. E. Oesterley and Dr T. H. Robinson, have collaborated. Is there any contemporary critic who would be prepared, *on the ground of internal evidence alone*, to say which parts have been written by Dr Oesterley, and which by Dr Robinson? Would he also care to affirm that he is able to distinguish Oesterley's distinctive idiom in the Robinson sections, and to find traces of Robinson's hand "working over" sentences here and there in the chapters that were written by Oesterley? And that would be a relatively simple achievement in comparison with the task of the critic who would attempt a similar analysis of the book in the far-distant future—in the day, let us suppose, when Macaulay's traveller from New Zealand will sketch the ruins of St Paul's, taking his stand on a broken arch of London Bridge; a contingency which rests, of course, on the assumption that the volume in question will be more enduring than St Paul's. But it is something closely analogous to this that Oesterley and Robinson themselves have been doing with regard to the text of *Jeremiah*.

[2] Oesterley and Robinson give a detailed analysis of the textual structure of *Jeremiah*, dividing it into three types—*A* (oracular Poetry), *B* (Prose in the 3rd person), *C* (Prose in the 1st person). The general result of their examination is summed up as follows: "It will be seen at once that in the

particular field, one man's theory is about as good as another's. Such at least is my conviction, although I realise that on so recondite a theme my judgment is not likely to carry a great deal of weight. I may be permitted, however, to adduce in its support the testimony of two witnesses whose views are entitled to the highest respect.

The late Sir William Robertson Nicoll devoted a great deal of attention to this question, and his judgment is of value, not only because of the extraordinary range of his literary attainments, but also because of his generally favourable attitude to modern Biblical Criticism. In *The Church's One Foundation*, a small volume the worth of which must not be judged by its bulk, he deals with attacks on the New Testament Scriptures which, thirty years ago, were developing into a denial of the cardinal truths of the Christian faith. "No one," he declares, "who takes up Schmiedel or Dr Moffatt will read very far without asking himself, But how does the critic know this? Upon what principle are certain passages rejected,

earlier part of the book these headings occur most frequently at the beginning of prose passages which are followed by poetical pieces. Later, when the poetical pieces have practically come to an end, they occur in the course both of *B* and *C*. This *seems to imply* that the compiler had before him collections of *B* and *C* material, divided into sections, all of which had headings of some kind, many of them being dated. These headings were no part of the original pieces, since in more than one instance the heading of a *C* passage is in the third person, *e.g.* in xviii. 1, xxv. 1, xxvii. 1, and xxxv. 1. *It is possible* that some of the oracular sections had such headings, and *one may survive* from this source in xiv. 1. . . . These facts give us a clue to the methods of the compiler. He had before him a number of little collections of oracular material in poetry, some of which had prose appendices or expansions of no great length. He had also a collection of descriptive material from the hand of a biographer, and a similar collection of passages in the first person, mainly consisting of oracular material worked over into rhetorical prose form.

"His method was to take each small collection, or group of oracular utterances, and to prefix to it a suitable selection from one of the two prose collections. *We may safely assume* that if he had had but a single poetic collection, he would have made it more continuous, and the result would have been a book much more like that of Isaiah in general appearance. For this purpose he preferred passages of the *C* type, and used but little of the *B* class until the others were nearly all exhausted."

The italics in this passage—which are mine—indicate the hypothetical nature of the reconstruction.

certain narratives denied, certain conclusions drawn as to authorship ? . . . He will in fact soon come to the conclusion that there are few real principles in criticism, principles that can be depended upon. . . . We venture . . . to say with great respect that those who have studied the problems in English literature will be the first to hesitate as to the legitimacy and validity of the methods adopted by many Biblical critics." Dr Robertson Nicoll then passes in review a number of these problems—the letters of Lady Mary Wortley Montagu ; the forged Shelley letters ; the Logan-Bruce controversy ; the authorship of *An Englishwoman's Love Letters* ; the novels which were the fruit of the collaboration of Besant and Rice. His considered opinion is summed up in the Introduction to the volume.[1] "For our part," he says, "we have the deepest conviction that until the principles of criticism are established by an induction based on the phenomena of literature generally, little that is solid or certain can be established. It is past dispute that English Criticism is unable, as a rule, to assign authorship to an anonymous contemporary book. It is unable, as a rule, to distinguish between the work of two collaborators. It is unable, in short, to perform any of these achievements which are believed possible when the Scriptures are handled. . . . There may be probabilities ; but, as a rule, the likely interpretation is not the true explanation. In other words the answer to much sceptical criticism is to be found in showing, by a catena of instances, that Criticism is attempting a task of which it is fundamentally incapable."

It may be objected, however, that this line of argument is hopelessly out of date, because it deals with the problems of thirty years ago, and Criticism has made such progress since that time that to-day it is in a position to speak with much greater authority. To this it may be answered, with great deference, that, so far as the questions now under discussion are concerned, Criticism has made little real progress since the days when the Editor of *The British*

[1] p. 12 f.

Weekly uttered his telling protest. The problems of the Old Testament are essentially the same to-day as they were then. Of course there has been a great advance in knowledge: to deny this would be simply to proclaim one's own ignorance. With painstaking application in various fields, scholarship has succeeded in casting new light on many difficult questions. But with regard to the literary Criticism of the Old Testament as a whole, there has been little finality of achievement. Many theories which used to be proclaimed as "assured results" have had to be abandoned, and others, with an equally precarious tenure of life, have from time to time succeeded them. What has really happened is that the old positions have continually been reappearing in new forms. There have been revisions and restatements, but the conclusions of Criticism reveal to-day the same diversity, and therefore bear the mark of the same uncertainty, as they did a generation ago.

And this is not the whole truth. It is not too much to say that the clearly established gains that have been made in this department of knowledge have had the effect of confirming the accuracy of the Old Testament records. The results of archæological research—and these have been neither few nor unimportant within recent years—have been of incalculable value in strengthening faith in the trustworthiness of the Bible. And this fact leads directly to the second witness whose testimony I propose to quote.

Professor A. H. Sayce was an expert in a different sphere of knowledge from that in which Robertson Nicoll achieved distinction. He was one of the foremost archæologists of recent times, with a particularly intimate knowledge of the antiquities of Assyria and Egypt. At one time a Higher Critic himself, he changed his attitude entirely as a result of his studies in this field, and became a vigorous opponent of the views which he had once proclaimed. Especially was he distrustful of the methods of literary analysis applied by many critics to the Scriptures. In an article written little more than six years ago he condemns these misdirected activities with scathing severity. "The so-called 'literary analysis' of our documents," he says, "which has been the pastime of scholars and amateurs for so long a time is being superseded by the discovery and collection of objective facts. Long ago I protested against the waste of time and ingenuity which it involved, and challenged its advocates to apply the same process to a modern newspaper. When they were able to refer the unsigned leading articles in it to their several authors we might give some credence to their attempts to slice up an ancient Oriental document, assigning each small fragment to some imaginary author and date. If this cannot be done where the language is that of the critic and the mental outlook the same as his own, how can it be possible where he is dealing with a dead form of speech and an equally alien outlook upon the world? Those who have lived in the East of to-day know how impossible it is for the stay-at-home European to understand the mentality of the Oriental: still more impossible would it be if the Oriental were one who had lived and written more than two thousand years ago. Of one thing we may be certain: the literary and historical prepossessions and assumptions of the scholar in a European library will have little or nothing in common with the actual facts." [1]

The views of two men of such unchallengeable authority in their respective provinces of learning cannot be lightly brushed aside.

Another thing that needs to be said is that this method of handling the Scriptures cannot by any stretch of charity be reconciled with a true reverence. We are familiar of course with the position that the Bible must submit to the same critical tests as are applied to other kinds of literature. And in a certain sense this is no doubt a reasonable demand—although it should not be forgotten that the claims of the Bible to be something radically *different* from ordinary literature have been made good at the bar of history and of the religious

[1] *The Evangelical Quarterly*, October 1929.

consciousness of mankind throughout the ages. But leaving out of account meantime the question of Inspiration in the Biblical sense of that term; setting aside also, in particular, the significance of the fact that the Lord, in calling Jeremiah, put His words in the young prophet's mouth; renouncing in short for the moment every claim to differential treatment on the ground of supernatural considerations, both as to the origin and the preservation of the Scriptures, it remains unquestionably true that the kind of criticism to which reference has been made denies to the Bible the ordinary decencies of respect that are due to any kind of reputable literature.[1] Sir George Adam Smith deplores the activities of later writers who added to Jeremiah's original words, especially in the closing part of the Book. "How pathetic," he exclaims, "that even after his death he is not spared from spoiling, but that the last clear streams of his prophesying must run out, as we have seen, in the sands of those expanders."[2] The present writer confesses his ignorance of those industrious corrupters of Jeremiah's work. But he does know about a class of spoilers who are not expanders, but mutilators. They do not as a rule add to the prophet's words, but they take away from them. They cut and tear the text of the sacred oracles with a ruthlessness which can only be compared to the methods of Jehoiakim when he used his pen-knife so freely on Jeremiah's original roll. This, one ventures to say, is the real tragedy, for which the eminent scholar just quoted might well have reserved his exclamation of distress—Jeremiah is being "sawn asunder" in these modern days by the hand of a daringly irreverent criticism.

But his words endure in the energy of an imperishable

[1] The following are examples of the spirit in which Criticism sometimes approaches Jeremiah: "The oracle against Moab (xlviii.), besides being unpardonably diffuse, is essentially an imitation of the old oracle preserved in Isaiah xv., xvi." (Prof. J. E. M'Fadyen, *Old Testament Introduction*, p. 152); "The introduction 1-3a is an unintelligible piece of writing, and is evidently the result of repeated and careless editing" (Dr John Skinner, *Prophecy and Religion*, p. 98).

[2] *Op. cit.*, p. 316.

life, and his message has lost nothing of its timeliness with the passing of the generations. It is a message which the world would do well to ponder in this Twentieth Century. Jeremiah's teaching about sin, for example, is sorely needed in an age when the sense of guilt has well-nigh ceased to trouble the consciences of men. In days too when the note of judgment has to a large extent disappeared from the message of the pulpit, and God is represented as an indulgent Father, who is too good-natured to " mark iniquity " on the part of nations or individuals, we need to listen anew to the voice which proclaimed with such unwavering fidelity the holiness and righteousness of the Divine character. And perhaps our greatest need of all is that Jeremiah's doctrine of the New Covenant should be really understood and accepted by men, in a time when " another gospel " which speaks of salvation on the basis of character and of service is taking the place of the old evangel of the free grace of God.

I

THE MAKING OF A PROPHET[1]

JEREMIAH'S Call to the prophetic office has already been discussed in the opening pages of this volume. There it was considered in its immediate bearing on the young prophet's commission. In its main elements, however, Jeremiah's experience was by no means unique, but is shared to some extent by all God's servants. The same intimations of the Divine purpose ; the same authoritative commands ; the same heartening assurances ; and—not infrequently—the same hesitations in assuming the burden of responsibility which the heavenly vision implies—these are features which, with varying degrees of definiteness, are reproduced in the history of all those whom the Lord calls to the work of His kingdom. We shall therefore go over the brief, pregnant story again, and meditate for a little on the light which it casts on the processes which go to the making of a prophet.

I

FIRST OF ALL, WE RECALL THAT THE WORD OF THE LORD WHICH CAME TO JEREMIAH REVEALED TO HIM THE FACT THAT HE WAS A PREDESTINED MAN.—" Before I ever formed thee in the belly I knew thee, and before thou camest forth out of the womb I sanctified thee and I ordained thee a prophet to the nations"—this was the amazing communication which, by some mysterious channel, made its way into the young man's soul. God, he was told, had thought of him, and cared for him, and planned for him, before " He fashioned star or sun." As this fact became clear to his consciousness,

[1] i. 2-10.

many experiences of his earlier years would no doubt be invested with a new meaning for him. The outward circumstances which had shaped his course; the influences which had contributed to the formation of his character and to the development of his powers; the inner conflicts of his soul; the secret impulses of his heart; the very frustrations and repressions under which his spirit may sometimes have chafed—all would become luminous as indications of the controlling hand of God. It was indeed an overwhelming revelation of the Divine plan. Like a very different character in literature, and with an entirely opposite meaning inherent in the words, Jeremiah might say, "The spell of my creation is read backwards."

We must believe that this fact, in its essential features, holds good with regard to all God's servants in the world. "There is," says Miguel Unameno, the foremost man of letters in Spain to-day, "a certain characteristic common to all those whom we call geniuses or great men and other heroes. Each of them has a consciousness of being a man apart, chosen very expressly by God for the performance of certain work." [1] The saying is specially true of those who are chosen for the work of Christ's kingdom, and in its widest sense it applies to the whole company of believers. The Lord "knew" them from of old with a personal, distinguishing knowledge, and "ordained" them to their special tasks in His kingdom. When they do appear in the world, they may be long unconscious of their appointed mission. But with ceaseless care He shapes their earthly course, and directs the happenings of their life to the fulfilment of His purpose. And one day He calls them by His grace, and reveals to them their destiny. It is a day of far-extending illumination, which casts new light on many a strange experience, and gives rise to many a moving reflection. Above all, there is the thought of the everlasting love of God, and of the mysteriousness of His working in the lives of His people.

[1] Quoted in Miss J. T. Stoddart's *Great Lives Divinely Planned.*

Ere suns and moons could wax and wane,
Ere stars were thundergirt, or piled
The Heavens, God thought on me His child;
Ordained a life for me, arrayed
Its circumstances, every one
To the minutest . . .

Among the many temptations which agitated the soul of John Bunyan there was scarcely any that was more distracting than the fear that he was "too late for salvation"; so tossed was he with the tempest, indeed, that he was "scarce able to take one step more." But one day these words broke in on his mind with comforting power, "Yet there is room." "These words," he says, "were sweet words to me; for truly I thought that by them I saw there was place enough in heaven for me; and, moreover, that when the Lord Jesus did speak these words, He then did think of me; and that He, knowing that the time would come that I should be afflicted with fear that there was no place left for me in His Bosom, did before speak this word, and leave it upon record, that I might find peace from this vile temptation. . . . And the comfort was the more, when I thought *that the Lord Jesus should think on me so long ago*, and that He should speak these words on purpose for my sake."

In Bunyan's heart, too, the word which brought deliverance in the hour of sore distress gave rise to the thought of that "long ago" in which the love of his Saviour made provision for his need. And this reminds us of the message of abounding grace which Jeremiah himself was commissioned, on behalf of the Lord, to speak to his disloyal countrymen, "Yea, I have loved thee with an everlasting love; therefore with loving kindness have I drawn thee."

II

THE SECOND FACT TO BE NOTED IN CONNECTION WITH JEREMIAH'S CALL IS HIS OWN INITIAL RELUCTANCE TO FACE THE UNDERTAKING TO WHICH HE WAS SUMMONED.—At once he pleaded his youthful inexperience and his lack of the gift of speech which seemed necessary for the worthy discharge of the prophetic ministry. He was under no misapprehension as to the magnitude of the task which lay before him, even before its specific character had been revealed in the terms of his commission. Already he would have been well aware of the religious condition of the nation—how it was abandoned to idolatry and sunk in moral corruption; how priests and prophets, nobles and people, had all forsaken the living God. It was no easy road along which he was being asked to travel; it was indeed not difficult to foresee that a faithful prophet would be reviled and hated, and doomed to a life of loneliness and pain in the midst of such an apostate community. And Jeremiah was not naturally inclined to face so arduous and menacing an enterprise. He was constitutionally timid in disposition and sensitive in spirit, a gentle, tender-hearted man, with keen emotional sensibilities and little aptitude for controversy or strife. In any case when he looked at the task which confronted him on the one hand, and at the poverty of his own resources on the other, his first response was a short, sharp cry, at the heart of which we find the words "I cannot."

Many a time a similar reluctance has been manifested by the servants of God when first they heard His call. Especially has this been true in the case of men who were confronted with lofty and difficult undertakings, men, for example, who were summoned from obscurity to be deliverers of their people from civic oppression, or to be leaders in a work of religious reformation, or crusaders for their Lord against particular forms of social unrighteousness. Their first answer to the Divine call has been some kind of "I cannot." Not because they were indifferent to the claims of God's work, or unconscious of the honour which His service involved; it was in reality far from their hearts to be disobedient to God's call. Their shrinking was due to their lofty conception of the Divine commission on the one hand, and to their deep sense of personal unworthiness on the other. A right-hearted man cannot take up the work of the Christian ministry, for example, as one sets oneself to learn a trade or qualify for a profession. "No man taketh this honour unto himself but he that is called of God . . ."; and even when the call comes, the honour seems too overwhelming to be readily accepted. This is why the Lord has to thrust forth labourers into His harvest. Many indeed are ready to run who have not been sent, but those who are sent have sometimes to be impelled along the path of obedience by the constraints of an unchallengeable necessity.

And it is no doubt expedient that this should be the case. It is the worker who is most conscious of his own unfitness for the task that is also most dependent on the power of God for success. His weakness is a channel through which the Divine energy flows, and through which, accordingly, the Divine Name is glorified.

III

THE THIRD FACT OF GENERAL SIGNIFICANCE WHICH CALLS FOR ATTENTION IN CONNECTION WITH JEREMIAH'S CALL IS THE PREPARATION WHICH HE RECEIVED FOR HIS PROPHETIC WORK.—There were three distinct elements which entered into his equipment.

First of all, there was the Divine word of command: "Thou shalt go to all that I shall send thee, and whatsoever I shall command thee thou shalt speak." This was God's answer to Jeremiah's reasons for declining his appointment. It was an answer which brooked no kind of evasion. There were no bounds to the places to which he might be sent, and no restrictions with regard to the words which he might be asked to speak. Here was a decree which was charged with the authority of the Lord. It therefore demanded unquestioning obedience, and made an end of controversy.

There are men engaged in the Lord's work to-day because the "Thou shalt" of Heaven made itself in their conscience with a power which could not be gainsaid. Necessity has been laid on them to declare the Word of the Lord. They are bound to the horns of the altar with the cords of a loving but imperious obligation. Various are the means which may have to be used before the waverer is induced to yield to the Divine constraining; certainly the making of a prophet sometimes means a long and painful process. The discipline of Providence must do its work of conquest and severance before his early reluctance is overcome; the fires of suffering must fulfil their purifying ministry before he becomes a serviceable instrument for the Master's hand. One thinks, for example, of the devoted service of Josephine Butler on behalf of fallen women, and of her fearless crusade against the State regulation of vice—how she toiled in the work-houses and gaols of Liverpool, even to the extent of picking oakum with the unfortunate sisterhood of iniquity and crime, and how her clear, strong voice rang out in denunciation of social impurity established by decree, until it awakened the conscience of the nation. And then one recalls the tragic experience which lay behind that noble ministry, and gave it passion and direction and strength: the sudden death of a little child in the midst of domestic rejoicings; the pain and the desolation which followed that bewildering stroke; and then the vision of the way of peace—she must go out, she said, to find some pain keener than her own, to meet people more unhappy than herself. So it was with the cry of her dying child sounding in her ears that she went forth to her Christ-like task. And Josephine Butler is but one among a great company who have had to tread the wine-press of suffering in order to reach God's harvest-field. Sometimes it needs an urge no less insistent than the pain of a breaking heart to open a prophet's lips, and to transform the "I cannot" of perplexity and fear into the "I will" of lofty and courageous resolve.

And although the initial cost may be heavy, the gain in after years is incalculable. The man who goes out to his work because God will not let him remain at home is not likely to turn back when once he has put his hand to the plough. He knows, too, the joy of God's secret inspirations, and that enables him to set his task to the music of a song.

Sorrow is hard to bear, and doubt is slow to clear,
  Each sufferer says his say, his scheme of the weal and the woe ;
But God has a few of us whom He whispers in the ear ;
  The rest may reason and welcome : 'tis we musicians know.

In the second place there was the Divine word of promise. Jeremiah was given the assurance that God was behind him in his strenuous ministry. The sending and the commanding were both from Him, and so the prophet was to be under direct orders from his Lord. He was to be an ambassador of the King of Heaven, with whom the final responsibility for the success of his mission must lie. And the Lord was not only behind him, but was also to be *with* him in the discharge of his tasks. " Be not afraid of their faces," came the inspiring assurance, " for I am with thee to deliver thee."

Be not afraid of *their faces*. This was an encouragement which was specially adapted to the young man's inward fears. He was as yet untried in the business of public speaking, and shrank from the ordeal of conveying an unpalatable message to an undisciplined and turbulent people. Even men with a long experience of public discussion have often to fight down the fear which springs from the thought of the faces of their hearers, especially when they have to plead on behalf of an unpopular cause. The faces which confront a speaker may be a real inspiration to him ; they are so responsive to his message that they draw forth the best that he has to give. On the other hand, they may send a chill through his heart, and be a source of embarrassment and confusion. For even when there is no outward manifestation of disapproval, the face may be eloquent of dissent. It may register the blankness of sheer boredom, or wear the expression of scorn and resentment, or—and this is often harder to bear than any direct opposition—it may speak the biting language of ridicule. The promise given to Jeremiah was a pledge that the faces of his hearers would never cause his voice to falter in declaring the word of the Lord. In spite of his natural timidity, he proved himself worthy to receive in full measure the tribute which many centuries later was paid to another eminent servant of God: he "never feared *the face of man.*"

In the third place, there was the Divine communication of power. The Lord touched Jeremiah's lips, and thereby endowed him with the gift of prophetic speech. "Behold I have put my words in thy mouth," He said, in explanation of this significant action. Thus was the prophet furnished for the demands of his vocation. All the natural disabilities of which he was conscious were removed, and he was made a fit medium through which God would speak to the men of his generation.

The Lord still encourages His servants with gracious promises, and equips them for the duties of their high calling as they put their hand to His work. "Lo, I am with you alway," He says to the preachers of His word as they go forth at His bidding "into all the world." He anoints them, too, with His Holy Spirit, and there lies the secret of any true success they may achieve. Usually a man is ordained to the work of the ministry by the laying on of the hands of his brethren, but the supreme requisite of spiritual achievement is the touch of the hand of the Lord both on the heart and on the lips. When that quickening contact takes place the preacher will not only have a message to deliver, but freedom of utterance in making it known. This is the true "grace of Orders."

IV

LAST OF ALL, WE FIND IN JEREMIAH'S CALL A DISCLOSURE OF THE PARTICULAR NATURE OF HIS MISSION.—It was to be *extensive in its range*, embracing not only his own country, but all nations and kingdoms—Egypt, Ammon, Moab, Tyre and Sidon. It was to be *destructive in its immediate purpose*. His commission directed him in the first instance "to root out, and to pull down, and to destroy, and to throw down." This means that primarily Jeremiah was to be a prophet of Judgment both to his own people and to the heathen nations. There were evil growths of idolatrous worship that had to be rooted out, strongholds of error and pride that had to be pulled down, and poisonous things of impurity and vice that must be destroyed. Jeremiah must declare that the wrath of God is revealed from Heaven against all such ungodliness and unrighteousness of men. But his mission was to be *restorative in its ultimate aim.* He was also " to build, and to plant." The end of his activities was to be the reconstruction of the Church of God in the land, so that, in a purified nation, the fruits of righteousness might take the place of the evil growths of iniquity.

These three elements have a permanent place in the Lord's commission to His servants. The range of the Gospel ministry is as extensive as the world ; its immediate design is revolutionary ; but its ultimate purpose is constructive, for it means nothing less than the building of the Kingdom of God among the ruins of a world that has been turned upside down through the energy of the Divine Word. This is surely a lofty vocation. Who would not covet a share in its far-reaching ministries ? To sow the seeds of eternal life in a guilty soul, to plant the trees of righteousness in the wilderness of social corruption, so that, to some extent at least, the lost Paradise may be regained through grace in this sin-stricken world—that is one of the highest honours that God can confer on mortal men.

II

THE SPRING-TIME OF THE RELIGIOUS LIFE

FOLLOWING Jeremiah's call to office there came to him a communication from God which may be regarded as an Introduction to the whole body of his prophecies. As we have already seen, His message for the most part was to be stern with the note of judgment. The apostasy of the people, with its attendant corruptions, must be fearlessly denounced, and the punishment of their disloyalty must be faithfully declared. But the preface to these oracles of woe is radiant with the " most benignant grace " of God, and reveals to us the loving-kindness and compassion that lay behind all the warnings and threatenings which He found it necessary to address to His unfaithful children. "*I remember thee,*" He declares, "*the kindness of thy youth, the love of thine espousals, when thou wentest after Me in the wilderness, in a land that was not sown. Israel was holiness unto the Lord, and the first-fruits of His increase.*" [1] In these arresting words we find :

I. A TENDER RECOLLECTION OF ISRAEL'S SPIRITUAL YOUTH

God is calling to the remembrance of His people the beginnings of their religious history, and the description which He gives of that early dawn forms a singularly attractive picture. When men are advanced in years memory is often inclined to cast a glamour over the days of youth. In retrospect they seem to be days of almost unclouded happiness, when the sky was always blue, and the air was always warm, and the flowers were always in bloom. But what we have in this passage is

[1] ii. 2, 3.

not an instance of the tendency of men to idealise their own past. It is not man who is speaking at all, but God, and God is recalling the Spring-time of His people's life, and describing it as it appears to Him after many days.

He speaks of the Kindness of their youth. The reference is not to the kindness which He had shown to them, but to the kindness which they had manifested to Him. It is the warmth of attachment evoked by His gracious dealings, the generous disposition created by the revelation of His love. They had experienced at His hand a great deliverance. He had brought them out from the misery and the degradation of the land of Egypt, and thereby had exhibited both His mercy and His power. The mystery of the sheltering blood, the miracle of the Red Sea, the gladness of their song as they stood in safety on the further shore and realised that they were no longer slaves but men—all this marvellous sequence of events was still fresh in their memory. And all of it, they were well aware, was the doing of the Lord. That almost incredible Exodus was the outcome of His gracious intervention. So when they thought on their indebtedness to their Deliverer their hearts went out to Him in a great rush of kindness.

He speaks, too, of the Love of their espousals. In the heart of Israel on that memorable day there was not only a consciousness of deliverance but a sense of high privilege, arising from the new relation to Himself in which their Lord had placed them. He had made with them a gracious Covenant, and thereby had betrothed them to Himself for ever. And it was no mere external alliance, this new relationship. It was a union which rested on mutual love, and was therefore intimate and tender. The Lord was giving Himself to them in all the riches of His grace and all the wealth of His resources, pledging Himself to guide and sustain and bless them throughout the coming years ; and they were giving themselves to Him in unconditional surrender to His claims and whole-hearted dedication to His service. Israel in that day became the Bride of God, and her heart was filled with love, and her face was radiant with happiness.

He also speaks of the Loyalty in which their love expressed itself. They followed Him into the wilderness, and made light—this at least is the implication of the words—of the difficulties of that inhospitable region. It was "a land that was not sown," a barren, trackless waste, where they suffered weariness and hunger and thirst. But love gave them courage and endurance, and they pressed on in the steps of their Divine Leader.

And, finally, He speaks of the Holiness which was the fruit of their obedience. On that glad bridal day Israel was wholly consecrated to her Lord. Her heart was a sanctuary in which His image was enshrined. Her face was a mirror which reflected His beauty. She was the first-fruits of His increase, garnered with peculiar delight and treasured with special care, as the earnest of that inheritance which was to be the harvest of His redemptive toil. And as she was holy, so He was at pains to keep her inviolate, separating her from the world and hedging her about with His protecting might, that she might be His own undivided possession.

Kindness, love, loyalty, holiness—it was indeed a vision of appealing beauty that rose before the mind of God as He recalled the promise of that far-off day. And how poignant the remembrance must have been when He knew that the picture represented but the tender grace of a day that was dead, and would never come back to Him, at least in its original splendour!

II. A Moving Revelation of the Heart of God

In the things which He recalls in the history of His people the Lord is unveiling His own character to our view. He shows us, for example, that when He remembers His children, He thinks of them at their best. It is the time when their love was warm, and their loyalty was strong, and their life was fruitful, that He delights to dwell on, not their seasons of unfaithfulness and decay. He passes over the dark days, and lets His thoughts rest on the days when their sky was without a cloud. For His present purpose it is not their failings that He sets before their face, but their attainments. And in so emphasising the kindness of His people's love, He is revealing the graciousness of His own.

He shows us, in addition to this, that when He remembers them at their best, He forms a generous estimate even of those worthiest moments of their experience. We know—for the fact is writ large over their whole history—that Israel's kindness to her Lord was mingled with a great deal of churlishness, that her loyalty was marred by many lapses, and that her holiness was disfigured by many blemishes. She often murmured and complained in the day of adversity, and manifested an ungrateful and rebellious spirit. But God's assessment of her qualities is the generous evaluation of love. He pities them with the affectionate compassion that is stored in a Father's heart.

In human life we know how a father remembers his child as his mind goes back across the years, and the boy stands before him again, summoned to "the sessions of sweet silent thought." He sees him in the freshness and beauty of his youth, with the light of the morning on his face. He thinks of the days when the child looked up to him with trustful eyes, and ran with ready feet to do his slightest bidding. He recalls every act of devotion, and treasures every word of affection. Little nameless incidents of everyday life they may in reality have been, but they are transfigured by a loving memory into things of priceless value. There is a moving little story of a mother whose son made slight excursions into the realm of poetry. During his lifetime the good woman, in a half-disparaging tone, used to refer to his efforts as "verses." But when he passed away—for he died when still young—the things he had written were no longer called "verses": they became "poems." The generous appreciation of love invested them with a new dignity. Israel's "first works" were poems in the eyes of her God.

Our gracious Lord is never niggardly in His estimates, or grudging in His praise. He places a value on the character and work of His children which goes far beyond either their expectations or their deserts. One thinks, for example, of Christ's tribute to Mary of Bethany on the occasion when she anointed His feet with her precious ointment. First of all, He put a generous construction on her loving deed. "She hath anointed my body for the burial," He said. Christ read into her homage a deep and spacious meaning, which beautified and ennobled it beyond her own recognition. Mary had done what she could; but how generous was her Lord's interpretation of her best. And then how magnificent was the recognition with which He repaid her kindness. He linked her action to His own redemptive work in a bond so intimate that the record of it goes ringing down the ages "wheresoever this Gospel shall be preached in the whole world." He credited her with seeking to embalm His body for the tomb; He recompensed her by making her deed of kindness a means of embalming her own name for ever.

And it is not in this world alone that He invests the attainments of His followers with a generous significance; His highest commendations and recompenses are reserved for the world to come. In His day of final reckoning He will dower the humblest service rendered for His sake with a surpassing dignity, and will reward it with a crown of glory. "Come, ye blessed of My Father," He will say, "inherit the Kingdom prepared for you before the foundation of the world. For I was an hungered and ye gave Me meat. . . ." And when they, in humble renunciation, cast their crowns at His feet, because they fail to recognise their own simple acts of kindness under the transfiguration of His grace, He will make plain to them His meaning, and reaffirm His judgment: "Inasmuch as ye did it to one of the least of these My brethren," He will answer, "ye did it unto Me."

In this matter of appreciation we are surely called upon to be imitators of God. It often comes easy to us to indulge in disparagement and detraction, but the more excellent way is to form generous estimates of our fellow-men. It is a more Christian thing to remember them in those moments

> When the spirit's true endowments
> Stand out plainly from its false ones,

than to recall the hours when achievement falls tragically short of aspiration. For if our judgment is determined by the charities of the Gospel, we shall believe that the heights to which a man is capable of rising are a fairer criterion of his worth than the depths to which he sometimes descends.

We should further bear in mind that in His recollections of Israel's youth God also shows us the things on which He sets most store in the life of His children. It is not the abundance of their sacrifices that He loves to remember, or their diligence in attending to the outward observances of religion. It is the homage of loving hearts, the obedience of consecrated lives. It is, in a word, the inner side of the religious life that He cherishes, rather than its outward forms. There is something deeply moving in the fact that God makes mention of the "kindness" of His children to Himself. He does not despise the simple ministries which reveal the warmth of their hearts. On the contrary He values beyond computation the thoughts and the words and the deeds which bear the stamp of love to His Name. And so the startling pronouncement of Rabbi Ben Ezra may not, after all, be far wide of the mark:

> Thoughts hardly to be packed
> Into a narrow act,
> Fancies that broke through language and escaped;
> All I could never be,
> All, men ignored in me,
> This, I was worth to God, whose wheel the pitcher shaped.

For, above everything else, it is the love of men's hearts that the Lord desires, and for the lack of that love there can be no compensation.

III. An Urgent Appeal to an Unfaithful People

There is nothing that stands out more clearly from the passage we are considering than that the love of God is wounded by the apostasy of His covenant people, and that His heart is yearning over them still. It is in order that they may consider their present position that He puts them in remembrance of their past. The kindness of Israel's youth has now faded; the love of her espousals has grown cold; she is no longer a faithful bride; the glory of her purity has given place to corruption. And He reminds her of the happy days of her youth in order that her conscience may be awakened, and her heart may be quickened; and she may come back once more to Himself in contrition and new obedience.

"What iniquity have your fathers found in Me," He asks, "that they are gone far from Me. . . ?" It is an affecting question: the love of God constrains Him to reason with men in patient expostulation. And the question is followed by a not less moving narrative—the story of how He had brought them *out* of the land of Egypt, and had led them *through* the wilderness, and had brought them at last *into* a plentiful country. The narrative in turn is succeeded by an indictment of the nation for their manifold transgressions, and then comes the crowning part of the appeal. Forth from the very heart of this record of Divine goodness and human iniquity there issue words which announce the resolve of God to follow on in His merciful pursuit of His erring children. "Wherefore," He declares, "I will yet plead with you . . . and with your children's children will I plead." Truly He is a God who "hateth putting away."

IV. An Abiding Message for the Followers of Christ

The Christian Church has had her own Spring-time of spiritual warmth and fruitfulness. One recalls, for example, the great days which followed the miracle of

Pentecost. Then indeed she looked "forth as the morning, fair as the moon, clear as the sun, and terrible as an army with banners." The warmth of her love to God was reflected in the mutual kindness which prevailed among her own members. They were of one heart and mind, and had all things in common. They followed the Lord with unflinching courage in the face of revilings and scourgings and imprisonments, rejoicing that they were counted worthy to suffer shame for His sake; they did many mighty works, too, in the power of His Spirit. But ere long the brightness of the morning began to fade into the light of common day. We have only to read the Epistles to the Seven Churches of Asia to learn how far the tide of spiritual attainment had receded before the death of the Apostle John. Ephesus has left its first love, and has therefore ceased from its first works. Laodicea is wretched and miserable and poor and blind and naked. In nearly all of them the leaven of erroneous doctrines and evil practices is doing its corrupting work. And the Lord is not silent with regard to these defections. As in the days of Jeremiah long before, He summons His unfaithful people to repent and return unto Himself, and His call is accompanied by a warning that continued disobedience will result in the removal of His candlestick from their midst. The Churches of Asia failed to benefit by His message, and centuries ago the light they had went out.

At the Reformation again—to take but one other example—the Church of Christ in Europe renewed her youth, for then she experienced a fresh deliverance from bondage. There had been long ages when priest-craft exercised its baleful sway over her life, but in the great movement of the sixteenth century she returned to the purity of New Testament doctrine and worship, and, in the consciousness of restored freedom and power, manifested once more the kindness of her youth, and recaptured the joy of her espousals. Our own country in particular is, like Israel, a covenanted land. There were days when Scotland formally pledged her loyalty to

Christ, and proclaimed that the furtherance of His Cause was her highest mission in the world. To-day there is an ominous falling away from these high attainments. It would take too long here and now to discuss the causes and symptoms of this declension, but the main facts are sufficiently plain to every serious observer. But the old pleading call is still sounding forth from Heaven, and it is because the risen Christ is enthroned at the right hand of the Father in fulness of grace and power that His servants continue to deliver that call without losing hope.

The words we are considering have, of course, a special application to the individual soul. To some indeed who read these lines they may be a direct message from God. For there are believers for whom the kindness of their youth and the love of their espousals are at once a fragrant and a bitter memory. In a more or less definite form they had their day of deliverance, when they were set free from the bondage of sin and were made a new creation in Christ Jesus. Their feet were set on the Rock, and a new song was put in their mouth. It was a day of clear vision, of purified affections, of high resolves, and of bright hopes. For a time they followed the Lord fully and brought forth fruit to the praise of His Name. But there came another day when their love waxed cold, and their feet strayed from the path of obedience. Whatever the cause, there has been a sad declension. But the Lord who redeemed them and called them by His grace is grieving over their unfaithfulness. He remembers the tender grace of their spiritual youth, and pleads with them to return to their early allegiance. And to His merciful call He links a gracious promise. " I will heal their backsliding," He says, " I will love them freely." There is no more encouraging assurance than that within the whole range of the Bible.

III

THE FOUNTAIN AND THE CISTERNS

JEREMIAH'S denunciation of Israel's iniquities appropriately begins with an account of the root evils from which all their corruptions had sprung. The voice which speaks is still the voice of love, but as the recollection of past fidelity is followed by a survey of present unfaithfulness, the tenderness of the opening appeal inevitably gives place to a sterner note. There were two radical evils of which the nation had been guilty. "*My people,*" says the Lord, "*have committed two evils: they have forsaken Me the Fountain of living waters, and hewed them out cisterns, broken cisterns, that can hold no water.*"[1] This was an apostasy so astounding that He calls on the very heavens to be "astonished" at it, and to be "horribly afraid," and "very desolate." It was something too that had no parallel in human life. The heathen nations who bowed down to gods who were lacking in every attribute of deity, were more steadfast in their religious loyalty than God's Covenant people. "My people," He declares, "have changed their glory for that which doth not profit." The direct reference of the words is of course to Israel, but they may be said to embrace within the compass of a single sentence the history of a sinful world.

The two evils complained of in the indictment are the departure of men from the living God and their endeavour to replace Him by resorting to earthly satisfactions. The first of these offences sets forth their guilt; the second describes the folly which is both the fruit and the aggravation of their apostasy. The substitute is not an equivalent; the cisterns cannot take the place of the

[1] ii. 13.

Fountain; hence the misery and disappointment which are inseparable from a godless life.

I

Let us think first of all of the evil of forsaking the Fountain. It is God Himself who is represented by this beautiful and suggestive figure. It speaks of the "absolute existence, the essential, independent, necessary being" of God. And as He has "life in Himself," so He is the source of life to all created things. By Him all things were made that are in Heaven and that are in earth. From Him in particular is derived the physical, intellectual and spiritual life of men. One thinks of ceaseless streams of creative energy flowing forth from the unfathomable depths of the being of God. And as He is the source of life so is He also the Fountain of Love. The Creator of men is the Divine Lover of their souls. He is the God who so loved the world that He gave His only begotten Son that whosoever believeth in Him should not perish but have everlasting life. He is a God of infinite goodness who is continually pouring out His gifts on the children of men. His mercy is a great deep; His compassion exceeds all our human calculations; His grace stoops to the lowest depths of our need.

The life with which He endowed the children of men in the beginning was in reality an outflow of His own. For He created man in His own image—in the beauty of holiness, with pure thoughts, warm affections, and lofty desires; in fulness of knowledge also, with clearness of spiritual vision and keenness of moral perception; and, not less surely, in wealth of happiness, for the waters of the Fountain were unspeakably gladdening. But the departure of men from God meant the deliberate forsaking of all this blessedness which the Fountain represents. In making such a statement one of course proclaims oneself to be old-fashioned enough to believe in the Fall of man, and also to regard that event as a Fall downwards and not upwards. And that first apostasy has many a time been repeated in the history of our race. The particular charge which Jeremiah brings against Israel is, of course, their idolatry. They had forsaken the worship of the living God and were bowing down before stocks and stones " upon every high hill and under every green tree." The most highly favoured nation under heaven had been guilty of the grossest treachery. They had been planted a noble vine—Jeremiah adopts a variety of figures to set forth the tragic fact—but had turned into a degenerate, barren plant. And this religious unfaithfulness had been accompanied by a scarcely less heinous form of practical disloyalty. They not only rendered homage to the gods of the heathen ; in their times of need they invoked the help of the heathen. " What," asks the prophet," hast thou to do in the way of Egypt, to drink the waters of Sihor, or what hast thou to do in the way of Assyria, to drink the waters of the river ? " Too often in hours of national emergency had Israel trusted in the arm of flesh instead of putting her confidence in the God who had done such mighty works on her behalf in the days of old. In this respect also she had forsaken the Fountain and resorted to the broken cistern.

And down through the generations since then the offence of Israel has continually been repeated. " All we like sheep have gone astray ; we have turned every one to his own way "—Isaiah's familiar words are an epitome of human history. Round about us every day there are multitudes of men and women who have no place for God in their scheme of life. They are separated from the Fountain, passing their days without the inspirations or the hopes of religion, immersed in the cares and the pleasures of this passing world. And this alienation from God is an evil thing. It involves rebellion against His will, as well as ingratitude for His abundant mercies. It also means, in a profound sense, the death of the soul. Separation from the Fountain carries with it not only guilt but spiritual corruption. " Out of the heart " in which God does not dwell—let us listen to the testimony of the faithful and true Witness—" proceed evil thoughts, murders, adulteries, fornications, thefts, false witness, blasphemies." Beyond question it is an evil thing to forsake the Fountain of living waters.

II

The second evil of which Jeremiah speaks is the sin of choosing the broken cisterns in place of the living Fountain, the sin, that is, of substituting the creature for the Creator, of preferring earthly satisfactions to the delights of fellowship with God. Some object of trust and desire we must have, and when that object is not God, we are under the necessity of creating one of our own. This is, of course, an aggravation of the original offence; it means the setting up of a rival to God in the allegiance of our heart and life, and for that reason constitutes nothing less than an insult to the majesty of Heaven. Apart from this root iniquity, however, there are fundamental differences between the cisterns and the Fountain which may serve to illustrate the evil of substituting the one for the other.

To begin with, *the Fountain is one, while the cisterns are many.* There is one living and true God, but there are many false gods. There is no need for more than a single Fountain, because its living waters are sufficient to meet all the needs of humanity. The thirst of the understanding for truth, the longing of the heart for love, the cry of the conscience for peace, all those deep necessities of sinful men—and they are essentially the same among every race and tribe on the face of the earth—find a satisfying answer in the God of our salvation. But the cisterns need to be multiplied, because none of them is deep enough to answer the call which rises from that other deep of a human personality. The unity of the Godhead is an evidence of its absolute perfection. The variety of the world's idols is an equally convincing proof of their inadequacy. The devotees of mammon worship at many shrines, and the lovers of pleasure serve innumerable masters. Not all the cisterns in the world can take the place of the living Fountain ; not all the rivals of God in the allegiance of men can be His equal.

For another thing, *the Fountain is always open, but the cisterns must be hewed out.* The everlasting God is " not far off from every one of us." The bounties of His Providence are lavished upon men with impartial kindness, and the blessings of His salvation are equally free to all who are willing to become debtors to His grace. But the efforts of men to find a substitute for God involve ceaseless toil and an endless quest. Jeremiah, like his predecessor Isaiah, lashes his apostate countrymen with a biting irony because of the labour which they wasted on the making of their idols. The energy expended by the workman in cutting down a tree with his axe, of the carpenter as he fixes it in its place with nails and hammers, and of the skilled artificer as he decks the image with silver and gold—all this means sweat of brow and weariness of brain ; but, alas, it is labour in vain, for even when the gods of men's creation stand upright as the palm tree, they " speak not : they must needs be borne, because they cannot go ! " And this is but a figure of the toil and the weariness of a godless life. The world is a hard taskmaster, and pleasure is an insatiable exactor. The pursuit of earthly success, the scramble for position, the race for wealth, with all the competition and rivalry, " the weariness, the fever, and the fret " which these involve, are in truth a particularly debasing form of slavery. The builder of the cisterns is doomed to a life of ceaseless hewing ; his hammer and chisel can never be long out of his hand. It would not be difficult to prove that an upright life takes less toll of mind and body than the efforts required of a man who has a distaste for honest work and seeks to live by his wits.

Once more, *the Fountain is always full, while the cisterns can hold no water*. The workmanship of the God-forsaking hewer is defective. His efforts at the best can produce only a broken cistern, a cracked and leaking tank, which cannot serve its intended purpose, and therefore renders all his labour of no avail. He may pour water continually into it, but as continually it runs out again, and the cistern is left empty. This is an element in the prophet's figure which points to the folly of the irreligious life. The guilt involved in hewing out the cisterns is accentuated by the futility of the procedure. It is not only an evil but a bitter thing to forsake the living God. This is a fact which is amply verified in human experience. A man hews out some kind of cistern for himself with much toil and care. He expects it to provide him with a constant supply of water, and for that reason to be a source of unfailing satisfaction to his heart. But he is doomed to disappointment, for sooner or later he finds that he has been putting his trust in a broken cistern. "Thou fool" was the description applied by Christ to the man who thought that he could supply the needs of his soul from the contents of his barn. Material possessions are a sorry provision for heart hunger. Earthly success cannot secure real happiness: "the dream of the reality" is often better than "the reality of the dream." Pleasure affords no balm for a wounded spirit. "Whosoever drinketh of this water shall thirst again."

The best commentary on Jeremiah's words is surely provided by the parable of the Prodigal Son—the story of the young man who forsook the living Fountain by turning his back on the love and happiness and ordered freedom of his Father's house, and "went into a far country." His attempt to find satisfaction in the broken cisterns of this new land turns out a tragic failure. Ere long his resources are exhausted, and the last cistern to which he turns is a swine-trough. There we find him—and through the grace of God he finds himself—a broken, lonely figure, sunk low in degradation and shame, and dying of hunger. Well was it for him that in that hour of bitter disillusionment he thought of the home he had so arrogantly forsaken, and said, "I will arise and go to my Father."

And although even the cisterns of legitimate human satisfaction often become empty, the Fountain of Divine comfort never fails. Earthly joys are proverbially transient; friends sometimes disappoint us when we need them most; loved ones are removed from our side when we least expect it; and, as the years go by, we are increasingly conscious that the roots of our life in this world are being pulled up. But Jesus Christ is the same yesterday, to-day, and for ever, and His consolations are not as waters that fail. In the hour of trouble He draws near us in loving-kindness, and His whispered "Fear not" makes music in our heart when strength had almost gone. How moving, for example, is this entry in the Diary of Dr Andrew Bonar at a time when the strokes of affliction were falling thick upon him: "Memorable to me as the anniversary of my beloved Isabella's departure to be with Christ. And now my son's son, a child of three days old, has been taken from them. Broken cisterns, broken cisterns all around; but the fountain remains full."

Finally, *the water of the Fountain is pure and life-giving: the water of the cisterns is foul and poisonous.* A drink from the one means life everlasting: a drink from the other is a "mortal taste" which brings death into the soul and many a woe. Let us hear Thomson's vigorous description, in *The Land and the Book*, of the broken cisterns which he actually saw in Palestine: "The best cisterns, even those in solid rock, are strangely liable to crack, and are a most unreliable source of supply of that absolutely indispensable article, water; and if, by constant care, they are made to hold, yet the water, collected from clay roofs or from marly soil, has the colour of weak soap-suds, the taste of the earth or the stable, is full of worms, and in the hour of greatest need it utterly fails. Who but a fool positive, or one gone mad in love of filth, would exchange the sweet, wholesome stream of a living fountain for such an uncertain mixture of nastiness and vermin?"

But in the spiritual domain there are multitudes who are so "mad in love of filth" that they prefer the draughts of "nastiness" to the wholesome waters of the Fountain. Familiarity with the taste of the earth and the stable soon creates a depraved appetite, so that pure water seems insipid in comparison with those more strongly flavoured mixtures. Intellectual enjoyments, for example—to say nothing of spiritual satisfactions—appear tame beside the pleasures of the senses, and solid, wholesome literature provides no thrill compared with that which is furnished by the fleshly type of fiction. The hewing out of the cisterns is an evil thing because it involves a perversion of the moral sensibilities of men.

III

Is there any remedy for this two-fold evil which Israel had committed? There surely is; and Jeremiah spent a great deal of his strength in directing the attention of the disloyal nation to its nature and its efficacy. It was through a return in penitence and new obedience to the Fountain which they had so lightly forsaken that they could look for healing of soul. This way of restoration is still more clearly set forth in the Gospel of the New Testament. Let us recall the ringing proclamation of Christ "on the last day of the Feast" in Jerusalem, when He stood and cried, "If any man thirst, let him come unto me and drink." In these arresting words He declares that He Himself is the Fountain of Life. In Him dwells all the fulness of the Godhead. To Him belong all the resources of power, all the riches of grace, and all the depths of compassion which belong to God, for the Father hath given all things into His hand. In Him the thirsty soul finds satisfaction for all its needs—pardon for guilt, cleansing for defilement, power for impotence, and comfort for loneliness and dejection. When we come unto Him in faith we are not only forgiven for our past iniquities, but are so healed and renewed in our whole being that we ourselves become a spring of blessing to others. Out of the believer's heart "shall flow rivers of living water."

There is an Eastern legend of a fountain into which at some time an angel had infused so mysterious a quickening power that when a few drops of its waters fell on a parched waste a new fountain gushed forth from the barren soil and transformed the desert into a place of fruitfulness and beauty. For that reason the traveller who possessed a portion of this living water could travel without fear through the widest and most arid wilderness, for he carried with him the secret of unfailing springs, and could minister, at the same time, to the needs of his companions on the way. It is, of course, nothing more than a fanciful story, yet it shadows forth the great spiritual reality which we have been considering. The man who drinks at the Fountain of Life not only attains to personal satisfaction of soul, but becomes himself a living spring, from which others derive quickening and refreshment.

Beneath the Cross those waters rise, and he who finds them there
All through the wilderness of life the living streams may bear ;
And blessings follow on his steps, until, where'er he goes,
The moral wastes begin to bud and blossom as the rose.

Who is this who so confidently affirms that He is able to satisfy all the needs of a human spirit—its unrest and fear, its desires and aspirations, its cries from the depths as well as its longings for the heights ? Surely there is but one answer to that question : " Thou art the King of glory, O Christ, Thou art the everlasting Son of the Father."

IV

AN APPEAL TO THE HEART

THE third chapter of the Book of Jeremiah forms one of the most moving pages in the whole volume of his prophecies. It is an appeal to the heart of an unfaithful people by a God whose love, indeed, has been wounded, but whose faithfulness to His Covenant engagements has never failed. In the background stands the appalling treachery of the entire nation. Israel had behind them a history of declension, the guilt of which was aggravated by a variety of circumstances. By an act of amazing condescension the Lord had entered into a gracious Covenant with them, although they were a people who had no inherent claim to such a distinguishing favour. It was a Covenant that, as has already been stated, involved mutual obligations. On His part there was the undertaking embodied in the words, "I will be your God." That assurance was the charter of incalculable privileges. It was a pledge that God would do for them all that Almighty power directed by infinite love was able to accomplish. On their side there was the promise of loyalty contained in the words, "Ye shall be my people" —words which not merely express the fact, but—coming from the mouth of God—impose the obligation of obedience. But Israel, as we know, failed to honour their bond. They departed from the living God, and abandoned themselves to idolatry and, as a result of that, to various forms of corrupt living. The sad story of their apostasy is summed up in the indictment which has formed the subject of the preceding chapter: "They have forsaken Me, the Fountain of living waters, and have hewed out for themselves cisterns, broken cisterns, that can hold no water."

But God did not annul His Covenant because of the treachery of His people. He did not give them "a bill of divorcement," and cast them off for ever. Instead of that, He used every endeavour to win them back to their former allegiance, mingling warnings directed to their conscience with appeals addressed to their heart. Year after year, day after day, He continues with unwearying persistency to remonstrate and to entreat. In the message we are now to consider, which belongs to the earlier period of Jeremiah's ministry, He plies them with invitations and promises, and by sheer tenderness of appeal seeks to rekindle within their fickle hearts the flame of a love that had long since waxed cold. "*Turn, O backsliding children . . . for I am married unto you. . . . Return . . . for I am merciful. . . . Return . . . and I will heal your backslidings.*"[1]—that is the constantly reiterated call. Truly He is a God whose compassions fail not, and from whose love neither life nor death can separate.

I

Believers often fail in loyalty to their God. For one reason or another they forsake the Rock of their strength, and live in a state of real, if not always visible, estrangement from Him. Sooner or later—because "the foundation of God standeth sure"—they will be brought back to their former allegiance, but not without grievous loss and pain. They forfeit that sense of freedom which is the heritage of the sons of God; they are bereft of the peace and the joy of salvation; they are shorn of their strength in the service of their Lord; and their whole spiritual life is impoverished and blighted. It may be a long time before they recover the lost ground, and it is possible indeed that they will go halting throughout the rest of their journey to the grave.

The immediate causes of backsliding are many, but, one and all, they have their roots in the deceitfulness of the human heart. God's announcement to Israel regard-

[1] iii. 14, 22.

ing the enemies who were to meet them in the land of promise has an abiding message for His people. "I will not," He said, "drive them out from before thee in one year. . . . By little and little I will drive them out, until thou be increased, and inherit the land." Believers must carry on a long warfare with indwelling sin in order to gain full possession of their inheritance, a warfare in which they must steadfastly refuse to make terms with the enemy. But, as Israel eventually entered into compromising arrangements with the foes whom they were enjoined to conquer and expel, so the children of God often fail to keep in subjection the corruptions which dwell in their own hearts. Sometimes it is the appeal of the world that lowers their spiritual temperature, and causes their sword to sleep in their hand—the deadweight of some hurtful companionship, the snare of some unhealthy amusement, or the lure of some selfish ambition. Or it may be the uprising of some old sin, which seeks to regain its former dominion over them. The beginnings of the assault may be insidiously gentle, but the end is an onset which breaks down the defences of the soul and brings it into captivity.

Occasionally, too, the declension may be due to a shortcoming of a somewhat different order. In the *Life* of C. T. Studd, one of the famous "Cambridge Seven," we are told that "for six years he had been a backslider." The reason for this falling away is given in his own words: "Instead of going and telling others of the love of Christ, I was selfish, and kept the knowledge to myself. The result was that gradually my love began to grow cold, and the love of the world began to come in. I spent six years in this unhappy backslidden state." This is a searching testimony. It reminds us that there is a silence which is disloyalty, and that there is an inactivity in Christ's service which brings leanness of soul. The flame of devotion, like the Bush in the desert, burns, and yet is not consumed, through the outflowing of love for the souls of others.

II

But whatever the cause may be, the backsliding of a believer in the Lord Jesus Christ is a spiritual tragedy. "Believers," said Rabbi Duncan once, "should live like restored princes"; it is one of the saddest spectacles under the sun, when like Samson in the hands of his enemies—

> Eyeless in Gaza, at the mill with slaves,
> Himself in bonds under Philistian yoke,

they degrade their sonship, and thereby dishonour their Lord. Of course, behind all outward causes, the declension must be traced to unwatchfulness of soul. There is no hour of the day, or of the night, when a Christian can afford to be off his guard. So deceitful is his own heart, and so insidious is the approach of temptation, that sometimes it is directly after an experience of the kindness of God that he falls into the snare of the devil. Emotional uplifting is often followed by an ebb-tide which brings to light not a few slimy and unsavoury things. Success, too, often leads to spiritual pride. Of course we must distinguish the lapse of one who is "overtaken in a fault" through temporary weakness, from the offence of one who follows a course of declension with deliberate persistency. But in any case the old familiar counsel is always a word in season: "Watch and pray lest ye enter into temptation."

How then shall we fortify our souls against a danger which is always imminent? In the recently published biography of Dr John R. Mott mention is made of certain great guiding principles which he has been in the habit of setting before young men for the strengthening of their Christian life. The first is, Burn the bridges behind you; that is, give up definitely everything that reason, conscience, and experience show to be questionable. The second is, Build up a life-habit of studying the Bible. Burn and Build—the soundness of these two complementary maxims cannot be questioned. There can be no security when we do not make a clean break with our sinful past; and no soul can maintain its health and strength which does not find in the Bible its daily bread. To these two principles a third may be added. More and more as the days and the years go by, realise your absolute indebtedness to the grace of God, and let your dependence find expression in the habit of prayer.

III

There are three main considerations with which the Lord reinforces His appeal to the heart of His unfaithful children. The first—"for I am married unto you"—is a reminder of their Covenant relationship to Himself. It proclaims the dignity of their standing as the chosen people of God, and aims at awakening within their souls the tender memories of the love of their espousals. They had been guilty of gross infidelity, but He remained faithful to the Covenant bond. And so He stands before them with hands that are outstretched in entreaty and words that glow with the fervour of an unchanging love.

This is a form of appeal which is still addressed to the backsliding Christian. To him also the figure of the marriage bond represents a great reality. In the day in which He puts his trust in the Lord Jesus Christ there is effected between him and his Saviour a spiritual union which death cannot sever. "They two," says Paul, speaking of the conjugal tie on the human plane, "shall be one flesh." "This," he adds, "is a great mystery, but I speak concerning Christ and the Church." And just as a man and his wife pledge their troth on their marriage day, so also in the hour of a soul's espousal to Christ there is a promise of mutual loyalty. On the one side, as we have seen, the covenant is often broken, but on the other it is kept inviolate throughout all the years. Christ betrothes His bride to Himself "in faithfulness," and as He takes her by the hand He declares—according to Weymouth's vivid rendering of the great promise in

Hebrews—"I will never, never let go your hand; I will never, never forsake you." Even "if we believe not," that is, if the exercise of our faith should temporarily be suspended, "He abideth faithful, He cannot deny Himself"; so runs one of the profoundest assurances in the New Testament. It means that our Lord cannot go back on His word without dishonouring His own Name; He cannot be false to us without at the same time being false to Himself. But unfaithful to any of His engagements He never will be. His promises are the "Yea" of everlasting certainty in Christ Jesus; His love is an undying flame; the Covenant of His peace will never be "removed" from the soul that has once been brought within its bond. And so His call to His backsliding children is, "Turn . . . for I am married unto you."

The second plea which is attached to the call has reference to the mercy of the Divine character. "Return . . . for I am merciful." This again is an affirmation which sounds a great deep. It is designed to meet the consciousness of guilt which springs up within the penitent soul. When the summons to repentance makes itself felt in the slumbering conscience, then is an awaking, more or less intense, to the fact that it is indeed "an evil thing" to have forsaken the living God. There follows the sense of fear which in some degree usually follows upon conviction of sin. Will the Lord cast off for ever the soul that has so shamefully dishonoured His Name? Will He receive the wanderer in the far country when he sets his face again on the Father's House? In the wrath which guilt deserves will He remember mercy? These are the questions with, for the time being, most insistently press for an answer. The answer is furnished by the gracious declaration which sounds forth from the lips of God, "I am merciful." It is a declaration in which deep calls unto deep. The mercy of God is the supreme attribute of His character, and especially His mercy to His disloyal people. It is this readiness to pardon until seventy times seven that constrained the prophet Micah long ago to place on His head the crown of pre-eminence. "Who," he exclaims, "is a God like unto Thee that . . . passeth by the transgression of the remnant of His heritage? He retaineth not His anger for ever, because He delighteth in mercy." In calling the transgressor to return, therefore, God offers him the encouragement of an abundant pardon.

The third consideration is a promise of spiritual renewal: "Return . . . and I will heal your backslidings." And here, beyond question, the grace of God reaches its highest manifestation. For there is perhaps nothing that seems more precious to the wanderer who, in coming to himself, realises that his departure from God involves corruption of soul, than the assurance of *healing*. It implies forgiveness, of course, but restoration of health is more than remission of guilt. It means the curing of disease and the renewal of life. It means that the lost energy is recovered, and the first love revived; that "the voice of rejoicing and salvation" is heard anew within the soul; that the perverse desires and inclinations are directed again towards the things that are lovely and of good report; that the palsied hand regains its strength, and the erring feet are established once more in the paths of righteousness. Beyond question the healing of a soul that has relapsed into the madness and folly of sin is one of the crowning mercies of the God of salvation.

IV

The answer of Israel to the Divine appeal has every appearance of genuine repentance. "*Behold,*" they cry, "*we come unto Thee, for Thou art the Lord our God.*" And following that resolve there are words which speak of sorrow, renunciation, and conscious shame. The event, however, too clearly proved that the penitence of this wayward people was superficial and short-lived. It did not issue in a reconsecrated life, and appears indeed to have been little more than a temporary emotional reaction. In themselves, however, the words describe the experience of a sincere repentance, and regarded in that light they are entitled to our earnest consideration.

First of all, it behoves us to remember the terms upon which God declares that He is ready to restore His backsliding children to His gracious favour. One stipulation, and only one, He lays down as a condition of reinstatement. That is a simple but honest confession of wrong-doing. " Only acknowledge thine iniquity that thou hast transgressed against the Lord thy God "—that is all that God requires. It is surely not an exacting demand. There is no word of reparation for the evil committed, no mention of any form of compensating penance. But here, as elsewhere throughout the Scriptures, God insists on confession as the pre-requisite of reconciliation.

And Israel, certainly, are represented as making the acknowledgment required. " We have sinned," they cry, " against the Lord our God." This admission, too, has in it the element of sorrow. " A voice was heard upon the high places "—notice how the scene of transgression becomes the place of repentance—" weeping and supplication of the children of Israel : for they have perverted their way. . . ." Confession in turn is followed by renunciation : " Truly in vain is salvation hoped for from the hills, and from the multitude of mountains." Every ground of earthly confidence, let it be as imposing in appearance as the mountains and the hills, is abandoned ; every source of creature satisfaction is forsaken ; in God alone is the hope of a penitent soul. And, lastly, renunciation is accompanied by a feeling of shame : " We lie down in our shame, and our confusion covereth us." Without doubt the language of Israel represents the actings of a whole-hearted return to God.

Confession, contrition, renunciation, shame—these, in a greater or less degree, are abiding elements in the experience of the penitent. It is more than possible that there are readers of these lines who have left their first love and failed in keeping covenant with their Lord. Well for them if they adopt the language of

Israel in more than mere lip profession. When the words are translated into corresponding action; that is, when they are followed by a return, in sorrow and shame, from the ways of transgression, the restoration which God so emphatically promises will surely become an accomplished fact.

V

THE LIKENESS OF A MAN

It was not only to the heart of Israel that Jeremiah's appeals were addressed in his effort to win them back to God ; he also strove to pierce their conscience with words that flamed in vehemence of denunciation and sternness of warning. Of this character is the message which we find in the opening words of the fifth chapter : " *Run ye to and fro through the streets of Jerusalem, and see now, and know, and seek in the broad places thereof, if ye can find a man, if there be any that executeth judgment, that seekest the truth ; and I will pardon it.*" [1] This is one of the most scathing passages in the prophet's whole exposure of the national iniquity ; it furnishes at the same time one of the most striking manifestations of the mercy of God within the entire range of the Scriptures.

I. The Words first of all present a Challenge

As a consequence of religious declension the life of the nation had become so diseased that there was no purity or justice or truth in the land : so intimate is the connection—notwithstanding a great deal of superficial talk to the contrary—between religious belief and practical conduct. The prophet, accordingly, challenges his countrymen to find in the whole of Jerusalem a MAN. The moral pestilence, he declares, had spread so widely that none had escaped its foul contagion, and in all Jerusalem, therefore, there was not a single honest man. It is without doubt an arresting and a biting challenge. Let search be made,

[1] v. 1.

says Jeremiah, in the holy city, the place where good men should be most easily found; let it be conducted with the utmost diligence and thoroughness, so that the seekers shall "run to and fro" among the narrow streets and the public squares; let it include within its sweep every aspect of the city's life, the sacred as well as the secular, so that priests and people may undergo a common scrutiny; and then, when your comb-out is completed, produce—a man. One inevitably thinks of Diogenes with his lantern searching for an honest man among the streets of Athens, and indicating thereby his conviction that uprightness had fled the land; but the attitude of the Greek cynic to his country's condition would probably have little in it of the grief and the compassion which filled the heart of the Hebrew prophet as he brooded over the corruption of Jerusalem.

To what a pass had religion come in those dark years which preceded the Exile! Even if Jeremiah's words are not meant to be understood in their strictly literal sense—in point of fact we know that there were at least a few faithful men in Jerusalem during the time of which he spoke—there remains a picture of religious and moral degradation which must have few parallels in the history of the Church of God. Believers in every age have a tendency to bewail the evils of their own time, and Coventry Patmore's familiar saying, that "Christianity has always seemed to its contemporaries to be in a state of decay," is profoundly true. In our own day we can see a widespread laxity in matters of faith as well as in morals, and in both directions there is undoubtedly good reason for concern. But a review of the past is often a useful corrective for a despondent mood. In any case we may well thank God when we compare our own generation, in spite of all its faults, with the days in which Jeremiah poured out his soul in lamentation before the Lord. To-day there are multitudes of men and women throughout the length and breadth of the world who fear God and keep His commandments.

II. In the second place the Words provide a Description

It is the description of one whose character entitles him to be called a *man*. Most people are ready to honour a real man when they meet him, and all of us would covet for ourselves the tribute paid to "the noblest Roman of them all," after his troubled course was finished :

> His life was gentle, and the elements
> So mixed in him, that nature might stand up
> And say to all the world, This was a man.

It is necessary, however, to have a true conception of what real manliness involves. There are widely differing estimates of worth to be found in the world ; what is counted greatness in the view of some people may be a very paltry thing in the judgment of others ; and the heroic figure in each of them may shrink to sorry dimensions when measured by the standards of God. In the world, for example, the financial standard is often the supreme test of human values. It is used, of course, by those who do homage to earthly success. You are no man at all in their eyes unless you are a prosperous man. Your worth as a man is determined by your balance at your banker's. It need scarcely be said that this is a poor and sordid criterion. A man's life consisteth not in the abundance of . . . *things*. Strip many a one of his outward possessions, and there is not much manhood left.

Then there is the social standard. This is the test applied by those who worship rank. In their view the question of first importance is the grade of society to which a man belongs ; the visiting lists on which his name has a place ; the "set" in which he lives and moves and has his being. This again is an essentially paltry standard. Membership in the most exclusive social circles is no guarantee of nobility of soul. Again, there is the physical standard. It is used by those who attach paramount importance to bodily strength. The hero with them is the conqueror in the athletic arena—the outstanding performer in the realm of sport, the prolific scorer of goals, the brilliant compiler of centuries, the man whose frame is so well-proportioned and well-developed that it becomes an instrument of surpassing endurance and skill. But this too is in itself a totally inadequate criterion. It is, of course, a good thing to have a sound physical frame, and it is a Christian duty to attend to the laws of health ; but many a time the soul of a man has dwelt in a frail body.

Or, once more, there is the intellectual standard. It is the test applied by those who declare that " the mind's the measure of the man." According to them the creative genius in the realm of intellect—the brilliant scholar, the successful author, the eminent scientist, the world-famous inventor—he is the real man. Now this is undoubtedly a loftier standard than those that have already been mentioned ; but it is not God's standard, and, when accepted as the determining factor in forming our judgments, it may be utterly false. The clever man is not always a good man ; in fact he is often a rogue. The scholar is not always a saint ; too often, alas, he is a notorious sinner. The head may be splendidly right while the heart is fatally wrong.

What, then, is God's standard ? Let us listen again to Jeremiah's description of the true man. He " executeth judgment and seeketh the truth." Here we have the man stripped of every adventitious feature, and left with those qualities which will survive all changes of outward circumstance. A doer of judgment and a seeker of truth : the broad fact disclosed in these words is that God assesses a man's worth in terms of moral and spiritual values. It is not a lengthy description, for it consists of only two terms. Taking the latter phrase first, we find that the true man is " a seeker of the truth." The words reveal the bent of his soul. He is a lover of truth, and therefore he has truth in his heart as well as on his lips and in his life. His character bears the stamp of sincerity and reality. He is, in short, a man to be trusted. But he also executeth judgment, that is, he is a doer of that which is right. This means that he applies the truth which he seeks to the art of every-day living. Right thinking is accompanied by right conduct. And this practical uprightness, whenever it goes deeper than mere outward propriety, is guided by the will of God. In all the relationships of life this man seeks to walk in the paths of righteousness. "Who," asks George Herbert, "is the honest man?" This is the answer which he gives to his own question:

> He that doth, still and strongly, good pursue,
> To God, his neighbours, and himself most true;
> Whom neither force nor fawning can
> Unpin or wrench from giving all their due.

It will be seen that the brevity of Jeremiah's description is equalled by its comprehensiveness. Viewing the words in their most general sense, we may say that the character of the upright man is marked by several definite qualities. First of all, he is a strong man. Strong in body, if that is possible, though not necessarily an athlete; vigorous in mind, too, though not necessarily a scholar; but certainly strong in soul, a man of courage, hating "the cowardice of doing wrong," and ready to stand up fearlessly in defence of the right. The true man has a certain bigness of soul, an unmistakable nobility of spirit which carries with it a scorn of everything that is false and mean and petty. "There is indeed"—it is Hazlitt who is lauding the character of Charles James Fox, and we can admire the justness of his sentiments, as well as the beauty of his tribute, without, for the present, inquiring too closely into the claims of his hero to such glowing praise—"there is indeed a purity, a rectitude, an integrity of heart, a freedom from every selfish bias and sinister motive, a manly simplicity and noble disinterestedness of spirit, which is in my opinion to be preferred before every other gift of nature or art. There is a greatness of soul which is to be preferred to all the brilliancy of the understanding. This strength of moral character, which is not only a more valuable but a rarer quality than strength of understanding . . ., Fox possessed in the highest degree. He was superior to every kind of jealousy, of suspicion, of malevolence; to every narrow and sordid motive. He was perfectly above every species of duplicity, of low art and cunning. He judged of everything in the downright sincerity of his nature, without being able to impose upon himself by any hollow disguise, or to lend his support to anything unfair or dishonourable." This lofty estimate may be accepted as a legitimate expansion of Jeremiah's brief description of the righteous man.

In the second place, he is a gentle man. Though strong, he is tender and compassionate, considerate to the weak, hating every kind of cruelty and oppression, and courteous in speech and behaviour. He is not overbearing in his attitude to others, or loud-voiced in expressing his opinions. He is no boaster and no bully. The real man is always a gentleman. In addition to this he is a clean man. "Who," asks the Psalmist, "shall ascend into the hill of the Lord? He that hath clean hands and a pure heart." The righteous man seeks to conform his life to this lofty ideal. He endeavours to keep his manhood clean by guarding his heart against the defilement of evil, and setting his thoughts on the things that are pure and honest and lovely and of good report. And all this implies that he is a God-fearing man. His strength of soul is rooted in his religious faith.

Does any one ask, How can I attain to a true manhood—strong, courageous, gentle, and pure? The final answer to that question is that it is by faith in Jesus Christ. Through faith we are united to Him, and receive of His Spirit, and are conformed in some real degree to His likeness. In Christ Himself we find all the qualities that constitute "the highest, holiest manhood" revealed in perfect degree and harmonious combination—righteousness and mercy, majesty and meekness, holiness and love, gentleness and strength. Only when we become "new" men in Him do we begin to grow up unto the stature of real men. There is nothing in Christianity that is incompatible with true manliness. The Christian is gentle, but he is not soft. His meekness is not another name for weakness. His spirituality of mind does not mean a devitalised and anæmic humanity. His affections are set on the things that are above, but he is not insensible to the joys of a pulsating life in this present world. He is a stranger and a sojourner in the earth, but he does not stand apart in morose aloofness from healthy human interests and attachments. Some of the finest specimens of young manhood in the world to-day, youths who have borne the palm in every form of wholesome rivalry with their fellows, are also Christians of the most earnest type, strong in moral conviction no less than in physical prowess, and filled, not simply with the joy of living, but with zeal for the glory of Him whom they call Master and Lord.

III. Finally, the Words convey an Assurance

That is the assurance of pardon to the guilty city if a righteous man should be found within its walls. This is a promise which, as has already been indicated, constitutes an amazing revelation of the grace of God. Ten righteous men would have delivered Sodom from destruction, but one would have sufficed to save Jerusalem. It may be that sometimes we are tempted to regard the punishment of Israel's unfaithfulness as unduly severe. We think of Zion turned into a wilderness and Jerusalem into a desolation ; of the holy and beautiful house which was the centre of the nation's religious life burned up with fire ; of the ravages of successive invasions, the horrors of the final siege, and the sorrows of the seventy years' captivity. But over against all those sufferings let us place the longer years of the patience of God. Years they were that were filled with remonstrances and reproofs, with faithful warnings and tender appeals, all of which showed His reluctance to lift the rod, and His willingness to save. " Run ye to and fro through the streets of Jerusalem . . . and seek . . . if ye can find a man . . . *and I will pardon it*"—so reads the Divine promise of mercy.

One obvious inference from this assurance is that righteous men serve a purpose of vital importance in the world. Unknown perhaps to themselves, and almost certainly unknown to others, they are public benefactors. This is especially true with regard to the function which they fulfil as moral preservatives in the community in which they live. In this sense they are the salt of the earth, preserving it from being wholly consumed of its own corruptions, and thereby averting the Divine judgment which its iniquities deserve. By their example, by their teaching, and by those good deeds which shine in the darkness of an evil world—even as the little candle flings its beams into the encircling gloom—they exercise a restraining and purifying influence on the lives of their fellows. Often, too, they act the part of national deliverers. Time after time in seasons of emergency, when the call of the hour has been for wise and fearless leadership, God has raised up a man whose qualities matched the occasion, a man endowed with vision and courage and spiritual energy—a Moses in Egypt who delivered the chosen people from the yoke of the oppressor; a Luther in Germany and a Knox in Scotland who saved the Western world from the bondage of a corrupt religious system. Beyond question our country needs such men to-day, men of vision and of action, endowed with wisdom and courage, and filled, above all, with a passion for righteousness and truth.

Righteous men are also useful in the capacity of intercessors. God's remembrancers who plead with Him night and day, in earnestness and importunity of supplication, are of more value in the world than multitudes of its nobles and mighty men. It is not always those who occupy the high places of the earth, and command the applause of listening senates, and exercise the arts of diplomacy at Conference Tables, that play the most effective part in guiding a nation's destinies. An aged saint in a garret, who has the ear of God, may exercise a more powerful influence on a country's public affairs than all its Cabinet ministers. So true is it that prayer brings the power of God into action in every sphere of human life.

And all this brings us back again to Jesus Christ. A man could have been the saviour of Jerusalem in the days of Jeremiah; and another prophet has declared that "A MAN shall be an hiding-place from the wind and a covert from the tempest, as rivers of water in a dry place, and as the shadow of a great rock in a weary land." It is to the Man who is God's fellow that, in the fulness of their meaning, those majestic words apply, and every other man who in any sense becomes a deliverer of others fulfils that function in virtue of His redemptive grace.

VI

A BARRIER OF SAND

There are few more suggestive words in the Book of Jeremiah than those which declare that God has "placed the sand for the bound of the sea." The fact there affirmed is adduced as a reason why men should fear the Lord, and the point of the statement will be seen only when we recognise that the emphasis is to be placed on the word "sand." God restrains the inroads of the sea with such effortless ease that He makes a barrier of sand suffice to keep it in check. He has not, as a general rule, erected a rampart of flinty rocks or of towering hills with which to subdue its pride; He keeps the sea in its place by surrounding it with a strip of sand. And that is an illustration of the general fact that God secures great ends by weak means, and thereby reveals the greatness of His power. This is the main consideration which, in the present instance, underlies the Divine appeal to Israel: A God so great in power may well be feared. "*Fear ye not Me? saith the Lord: will ye not tremble at My presence, which have placed the sand for the bound of the sea in a perpetual decree that it cannot pass it. . . .*"[1] What may we learn from the fact that the Lord has endowed the sand with this victorious strength?

1. It speaks, first of all, of the resistless Power of God.—The sea, it need scarcely be said, is one of the mightiest forces in Nature. When the winds lash it into a fury, it can be terrifying in its rage and majestic in its might. Its waves dash themselves against the shore as if to overwhelm the earth, and though baffled in each successive effort they return again and again to the attack, tossing their crested heads as though in conscious pride, and

[1] v. 22.

roaring like angry beasts of prey. And even when there is no such crash of billows the sea invades the land with assaults that are not less dangerous because they are insidious. It is not only " the league-long roller thundering on the reef " that is menacing, but also the stealthy, almost imperceptible advance of " the cruel hungry foam " which, one tragic day,

> Crept up along the sand,
> And o'er and o'er the sand,
> And round and round the sand,
> As far as eye could see.

And yet the sea, whether in storm or in calm, is held in restraint by a barrier of sand. God takes something which seems to be the very symbol of unresisting weakness and makes it an effective guardian of the earth. Sand—you scoop up a handful of it, and it pours through your fingers like water. Unstable as water it appears indeed to be, but it is the Divinely appointed means of resisting the encroachments of the sea.

The sand indeed is not so weak as to us it sometimes appears to be. Science tells us that it possesses an enormous resisting power; for the shock of the blows which fall upon it is distributed laterally, and so produces little effect. For that reason the pressure of waves which in course of time would wear down the hardest rock makes little impression on the sand. Be that as it may, we must remember that behind the narrow strip of sand there is the " perpetual decree " of which the prophet here speaks. To that decree we usually give the name of natural law. The sea, we say, is controlled by the Laws of Nature. That is no doubt true; but the Laws of Nature are simply the expression of the Will of a personal God, and it is by that sovereign Will that all the motions of the sea are governed. The ebb and flow of the tides, for example, are determined by the attracting power with which He has dowered the moon—that noiseless influence which " moves all the labouring surges of the world." And so, that silvery circlet which protects the earth from the devouring sea is a visible sign of God's mastery over His own universe. The sand is a bound of the sea because it is the chosen medium whereby God gives effect to His ancient decree: "Hitherto shalt thou come, but no further, and here shall thy proud waves be stayed."

The power of God as revealed in Nature should certainly beget within the heart of man a healthy reverential fear. It proclaims the greatness and majesty of the Creator, and emphasises by contrast the littleness and weakness of the creature. The power which quells, with so little effort, the turbulence of the waters, can break, with even greater ease, the feeble strength of men. And before the glory of that power what can a sinful man do but bow down in awe and lowly prostration of soul?

Israel indeed had good reason to fear a God who possessed such boundless resources. In the chapter which contains the words we are considering, Jeremiah uses great plainness of speech in denouncing their manifold iniquities, and in warning them of the consequences of their unfaithfulness. Once and again he uses words which might well have struck terror into their guilty souls: "Shall I not visit for these things, saith the Lord: and shall not My soul be avenged on such a nation as this?" It was his sense of the terribleness of this impending judgment that imparted such vehemence and urgency to the prophet's appeals. God's warnings to His treacherous people were no empty threats. Because they knew Him to be a God of power, they might have remembered that He was well able to execute His sentence of righteous condemnation.

II. In the second place, the words present us with a striking Contrast.—That is the contrast between the subjection of the sea to the will of God and the undisciplined corruption of the unregenerate heart of man. Mark the words which follow Jeremiah's description of the Divine control of the tossing billows: "*But this people,*" he says, "*hath a revolting and rebellious heart.*" The turbulence of the elements cannot prevail against God's thin white line of sand ; but Israel were up in arms against the authority of their Lawgiver. Their whole history bears witness to the accuracy of the prophet's description. They were a people of "a revolting and a rebellious heart."

Let us glance for a moment at this suggestive contrast. Man—and how feeble in one sense his strength is in comparison with the might of the sea—frail man refuses to obey the will of his God. "The carnal mind," declares Paul, "is enmity against God, and is not subject to the law of God, neither indeed can be." This is surely the darkest tragedy of our fallen condition. Man is in rebellion against his Maker ; the clay challenges the sovereign will of the Potter ; the creature of a day hurls defiance at the Throne of the Eternal ; the little king of our Lord's parable—it is of course an aggravation of the offence that the rebel is endowed with the royal qualities of intelligence and will and moral consciousness—matches his strength in unreflecting pride against the Lord of innumerable battalions. The deepest as well as the briefest definition of sin is that which describes it as lawlessness.

How terrible therefore it is in its nature ! We sometimes regard it as a comparatively trivial thing which we may commit again and again with impunity. But if we look deep enough we shall find that it aims its shafts at the very heart of God. Sin, if it could, would dethrone the Eternal. It is not only a transgression of His commandment ; it is an attempt to overturn His purposes. If we wish to get a view of sin in its true nature, sin "laid bare to the bone," let us come to Calvary, and see the hatred of men poured forth with relentless venom upon the head of Him who was none other than God manifest in the flesh. Infinite goodness was crowned with thorns, and after being vilified and scourged and spat upon, was at last nailed to the accursed tree.

And sin is also terrible in its power. The human heart is "desperately wicked," and its corruptions cannot be healed by any earthly remedy. Many restraining and refining influences may be brought to bear upon it—education, home training, a healthy social environment—and these doubtless have a certain repressive effect; but none of them goes down to the roots of the disease. George Herbert writes of still more potent ministries which God uses as "fine nets and stratagems to catch us in." But neither the discipline of Providence nor the appeal of Religion can of themselves tame the contumacy of the natural man.

> Blessings beforehand, ties of gratefulness,
> The sound of glory ringing in our ears;
> Without, our shame; within, our consciences;
> Angels and grace, eternal hopes and fears.
>
> Yet all these fences and their whole array
> One cunning bosom-sin blows quite away.

This, then, is the contrast to which the prophet draws special attention: on the one hand, the obedience of inanimate Nature to the decree of God; on the other, the rebellion of men against His sovereign rule. And here surely is a sufficient reason for the Divine challenge, "Fear ye not *Me*, saith the Lord: will ye not tremble at My Presence?"

III. Further, the words furnish us with a pledge of God's ultimate victory over every force that opposes His Will.—His unchallengeable supremacy over the raging elements is a guarantee of His triumph in every field in which He has to contend. It is not too violent a transition, therefore, to turn our thoughts from the sphere of Nature to the realm of Grace. The God who is a Controller in the one domain is not less surely a Conqueror in the other. So we may justly claim that the victory of the sand over the sea is an assurance—it may even be said to be an appropriate figure—of the conquests of the Gospel in a sinful world. The wicked are fittingly compared to "the troubled sea," because of the foul corruptions which they are both wont to "cast up." It has already been indicated that the pollution of the unregenerate heart cannot be cleansed by any human agency ; its rebellion cannot be subdued even by the restraints of the Divine Law. But what the Law cannot do, because it is " weak through the flesh," the Gospel of the grace of God can accomplish. Look, for example, at that man who is the slave of unbridled lust ; or at his neighbour who is the devotee of worldly pleasure ; or at that other, again, who is the victim of strong drink ; or once more at those unhappy men and women who are in bondage to an ungovernable temper—we have seen them all transformed into trophies of the grace of God, and enabled to deny ungodliness and worldly lusts, and to live sober, upright, and pious lives in this present world. " Such were some of you," says Paul to the Corinthian Church, " but ye are washed, but ye are sanctified, but ye are justified in the name of the Lord Jesus and by the Spirit of our God." And the word " such " refers back to some of the foulest sins of which a man can be guilty in this world.

The parallel can be carried further still. God secures the victories of His grace by means that to human wisdom often appear to be as futile as the sand might be regarded, when judged by that same wisdom, as a defence against the sea. It is by the foolishness of preaching that, ordinarily, He saves them that believe. Let us recall what happened on the day of Pentecost. One sermon was preached, and three thousand miracles happened ! And this " silent awakening of the spirit of man " is a more wonderful manifestation of the power of God than the most impressive phenomenon of the material universe. The breaking down of its enmity is a more notable achievement than the bridling of the ocean's fury. Think of Saul of Tarsus as he sets out on the road to Damascus—the proud, confident, zealous Pharisee, breathing out threatenings and slaughter against the Church of God, every breath a threat, and every threat a menace of death to some Christian man or woman. But the Lord Jesus met the ruthless persecutor in the way and conquered him. It needed but a flashing forth of the glory of His face and the victory was won. Truly He quells the raging sea in human life as completely as He does in the material creation.

Once more, the soul that is conquered by the power of Divine grace is controlled thereafter through the gentle sway of love. The man who has been set free from the guilt of sin, and has received the gift of life, is not without law to God, he is under law to Christ. But the yoke of that law is as easy and gentle as the sand that is placed for the bound of the sea. For restraint in this case is accompanied by constraint; the inward incentives and inspirations of love are added to the outward discipline of law. Christian loyalty, for that reason, does not consist in the forced subjection of slaves, but in the gracious submission of children to a Father's will. The yoke of Christ is easy because it is the will of a loving Redeemer.

IV. Finally, the words remind us that the Lord restrains the wrath of His people's enemies as easily as He subdues the violence of the sea.—The believer often has special trials to endure in an unsympathetic and sometimes hostile environment. "Marvel not," said Christ to His disciples, "if the world hate you"; and the application of His words is not confined to those to whom they were directly addressed. The ungodly man, who is the avowed enemy of all religion, and denounces the whole race of Christians as hypocrites; the worldling, whose careless living is rebuked by the faithful witness of a Christian walk and conversation; "the little tyrant" of a community, who resents every resistance which a sensitive conscience may be compelled to offer to his authority; the sectarian zealot who takes exception to the accent with which you pronounce his particular shibboleth; and, not least, the man who makes a profession of the Christian name, but is totally ignorant of the power of living religion—all these constitute a brotherhood of hate who are not slow, when opportunity offers, to vent their malice on the loyal followers of Jesus Christ. But the eyes of the Lord are over the righteous, and, in ways that often appear strange in their noiseless simplicity, He sets a bound to the sea of their wrath.

Browning's little poem entitled *Instans Tyrannus*, for example, describes the mysterious power with which the prayer of faith clothes an otherwise weak and defenceless man. It is the story of a ruthless tyrant and a poor, feeble underling of his who somehow had fallen under his displeasure, and whom in sheer lust of cruelty he resolved to crush beneath his feet. With sleepless malice he strove to torture his victim, but all his efforts failed to yield him complete satisfaction, for the man's very insignificance and friendlessness were a kind of protection to him. At last, however, the tyrant prepared a master-stroke of vengeance, and, having laid his train, was ready "to enjoy the event." Then a strange and disturbing thing happened. The man who seemed so puny and friendless was all of a sudden surrounded with mysterious and terrifying defences. The very sky above him became his shield, and a mighty Arm was flung about him to ward off his enemy's blow. The tyrant himself provides the explanation :

> Just my vengeance complete,
> The man sprang to his feet,
> Stood erect, caught at God's skirts, and prayed!
> So *I* was afraid.

With what amazing ease the miracle of deliverance seems to us to have been accomplished! A face lifted up to Heaven, and immediately the rage that seethed in the oppressor's heart gives place to fear, and the hand that was ready to deliver the final blow is hanging in pathetic impotence by his side : God had placed the sand for the bound of the sea.

Then there are attacks that are directed against the Word of God. It would be an interesting thing to know, if it were possible to discover, how many copies of the Bible have been burned in the history of the Christian Church through sheer hatred of the sacred volume. But God has placed a bound to the devouring flame as surely as to the raging sea. The Word of the Lord endureth for ever, and every attempt of its enemies to put out its light is fore-doomed to failure.

Or it is the Church of Christ as a visible organisation in the world that is the object of attack. Again and again throughout the centuries the waves of persecuting rage have broken over her head, but her Lord on high has always proved Himself to be "mightier than the noise of many waters." One remembers the conflict between Herod and Peter in the early days of Christianity, or—as it really was—the conflict between the petty King of Judea and the exalted King of Sion. Herod's efforts were directed against the whole Christian community, and the imprisonment of Peter was designed to be a master-stroke in this war of extermination. It is not necessary to dwell on the details of the conflict; we shall pass on to its dramatic close in Cæsarea when the proud king was smitten by the angel of the Lord and died an ignominious death. "*But the Word of God grew and was multiplied.*" That simple statement discloses the real nature of the struggle, as well as its issue. Herod had launched an attack against the Church of Christ, and the Lord once more had His enemy in derision, and left his stricken body to be a prey to the devouring worms.

I like to recall that moving story of old Alexander Peden—the man who was so far ben in the life of fellowship with his Lord that he came to be known as "Peden the Prophet"—which has come down to us from the dark days of persecution in Scotland, when our Covenanting forefathers were compelled to worship God in some secluded hollow among the Ayrshire and Galloway hills. One day, when a great congregation was assembled in some such retreat, the watchers on the surrounding heights gave the signal that the enemy were approaching. A great silence fell upon the company, for there seemed to be but a step between them and death. Flight was impossible, for there were aged men and feeble women among the congregation, and the soldiers were men of ruthless heart. Then the voice of Alexander Peden broke the stillness as he lifted up his heart to God in prayer. "Lord," he cried, "this is the day of Thine enemies. Hour and power are allowed to them. Send them after those to whom Thou hast given strength to flee, for our strength is gone. Twine them about the hill, O Lord, and cast the lap of Thy cloak over auld Sandy and thae puir things, and save us this one time." And then "something happened." From behind the ridges of the Duchrae and Drumglass there rose a great sea of mist which enveloped the whole company, and completely hid them from view. Scarcely daring to breathe, as we may well suppose, they could hear the sound of the troopers' voices, the jangling of bridles and spurs, and the noise of horses' hoofs as they struck the hard mountain stones. But Peden and his company were shrouded in the cloak of the Lord, and the dragoons were unable to find their prey. And I would fain believe that that whole company, from the youngest to the oldest, as they lay down that night to rest, sang—it may well have been, with voices that were soft and not always steady, but with hearts that were aflame with gratitude to their strong Deliverer—

> The raging streams,
>   With their proud swelling waves,
> Had then our soul
>   O'erwhelmed in the deep.
> But bless'd be God
>   Who doth us safely keep,
> And hath not giv'n
>   Us for a living prey
> Unto their teeth
>   And bloody cruelty.

A screen of gentle mist as a bulwark against the fury of religious persecution! Surely it was as if God, on this memorable day, had "placed the sand for the bound of the sea."

VII

THE GOODNESS OF GOD AND THE FEAR OF GOD

It is not alone the thought of the Power of God that should give rise to fear in the hearts of men. His Goodness also is designed to produce a similar result. His loving-kindness to the undeserving is " so amazing, so Divine," that when it becomes a fact of experience it begets within the soul an almost overwhelming sense of awe, and becomes a powerful incentive to holy living. The prophet Hosea, for example, declares that the result of the " return " of the children of Israel, through the redeeming grace of their God, will be that " they shall fear the Lord and His goodness in the latter days." Jeremiah also, in more than one striking passage, shows that an experience of the Divine mercy produces in the souls of men that godly fear which is one of the chief inspirations of an upright life. In one [1] of several great chapters in which, with unmistakable plainness, he foretells the Restoration of the exiles to their own land there is a glowing account of the goodness which the Lord is to manifest to them in that glad day of deliverance. Pardon and cleansing from all their iniquity ; " health and cure " for their spiritual diseases ; abundance of " peace and truth " in place of unrest and falsity ; " a name of joy, a praise and an honour before all the nations of the earth "—these are among the blessings which He will lavish upon them in the greatness of His love. And the Lord Himself describes the effect which this wealth of kindness will have on His penitent children. " They shall fear and tremble," He declares, " for all the goodness and for all the prosperity that I procure unto it." To

[1] xxxiii.

the same purpose are the words which are now to engage our attention, and which are closely related to the appeal and complaint which came under consideration in the preceding chapter. The people whose "revolting and rebellious heart" regarded with unconcern the manifestation of God's Power in Nature were equally unimpressed by the experience of His Goodness in Providence. "*Neither say they in their heart,*" declares the prophet, "*Let us now fear the Lord our God, that giveth rain, both the former and the latter, in his season: He reserveth unto us the appointed weeks of the harvest.*" [1]

Primarily, of course, the words are to be understood in their literal sense, as a testimony to the Divine goodness in Providence. The local background is that of the East, where the rains in their season are specially recognised as the gift of God. He sends the former rain at seed-time, when the refreshing moisture is needed to make the earth "bring forth and bud." Then come the days of heat and drought, when the fruits are in danger of withering, and of failing to reach maturity. It is at this season of need that He sends the blessing of the latter rain. It comes in time to avert the tragedy of blighted fields and empty storehouses. The earth is once more refreshed and revived; the fields become white unto harvest; and so when "the appointed weeks" arrive, the reaper goes forth to his joyful task. It surely becomes us to acknowledge, with that "fear" in which there is humble gratitude, the goodness of God in providing us with the sustenance which our earthly life requires. It is He who gives us "the rains and the fruitful seasons, filling our hearts with food and gladness." With unfailing regularity He has been fulfilling His promise of "seed-time and harvest" throughout the revolving years, and the very uniformity of His providential operations accounts in no small degree for our insensateness and ingratitude. But Christ Himself taught us the duty of dependence on the bounty of Heaven when He put into our lips the petition, "Give us this day our daily bread"; and the

[2] v. 24.

gifts with which He answers that prayer ought surely to be received with appropriate thanksgiving.

The temporal mercies of which Jeremiah speaks, however, were a figure of higher blessings, and the seasonable refreshings which meant so much for Israel in the realm of Nature have their counterpart in the religious life. There are seasons in the Christian life when the believer renews his strength and makes a fresh start in the spiritual pilgrimage. Without such repeated restorations he would soon faint and be weary, and his strength would utterly fail. But his gracious Lord restores his energies at the opportune time, and enables him to hold on his way with fresh hope and courage. In the prophecy of Joel, indeed, the former and the latter rain are directly linked on to the miracle of Pentecost. We shall meantime consider the words as a kind of parable of spiritual experience.

I

First of all, we have the Former Rain with its mighty quickening. The coming of the Former Rain marks the beginning of the Christian life, and ushers in the freshness and the glory of spring. The "precious seed" of the Gospel has been sown in the heart, and God gives the increase through the might of His quickening Spirit. The Spirit descends like the gentle rain from heaven, and makes all things new. He brings light into the mind and life into the will. The result is an experience of spiritual power which means nothing less than a resurrection from the dead. In that glad morning of the religious life the world is shining with a wondrous glory. Heaven lies about the young believer in his daily path. The old bondage has passed away, and there is an inspiring sense of freedom. There is a new inrush of joy into the heart, and a new song of praise on the lips; for the soul is brought near to God in the consciousness of sonship. It may perhaps not be without hesitations and fears and many tossings to and fro, because of the backward pull of old associations, that the hour of final surrender is reached, but when once the vital decision is made, there is an enlargement of experience which is like the discovery of a new world. What a wealth of meaning is compressed into this one flaming sentence which describes the conversion of Francesca French in *Something Happened.* " By an act of faith she cast herself on grace, and found herself on the breast of God." This is the miracle which results from the sending of the former rain. It marks for ever the hour when first the soul

> Saw and heard
> Spring's light reverberate and reiterate word
> Shine forth and speak in season. Life stands crowned
> Here with the best one thing it ever found. . . .

Now this experience brings with it a vision of the Divine goodness which is so moving in its appeal and so extensive in its range that it creates in the heart a godly fear which is more than a passing emotion. And if there is one thing more than another which gives rise to this attitude, it is the new conception which dawns on the soul of the greatness of God's salvation. God so loved the world, that He gave His only-begotten Son, that whosoever believeth in Him should not perish, but have everlasting life—that is beyond question a fact which should move the heart to joyous adoration. But when the magnitude of the fact is realised—the wonder of the love revealed, the greatness of the gift bestowed, the vastness of the issues involved—there rises within the soul a deep reverence and holy fear. No man can really believe that God loved him from all eternity without being humbled in the dust even when the new song is on his lips. No man can stand before the Cross of Calvary, and realise that the Son of God was there wounded for his transgressions and bruised for his iniquities, without being conscious of a sense of awe which causes him to tremble in the very hour at which he joys in God through whom he has " now received the atonement."

It is this consideration which the Apostle Peter has in view when he exhorts the readers of his First Epistle to pass the time of their sojourning here "in fear." The fact on which he bases this unexpected appeal is the greatness of their redemption: "Forasmuch as ye know that ye were not redeemed with corruptible things such as silver and gold . . . but with the precious blood of Christ." Christianity is too big a thing—in its origin, its central facts, and its ultimate issues—to warrant any jauntiness of bearing on the part of those who have beheld its glory and experienced its power. The riches of God's mercy, the majesty of God's righteousness, and the grace of God's forgiveness, together with the stupendous cost of redemption and the everlasting destiny of human souls—these are facts of revelation and experience which should impart an element of seriousness to Christian thinking and of gravity to Christian living. We need to-day to recapture in our religion what an eminent Christian thinker referred to, not so very long ago, as "the lost fear of God"—not less joy in our Christianity, but greater moral seriousness; not less singing in our devotional life, but a deeper note in our song; not less definiteness in the proclamation of our happiness as believers, but a more humbling sense of our indebtedness as sinners—unworthy sinners who are saved by the grace of God through the death of His Son on the accursed Tree. Without doubt, personal knowledge of the goodness of God should lead to a practical manifestation of the fear of God.

The believer, however, cannot always live on this initial experience. It is indeed true that the life which springs from that first watering of God will never perish. But it is equally true that if it is to be maintained in health and fruitfulness its energies must be continually renewed. In other words, it needs the latter as well as the former rain. Without constant replenishings of grace the brightness of the early vision will fade into the light of common day; love will lose its fervour, and faith will be shorn of its vigour; the eye of hope will grow dim, and the edge of conscience will become blunted. There are evil influences from without which continually war against the soul. The world is constantly knocking at the door, and presenting its appeal in an endless variety of forms. And, what is more dangerous still, sin is ever seeking to regain the ascendency in the secret chambers of the soul. So that without fresh supplies of strength there is bound to be spiritual declension. The Christian, no doubt, has his own part to do in maintaining the loyalties of his soul and the fruitfulness of his life through fellowship with God, but in order to endure in the path of obedience he needs the constant renewal of his inner life by the Spirit of Christ.

II

But the Lord, in due season, sends the Latter Rain with its gracious reviving. He revisits the souls of His children in restoring mercy, and enables them to make a fresh beginning. The refreshing showers descend on the parched and withered earth, and the tender grass springs up again "by clear shining after rain." The fainting believer is baptised anew with the Spirit of Christ. He receives a fresh vision of the glory of the Lord, and gains a fresh experience of His forgiving and restoring grace.

The latter rain comes when it is needed most. Perhaps in the time of strenuous toil, when one's strength is failing beneath the burden and heat of the day. Perhaps in the hour of temptation, when the defences of the soul are being swept away through the fierceness of the enemy's assaults. Often it comes in the season of sorrow, when the heart is wrung with pain. In the darkness of the night the soft rain of God's love and pity falls on the soul, and gives it strength to endure. Sometimes the latter rain is specially needed in the mid-time of life, when a man's moral enthusiasms may have largely faded, and the cares of this world and the deceitfulness of riches are making their influence felt. And it is certainly needed in the evening of old age, when the strength of the body is exhausted, "and the mind can only disgrace its fame." But in those testing seasons of experience the Lord will not forsake His children. They are an inheritance which, as Moses said to Israel regarding the land of Canaan, "drinketh water of the rain of heaven. . . . The eyes of the Lord thy God are always upon it, from the beginning of the year even unto the end of the year." He comes to them again and again in the riches of His mercy, and makes all things new in their experience. The blessing of the latter rain brings back the erring into the paths of righteousness, and enables them to sing as in the days of their youth. It brings fresh strength and courage to him that was ready to perish, and restores to the contrite the years that the locusts had eaten. The renewed life is dowered with even more than its original power and beauty. It gains

> From shower and shining, from the moulds and suns,
> Deep colours, odours, richer than of old.

The grace of the latter rain often seems more wonderful than the first experience of the mercy of God. It is in describing the joy of the Return from Babylon that Jeremiah's narrative rises to its loftiest height of lyrical beauty. In the chapter to which reference has already been made he declares that on this day of new deliverance there will be heard "the voice of joy, and the voice of gladness, the voice of the bridegroom, and the voice of the bride, the voice of them that shall say, Praise the Lord of hosts: for the Lord is good; for His mercy endureth for ever: and of them that shall bring the sacrifice of praise into the house of the Lord."

III

Finally, there comes the Harvest with its joyful reaping. This is the end for which the gracious rains are the preparation. It is the consummation to which all the gifts of the Divine bounty are designed to lead. The Christian life should yield a rich harvest when "the appointed weeks" of reaping shall have come. And beyond question the Lord of the harvest will gather in His "pleasant fruits" from every field which He has blessed. A

Christian old age should yield a rich harvest of grace. There are few things in the world more tragic than a hoary head, which is not found in the way of righteousness. "There is nothing," said Seneca, "more disgraceful than that an old man should have nothing to produce as a proof that he has lived long except his years." But the aged Christian can produce something which is an evidence of the mercy and faithfulness of his God. The Lord reserveth unto him the appointed weeks of the harvest. For one thing he has gained experience. His judgment has matured, and the rashness of youth has given place to a riper wisdom. He has grown, too, in humility. The passing of the years has subdued his pride, and he is willing to take a lowly place. He also bears the fruits of a deeper dependence upon the grace of God, a clearer detachment from the world, and a greater readiness to depart and be with Christ, than he had in the earlier years. And as he draws nearer to the end, he longs more intensely for the coming of Christ's Kingdom throughout the world.

With reference also to the believer's work for his Lord on earth the appointed weeks of harvest will surely be reserved. No faithful servant of Christ is willing to give place to the thought that his labour bears the character of the "wood, hay, stubble" that will be burnt to ashes in the flames of doom. Rather does he cherish the hope that his efforts—however weak and imperfect—to further the Kingdom of God in the world may bear the seal of everlastingness. Yet the most diligent labourer sometimes sees little fruit resulting from his toil, and in hours of dejection, when the eye of faith is dim, may be inclined to write "in vain" over the whole record of his service. But whatever appearance the present may offer to our view, we know that the future belongs to Christ—that future

> When there dawns a day,
> If not on the homely earth,
> Then yonder, worlds away,
> When the strange and the new have birth,
> And Power comes full in play.

On that day the believer will have his reaping-time, and God also will keep His harvest-home. Every kind of service that had been truly rendered unto the Lord, however little recognition it may have achieved at the hands of men, shall then receive its fitting recompense. The sower who wept, because his labour seemed to be so unproductive, shall appear before the Lord with rejoicing, bringing his sheaves with him. In this world there is often much effort expended that for various reasons never secures its appropriate return of love and gratitude from those who are benefited by it, but on that glad day when sower and reaper shall "rejoice together," it is not too much to expect that all the relations of inter-dependence and mutual helpfulness that ever existed between the redeemed on earth shall be completely revealed. Above all, there will be the Master's "Well done," and the meed of honour which will express the gladness of His heart. The servant shall enter into the joy of his Lord, and shall receive from His hand an unfading crown.

It is with his eye fixed on that promised inheritance that Paul assures his fellow-workers in the ministry of the Gospel that their labour is not in vain in the Lord. The Christian hope passes beyond this brief stretch of time, and embraces those unnumbered weeks of harvest which are reserved within the veil. And so "the quiet church-yards spread their graves to the sun," and the shadow of death is gilded by the Morning Star.

VIII

AT THE CROSS-ROADS

THE sixth and seventh chapters of Jeremiah set forth in realistic detail the conditions which prevailed in Israel during the earlier years of the prophet's ministry. It is difficult for us, indeed, to realise the ascendency which the forces of evil had gained in the land throughout that unhappy time. Jerusalem, we are told, was like a corrupt fountain, continually pouring forth its streams of wickedness. The noise of "violence and spoil" was continually heard within its bounds; "grief and wounds" were facts of ordinary occurrence; and men and women gave themselves over to "abomination" without any sense of shame.

In the sphere of religion conflicting influences were at work. Jeremiah, of course, was faithfully carrying out the terms of his commission. But he was faced with a hopeless task. As he realises this fact his voice takes on a sterner note of condemnation, and his predictions of approaching calamity become more vehement and startling. "I am full of the fury of the Lord," he cries; "I am weary with holding in." The reference to "fury" does not mean that his words were spoken in a wrathful spirit, for we have every reason to believe that his heart was wellnigh broken with the intensity of his personal anguish. But the message of wrath which was given him to proclaim was straining for utterance; repression was no longer possible; he *must* tell of that ruthless enemy from the north who is to be the instrument of Divine judgment on a people who had so completely sold themselves to iniquity.

There was an additional factor, too, which complicated the religious problem. There were other prophets in the land, whose "Peace, peace" gave the lie to Jeremiah's message of doom. And it always happens that those smoother voices, which declare that there is nothing far wrong with the existing order, find a readier acceptance than those which seek to rouse a nation from its inertia and to break in on its self-complacency with warnings of coming disaster. Of this fact the recent history of our own land furnishes some striking illustrations. In any case, the result of this conflict of testimony was a general state of uncertainty and bewilderment. There were many who were standing at the cross-roads—hesitating, perplexed, tossed between conflicting emotions, and unable to determine where the path of duty lay.

It was in such circumstances as these that Jeremiah addressed to his erring countrymen the appeal which is now to engage our attention: "*Thus saith the Lord, Stand ye in the ways, and see, and ask for the old paths, where is the good way, and walk therein, and ye shall find rest for your souls.*"[1] It was a heart-moving call, as reasonable as it was urgent. It summoned them to pause in the mad career of declension on which they had already travelled so far; charged them not to forsake their fathers' God or to break with religious traditions which were hallowed by the sanctions of antiquity; and promised them rest of soul if they walked in the good way of obedience to the Divine will. The answer which that call received was a churlish and defiant "We will not."

There are many in our own time who are at the place where various roads meet, and who do not know which way they should follow. We live in an age of ceaseless bustle, when the speed of our movements is considered to be of much greater importance than their direction. It is no libel on the present generation to affirm that comparatively few of its representatives take time to commune with their own soul. The result is that there are multitudes who never have, or who never give themselves, the opportunity of listening to those still small voices which are heard only in

> The soul's dumb watch,
> When spirits their fair kindred catch.

[1] vi. 16.

Our age too is a time of transition, when many of the ancient landmarks are vanishing out of sight. The thought of progress—the inevitable forward movement of humanity—still retains its hold on men's minds, although its grip is relaxing through the pressure of the stark realities of experience ; and institutions and observances which had maintained their position through the convulsions of many centuries are gradually yielding place to a new order. Christianity itself may be said to have been at the cross-roads throughout this twentieth century. The witness of the Church as a whole to the great truths which formed the very life-blood of the Apostolic testimony is to a great extent flabby and hesitating ; the old ring of triumphant confidence has largely disappeared from the message of the pulpit ; the Scriptures are more and more being divested of their regulative authority for Christian thinking ; liberty of judgment has degenerated into a licence which scarcely acknowledges any restraint ; and the Church, if I may adopt the words of an eminent living thinker, the very Church of God is almost dying of broad-mindedness.

It cannot but follow from all this that there is a great deal of unsettlement in the minds of the people. They are like travellers in a strange land who see in front of them a number of intersecting paths, and are unable to recognise among them the good way of safety. To such bewildered wayfarers Jeremiah's counsel is a word in season. Let us consider his appeal to the man at the cross-roads in its bearing on the special circumstances of our own time.

I. To begin with, it is a Call to Reflection

" Stand in the ways and see," is the prophet's first word of exhortation. " Stop and look about you," he says in effect, " lest you take the wrong road, and get lost in the wilderness."

The call is applicable, to begin with, to those who are

inclined to follow the path of least resistance through life, and have no liking for the road that winds up-hill all the way. Around us every day we see such followers of the ways of ease, cheerful pagans it may be, who take no thought for the morrow, although not in the Christian sense. To a great extent they spend their days on the level of a merely animal existence, allowing their decisions, when they take the trouble to choose at all, to be determined by their inclinations, and paying little regard to more serious issues. Their life is not fashioned by the inspiration of any special motive, nor is it directed to the attainment of any particular end. *Panem et circenses*—plenty to eat and " a good time " afterwards—this ancient slogan defines the ambit of their aspirations. When they have any religion at all, these irresponsible drifters, it is of a kind which involves the minimum of interference with their settled habits.

The prophet's exhortation is not less relevant to the condition of that parasite of the road who chooses the path that is followed by the multitude. This is the man who espouses the cause that has the largest number of adherents, and whose voice is nearly always the loudest among those that shout. He does not stop to think for himself at any decisive stage of his journey. It is enough for him that he is on the side of the big battalions, and his contempt for minorities is in inverse ratio to the intelligence of his opinions. One argument usually suffices to determine his loyalties—the majority must be right; and if at any time the majority should happen not to be right, it is at least more respectable to be wrong in company than to err in isolation. So he allows himself to be swept along in unreflecting submission to the sway of the crowd.

Closely akin to this unthinking class who are influenced mainly by the argument of quantity are those others who are always ready to respond to the appeal of novelty. They are the people who are " carried about by divers and strange doctrines," and from among whom, accordingly, the leader of every new " Movement " draws the greater number of his adherents. Seldom indeed has there been a time when the religious pedlar has carried on a more thriving trade among a credulous public than he does to-day, for, of course, the vacillations of the Church provide him with his opportunity. An astonishingly large number of people are easily imposed upon by enticing words—the implications of which they do not pause to consider—and are willing to be persuaded that they are in the van of spiritual progress. Few things can be more pathetic than the readiness with which they succumb to the infection of the very latest thing in religious fashions, or the eagerness with which they repeat its catch-words and proclaim its healing and emancipating virtues. This goes on until a collapse takes place somewhere, and then, when they have nursed their sores for a while, they transfer their enthusiasm to some new adventure in religious vagrancy.

Then there are the somewhat numerous company whose course is prescribed for them by some form of human authority. It may be the authority of a priestly order which lays claim to infallibility in the realm of truth. Or it may be the dictation of civil rulers who seek to extend their jurisdiction over that region of spiritual functions and relationships in which the human soul has always most passionately asserted its right to be free. More frequently it is the domination of scholarship in the sphere of religion. For the moment I am not thinking of the scientist who tilts at the Christian faith with the lance provided by his own particular department of learning; the fact is that in his attitude to religion the true scientist, instead of being a militant gainsayer, has nowadays almost become a mild-voiced pacifist. Nor have I in mind the more subtle attacks of the psychologist, who seeks to deny the reality of Christian experience by explaining it in terms of natural mental processes. I am referring to the scholar who assails the Christian documents and, as a natural consequence, some of the vital Christian facts, from within the Church itself, and whose pronouncements have not yet acquired the accent of humility which marks the utterances of the greater number of his colleagues in the realm of natural science. He is not, of course, animated by a deliberately hostile purpose ; his aim is to save *something* from the wreckage which appears to him to have been caused by the impact on Christianity of various forms of modern scepticism. But there are concessions which amount to betrayals, and there are scholars whose efforts to arrive at the irreducible content of Christian truth involve so complete a surrender of the Faith that they leave no Gospel for sinful humanity.

"Stand in the ways and see" is a call to the exercise of personal judgment in matters of faith and conduct. The ransomed of the Lord should not be like "dumb driven cattle" on the way to their promised inheritance. They must take time to reflect and to use their own eyes whenever they come to the cross-roads. It is not for them to be swayed by the multitude, or to yield to the seductive appeals of religious novelty. Nor must they render an unquestioning submission to the authority of scholarship when it claims to be the final arbiter of Christian truth. It would, of course, be the height of folly to think or speak of scholarship with contempt. It has its own record of noble achievement, and there is a province within which it holds legitimate and unchallengeable sway. When it is believing and reverent, it is indeed one of God's precious gifts to His Church on earth. But even when it is believing and reverent, its sphere is the outer Court of the Temple of Truth, and there are inner regions, spacious "realms of gold," that lie beyond its range. Sometimes, however, scholarship issues its decrees with respect to matters which it is not competent to decide. And when it establishes a kind of dictatorship in the commonwealth of spiritual truth, and sets itself up as a controller which doles out the very Bread of Life to the children of God, it must be quietly but firmly told to mind its own business. After all, there is a region of experience in which it is the saint who is the expert, and over which the scholar, as such, can lay no claim to special jurisdiction.

II. In the second place, there is the Call to Investigation

" Ask for the old ways," says Jeremiah, " where is the good way." The exercise of private judgment is a right and necessary thing, but it may be carried too far. Independence of mind may easily pass over into arrogance of spirit. The man who strikes out for himself in his religious thinking may become so enamoured of his own opinions as to invest them with final authority. But uncertainty at least should bear the fruit of humility, and conscious ignorance should be willing to learn. So the man who has reached the cross-roads is not only enjoined to stand, but also to ask.

And he is to ask for " the old paths." This however must not be understood to mean that antiquity is an absolute guarantee of truth. Error is old, as old as " man's first disobedience," and a blind submission to the authority of tradition may become a yoke of bondage. Investigation accordingly should be conducted with open-eyed discernment. But the assumption underlying the prophet's words is that it is among the old paths that the good way is to be found.

What, then, is this way that is " good " in a unique and pre-eminent sense ?

First of all, it is the way that answers to a man's consciousness of personal guilt.—Jeremiah's words are addressed to a people who had forsaken the living God. They were therefore wandering in a trackless waste, and had to find the way back—the way that leads from the far country to the Father's House. And the man who comes to himself in that condition of estrangement recognises that his most urgent need is the need of reconciliation to God. The question that presses most insistently for an answer within his soul is, How shall I find the way of peace—peace with God and peace within my own breast ? And assuredly he will find that good way among the old paths. For God's way of reconciling sinners to Himself is as old as the history of the human race. The Gospel of redemption was imbedded in the words of the first Promise, and was further disclosed in dim prefigurement through the sacrifices of the Old Dispensation. That same Gospel is revealed in noon-day clearness in the Cross of Christ. For us to-day the way of reconciliation passes by the hill of Calvary, and leads us straight to the mercy-seat of God. We stand at the cross-roads seeking wistfully for an answer to the problem of our personal guilt, and we see before us One whose pierced hands are stretched out in gracious invitation, in whose eyes there shines a light that bids us be of good courage, and from whose lips there comes a call to surrender which is accompanied by a promise of Rest.

No Gospel is adequate for sinful men which leaves out of account the demands of their own moral consciousness. The well-known London magistrate, Mr J. A. R. Cairns, used to pose the friends whom he invited to his house of an evening with the question, "Which would you prefer—to be guilty and be acquitted, or to be innocent and be condemned?" And most of them were wont to say that they would choose the former alternative. "You are wrong," the Judge would reply; "you forget conscience." There are many theories of reconciliation which are also wrong because of a similar forgetfulness. It is Christ alone who provides an answer to the demands of an accusing conscience, for the reconciliation which reaches us through His redeeming Cross is accompanied by a peace which has been kissed by the righteousness of God.

Again, it is a way which provides an answer to a man's experience of persistent moral failure.—As he stands at the cross-roads, it is not, perhaps, the sense of guilt that is uppermost in his mind; rather is it the consciousness of weakness and failure. He has been tried and found wanting. Again and again, in spite of resolutions and strivings, the defences of his soul have broken down, and he has known the humiliation of defeat. What he specially wants is a reinforcement of his moral energies that will enable him to stand and overcome in the day of temptation. In other words, he wishes to know the secret—if such a secret there be—of victory over sin. There *is* such a good way of moral and spiritual power. It is the old path that Isaiah spoke about, in words that to this day make the heart leap up in desire : " An highway shall be there, and a way, and it shall be called the way of Holiness ; the unclean shall not pass over it . . . the wayfaring men, though fools, shall not err therein." It is the way that is trodden by those who have not only heard Christ's word of forgiveness, but have received His gift of Life. That life means a new endowment of power through the renewing of the Holy Ghost. The power of God's grace releases a man from the bondage of corruption, so that he is enabled to walk not after the flesh but after the Spirit. It is indeed a good way which provides so radical a transformation.

Once more, it is a way which commands the allegiance of a believer's heart and enlists the energies of his new life.— Our traveller, let us suppose, has now found the good way, and has entered on a personal experience of reconciliation and renewal—surely these are blessings that are sufficient for all the needs of his pilgrimage. But no ; there is something more that is needed to meet the requirements of his personality. That is an outlet for the Christian desire for service. And this is to be found in love to a Person and devotion to a Cause—a Person glorious enough and a Cause big enough to make a conquering appeal to all his heart and soul and strength and mind.

Here again it is in Jesus Christ that we find the complete fulfilment of our aspirations. He is not only the Saviour of the lost but the Master of the saved, and His Lordship extends over the whole range of life. He loved me and gave Himself for me ; and I, when once I grasp that fact by faith, am bound to His chariot wheels for ever. And He confronts me too with a Cause which is worthy of my whole-hearted allegiance, for it is nothing less than the extension of His kingly rule throughout the world. Someone has said that the promise, "His servants shall serve Him," guarantees one of the brightest hopes of Heaven; it also unfolds one of the loftiest joys of earth. And that old path on which the privilege of service is found in combination with the blessing of pardon and the gift of life is surely entitled to be called "the good way."

How and where is our wayfaring man to carry out his task of Investigation? He is to "ask," surely, by searching the oracles of God. The Scriptures are that sure word of prophecy unto which we are enjoined to "give heed as unto a light that shineth in a dark place." It is the Bible that points us with authoritative direction to the good way of salvation, and that provides us with an unerring clue to the maze of this earthly life. But it is not every way of reading the Bible that will prove really fruitful. "The Bible," it has been truly said, "can only be read understandingly on the road of real life by a man who has become a problem to himself and is desperately in earnest about finding his way." Let us assume that our inquirer at the cross-roads is faced with this personal problem, and is in real earnest in his search for a solution for it; in that attitude of sincerity let him search the Scriptures, and then will he find that "unto the upright light ariseth in the darkness."

He is to "ask" also by consulting the records of Church History. There he will learn how God has been leading His people in the generations that are past; how He has been wont to chastise them for their departures from the good way; and how, in the riches of His mercy, He has brought them back, again and again, into the paths of righteousness. There too he will hear the voice of the Christian Church ringing down through the ages as she sings her *Credo*, and bears witness in death as well as in life to the truth which has become the master-light of all her seeing.

And should he not also "ask" by lending an ear to the testimony of Christian Experience? Multitudes of other souls have sought and found the way before him. How did they emerge out of darkness into the light of the Truth? What difficulties had they to overcome, and into what by-paths did they perhaps turn aside, before discovering the wicket-gate that opens into the way of life? What were the intellectual or emotional experiences through which they passed during the process of investigation, and what account do they give of the new world into which they entered when their search was ended? Not that Christian experience in matters of this kind conforms to any single pattern; but many a troubled heart has found comfort in its own perplexity through hearing or reading of God's dealings with the pilgrims of an earlier day. For this reason the seeker at the cross-roads will do well to scan the pages of Christian biography. And throughout his whole inquiry, from whatever source he seeks to receive enlightenment, he must ask above all at God's Throne of Grace, praying with uncreasing patience and sincerity that the Lord Himself will so vouchsafe His heavenly illumination as that his steps may be guided into the way of peace.

III. In the third place there is the Call to Submission.

"Walk therein," says Jeremiah in his final word of exhortation. It is the necessary climax of the Divine appeal. It is not enough to reflect or to inquire. Knowledge must yield the fruit of obedience. Investigation must be followed by submission. An intellectual apprehension of the way of salvation will not suffice unless it is accompanied by a practical surrender to the claims of Christ. It is nothing less than submission that the Gospel demands of sinful men, and the reality of our submission is attested by our walk. "If ye know these things," said our Lord one day to the people who listened to His message, "happy are ye if ye do them." There are many who have a sufficient knowledge of the Christain facts, but whose answer to God's call to obedience is a definite " We will not." And this, beyond question, is the final condemnation in this Gospel age. There is no sin so heinous in the sight of Heaven as the sin of rejecting God's remedy.

Jeremiah follows his three-fold appeal with a single assurance. " Walk therein," he says, " and ye shall find rest for your souls." It is an assurance which still rings in the ears of men to-day. Rest in this tumultuous world through believing on the Son of God—rest for the guilty conscience, for the troubled heart, and for the anxious mind; rest in the world to come, when the storms of life are over, and the saints shall enter into possession of their everlasting inheritance in God: that is one of the richest promises which the Gospel presents to a sinful world.

IX

LOST OPPORTUNITY AND CHANGELESS MERCY

THERE is a familiar passage in the eighth chapter of Jeremiah which gives poignant expression to the anguish that fills the hearts of men who realise that their day of opportunity is past, and that the door of hope appears to be closed against them for ever. Israel's persistent disloyalty to their God was not allowed to go unpunished. They were made to reap the fruit of their apostasy, and, for the time being, were left to be a prey to their approaching enemies. In their distress they looked for deliverance, but none came, and the prophet represents them as looking back on the lost days of privilege and lamenting their misuse of the Divine favours. "*The harvest is past,*" they cry, "*the summer is ended, and we are not saved.*" In the present instance, however, as in various other places in this Book, the cry of human distress is answered by the voice of Divine mercy. "*Is there no balm in Gilead?*" asks the God of Israel, "*is there no physician there? Why then is not the health of the daughter of my people recovered?*"[1] Regarded in their permanent application, the words confront us with:

I. THE TRAGEDY OF WASTED OPPORTUNITY.—In this woeful plight there is necessarily present the consciousness of past neglect. When spring and summer and autumn are past, it is not possible to deny that three-fourths of life are gone. Of some readers of these lines this is literally true. The springtime of youth is now a thing of distant memory; the summer of vigorous manhood and womanhood is over; even the fruit-gathering of an accumulated experience has ended in a despairing

[1] viii. 20, 22.

sense of futility. There is nothing left for them but the decrepitude of age. The snows of winter have now whitened their head, and the cold of winter has chilled their blood. And there are few things more pitiful in human life than the sight of an old man sinking down into his grave in a condition of stolid unconcern about the salvation of his soul.

There are many, however, who finish their course before they reach the stage of grey hairs. Their sun perhaps goes down while it is yet noon. And yet all the seasons of the year may be included within the compass of their brief life-span. Sowing-time and ripening-time and reaping-time all have been compressed into their day of privilege. Through the ministries of His Providence and of His Grace—I have in view, of course, those who are brought up under the hearing of the Gospel—God has given them opportunities of bringing forth fruit to His praise. For them too it is inexpressibly sad to look back from beneath the shadow of the end and have to say, "The harvest is past, the summer is ended."

And past neglect yields the result of present danger. "We are not saved," cried Israel in the agony of a belated recognition of the truth. When long-continued privilege has not yielded the fruit of salvation, a man's soul is obviously in grave danger. Its sin has not been blotted out, its diseases have not been healed, it has not received Christ's endowment of spiritual life. And to assert all that is to understate the truth. If there has been no improvement there certainly has been deterioration: that is an assured psychological and moral fact. If summer and harvest have not resulted in a movement upward, they have produced a declension along the ways that go down to death. Wasted opportunity means added guilt. The heart has become less impressionable and conscience more unresponsive. If there is no harvest of life, there is a terrible harvest of corruption. The nearer a man comes to his end in an unsaved state, the less likely is it that he will ever be saved at all.

Further, the consciousness of present danger, under

such circumstances, plainly suggests the dread of future doom. If the harvest is past and the summer is ended, then winter is coming. And winter is the time of chill winds and killing frosts, of bare fields and leafless woods, of raging tempests and angry seas—all of which may be regarded as a figure of coming judgment. It is seldom profitable to give rein to the imagination in discussing the destiny of an unsaved soul. But it is still more foolish to try to tone down, or to explain away, the plain teaching of Scripture regarding the awfulness of its doom. "He that believeth on the Son hath everlasting life, and he that believeth not the Son shall not see life, but the wrath of God abideth on him"; let that pronouncement —so overwhelming in the implications of its second alternative—suffice for the present. A careless past, a fruitless present, and a hopeless future—the man whose conscience has been stabbed awake to the reality of these three facts has a foretaste in this life of the torments of the damned.

One of the most terrible little poems in English literature—a sonnet by Dante Gabriel Rossetti, entitled "Lost Days"—gives expression to this fact in words which pierce the heart like the sound of the last trump. The poet asks himself what the lost days of his life would be like, were he to see them lying on the street as they fell. Would they be ears of wheat, sown once for food, but trodden into clay? Or golden coins, which were squandered, and for which a reckoning has still to be given? Or drops of blood dabbling the guilty feet? Or water which has been spilt, and which in dreams must cheat the undying thirst of throats in hell? And this is how he answers his own questions:

I do not see them here; but after death
God knows I know the faces I shall see,
Each one a murdered self, with low last breath.

"I am thyself—what hast thou done to me?"
"And I—and I—thyself," (lo! each one saith),
"And thou thyself to all eternity."

This is surely one of the most impressive sermons ever preached on the tragedy of wasted opportunity. To the same purpose is George Meredith's reminder that lost opportunity may prove to be "a mocking devil."

II. God's Message of Hope to those who are still "not saved."—"Is there no balm in Gilead?" He asks; "is there no physician there?" The words in all likelihood embody a proverbial expression. For Gilead, a district extending from the end of the Jordan to the Euphrates, had been noted, as far back as the days of Jacob, for a certain balsam which possessed remarkable medicinal qualities, and was particularly effective in the treatment of wounds and sores. The prevalence of this commodity in Gilead would also involve that in that region there would have been physicians who were skilled in its application. It is unnecessary to attach weight, as is sometimes done, to fanciful analogies—the piercing of the tree's side, for example, in order that the healing substance might flow forth—between the balm of Gilead and the Divine provision for the healing of men's souls. But Jeremiah's use of the phrase is clearly figurative, and does refer to a cure for the moral and spiritual "hurt" of his countrymen. For our present purpose, therefore, we shall extend the proverb to include the Gospel remedy for the wounds and bruises and putrefying sores of sinful humanity. "Is there no balm in Gilead, is there no physician there?" That is a question which the God of salvation still addresses to men and women who have neglected many seasons of opportunity.

It is a question in which we can detect the accent of surprise. You are not yet "saved"; is it because you have never heard of a Saviour? Your soul remains diseased; is it because there is no healing for its corruptions? You are still in a state of alienation from God; is it because there is no way of reconciliation? The question may well be charged with astonishment, for, with regard to the privileges which He has bestowed on His people, God may justly say, "What could have been done more to my vineyard that I have not done in it? "Wherefore," then . . . "wild grapes?"

It is also a question in which we can discover a note of reproach. Israel had despised a proffered deliverance, and had turned a deaf ear to reiterated warnings and appeals. That same charge can be brought against impenitent men and women to-day. They have rejected the healing balm which has been brought to their door, and have refused to recognise the worth of the Divine Physician whose glory is the light of Heaven and the theme of angels' songs. They have made light, too, of the cost at which the Gospel balm has been provided, and have regarded the sacrifice of Calvary as a thing of little account. It is nothing to them that in order to be a Physician the Son of God had first to be a Redeemer, and that the securing of redemption involved the shedding of His blood. God has surely just cause for reproaching men for their neglect of so great a salvation.

But, above all, the question contains a message of Hope. It is a question which obviously expects an affirmative answer. There *is* a Balm in Gilead, and there is also a Physician who knows how to make it work. The one efficacious remedy for the "hurt" of sinful men, as has already been indicated, is the provision of God's grace revealed in the Gospel, and the only Physician of human souls is the Son of God who was crucified on Calvary, and is now alive at the right hand of the Father in Heaven. The virtue of the balm is inseparable from the art of the Physician.

He is a Physician who possesses infallible Skill. In the days of His flesh on earth He performed many mighty works of healing, manifesting His power, as a rule, when the resources of men had proved of no avail. He cleansed the lepers, opened the eyes of the blind, cast out devils, and raised the dead. In the region of spiritual disease He exercises to-day a sovereignty of grace and power which is not less absolute. The balm which He administers is a panacea which embraces "all sin" within its range, and its curative effect is no mere temporary relief, but salvation "unto the uttermost." On the one hand, there is no sin so black that He cannot blot it out, and no corruption so deep-seated that He cannot overcome its power. On the other, the glory of His completed "health and cure" is greater than the mind of man can ever fully conceive. It is no maimed and disfigured life to which He restores those whom He rescues from the power of death. The Bride of Christ will stand beside Him at last in the beauty of perfect holiness. "He loved her foul that He might make her fair," says Augustine, and her fairness will be nothing short of full conformity to His own likeness.

He is also a Physician who manifests an unfailing Tenderness. An outstanding feature of His character is the quality of mercy. He is full of compassion for the erring and the suffering. When He sojourned among men in this world He associated with the outcasts and laid His hand on the untouchables. He is now exalted to the Throne of the majesty on high, but His heart still goes out to those who are ignorant and out of the way. He still raises the poor from the dust and the beggar from the dunghill; He still remembers our human frailty, and is touched with the feeling of our infirmities. Not that His tenderness is of that indulgent kind which shrinks from inflicting pain even when suffering is recognised to be an essential condition of healing. Every physician must sometimes hurt before he can cure. It is necessary for him to probe deep in order that he may reach the seat of the disease. Christ searches into the secret things of men's guilt and shame—their pride and selfishness, their malice and envy, their turbulent passions and impure desires—so that they themselves may recognise that their sores are malignant, and can be overcome only if they place themselves unreservedly in His hands.

> He took the suffering human race,
> He read each wound and weakness clear,
> And struck His finger on the place,
> And said, *Thou ailest here and here.*

We may change the tense of Matthew Arnold's lines from the past to the present, for our Lord still follows the same method in healing the souls of them that are sick. But even His probing of their wounds has in it the touch of gentleness. He heals the broken in heart, and preserves the bruised reed from being broken. And we shall never realise the wonder of these affirmations unless we remember who He is who stoops to such gracious ministries. It is the Creator of the ends of the earth who is the Healer of a sin-stricken soul, and it is the Hand that "meted out heaven with the span" which measures, with the same unerring exactitude, the distance between bruising and breaking in the heart of His afflicted child.

And this Physician, too, is always Accessible. He is never too far off to hear our cry. We do not need to ascend into heaven to bring Him down from above, or to descend into the deep to bring Him again from the dead; in the word of the truth of the Gospel He is ever at our side, and His healing resources are as available to the poor as they are to the rich. The Balm of Calvary is free to the chief of sinners, and the Divine Healer never casts out the meanest suppliant that knocks at His door. I do not forget that, in the bitterness of some great sorrow, men and women have sometimes charged Him with being indifferent to their need, but that is not the witness of any soul that has ever really become a debtor to His grace.

III. An Appeal to the Reason and Conscience of Men in View of that Hope.—"Why then," God asks, "is not the health of the daughter of my people recovered?" It is a question which must have left Jeremiah's hearers dumb with conscious guilt, and which also closes the lips of every unbeliever in our own day who has heard the message of salvation. For if the sinner who has had a summer and harvest of opportunity is still unsaved it is not because he has not been told of his disease, and neither is it because he has never heard of God's remedy. He cannot plead that the Gospel provision is not adequate to his need, or that the

Divine Physician is not available to apply the balm to his wounds. He can offer no excuse that will be accepted as valid even by his own reason and conscience. Still less can he justify himself before the bar of God. The man in our Lord's parable who was discovered at the marriage feast without the necessary wedding garment—which, presumably, he could have obtained as a royal gift—had not a word to say in answer to the challenge of the King. And this speechlessness of self-condemnation may be experienced in this life as surely as in the judgment to come.

That is true at least when the hour comes in which a man realises the truth about himself with a definiteness which makes evasion impossible. Up to that point he is usually ready, like the guests who were invited to the Great Supper, "to make excuse" for himself with a remarkable facility of invention. The reasons which led to the hopeless plight in which Israel at length found themselves are typical of the causes of unbelief throughout the ages.

To begin with, there is the natural tendency of the human heart to depart from the living God. That is the radical disease from which there is no deliverance apart from the washing of regeneration and the renewing of the Holy Ghost. Then there is the lure of worldliness, which in turn is closely related to the snare of false confidence. Israel were lulled to sleep by the assurance of "Peace, peace," which continually fell from the lips of their religious teachers. "Is not the Lord in Zion," they cried when the enemy were approaching the gate; "is not her King in her?" There are multitudes of people still who are buoyed up by the same groundless hope, imagining that a nominal connection with the Church of God is a pledge of everlasting security. And finally there is the fatal habit of procrastination. It is a habit which slays its tens of thousands. The duty which men neglect in spring, they resolve to fulfil in summer, and when summer days are over, and their loins are still ungirt, they promise once again that harvest will see their task accomplished. But, alas, it too often happens that the end of harvest finds them held more securely in the grip of sloth, and they are confronted with the closed doors of winter. " To-day," says our Divine Counsellor, " if ye will hear His voice, harden not your hearts."

X

THE LONGING FOR ESCAPE

JEREMIAH, like that greater Prophet whose experiences his ministry to a certain extent foreshadowed, was acquainted with grief in some of its sorest forms. Of these sorrows his outward sufferings formed by no means the greater part. Much more bitter than the personal trials which fell to his lot was the grief that he bore on account of his countrymen. "Oh," we hear him crying, "that my head were waters, and mine eyes a fountain of tears, that I might weep day and night for the slain of the daughter of my people." Jeremiah's sorrow, alike in its intensity and in its loneliness, was akin to the "great heaviness and continual sorrow" which oppressed the soul of Paul in a later age:

> Desperate tides of the whole great world's anguish
> Forced through the channels of a single heart.

Following this impassioned exclamation there breaks from the prophet's heart another cry which shows how near he had come to the limit of his endurance: "*Oh that I had in the wilderness a lodging place of wayfaring men, that I might leave my people and go from them!*"[1] These are words which express the longing for escape which, in that hour of inward tumult, sprang almost involuntarily to his lips. Jeremiah had no real intention of running away from his troubles and leaving his people to their doom. When put to the test at a later stage in his history, he showed that he was not the man to act the coward's part in time of danger. It was not ease or security that he coveted, but rest in some distant house of quiet, a respite from the load of pain which pressed

[1] ix. 2.

so heavily on his soul. And this revelation of natural human feeling is one of the things that make us feel that Jeremiah is kin to ourselves who are but common men.

There is a longing for escape which is not resisted, but passes over into some unworthy attempt at flight. There is another which sometimes enters into the experience of the most heroic souls, and which is overcome by a more compelling sense of obligation. This yearning for repose, it has been said, is deepest in those who stand most unflinchingly at their posts, and crush it down at the command of duty. " The greatest of all heroes is One " who was tempted in all points like as we are, yet without sin. We see Him in Gethsemane, standing under the shadow of Calvary, and confronted with the cup into which was compressed all the bitterness of that death which was the sinner's due. " Father," we hear Him cry, " if it be possible let this cup pass from me." That was the first word which He uttered in the terribleness of His agony. It expressed the instinctive shrinking of His human soul from the unutterable woe which was His appointed lot, and it rose as high as the very Throne of God, sweeping the whole range of possibility in its search for a way of escape. But it was not His last word. " Nevertheless," He adds, in meek submission to the inevitable, " not *My* will but Thine be done." The sacrifice of Calvary was no reluctant victim. Our Redeemer bound Himself willingly to the horns of the altar. And Christ's disciples have to drink their own cup and bear their own cross as they follow Him in the way, and for them too, whatever the longing of their heart may sometimes be, there is no legitimate way of escape.

I. There is a longing for escape from the Conflict of Life.—All life is in some degree a battle, " a long holding out " to endure, a more or less continuous effort to prevail, a struggle even to survive. And the Christian life especially is a persistent warfare. The believer lives in a world in which evil is one of the plainest facts of experience—moral evil which is sin, physical evil which is suffering. For the present let us confine our attention to the element of sin. With this ruthless enemy the follower of Christ must wage war to the end. He dare not relax his efforts; it is a fight for life. He must stand continually on guard, panoplied in the armour of God, defending himself with the shield of faith, and smiting his foes with the sword of the Spirit.

These foes are both numerous and powerful. Sometimes the most dangerous of them are lodged within a man's own heart. There are fleshly lusts which war against the soul, and there are lusts of the spirit which are even more insidious in their assaults—malice, and envy, and covetousness, and pride. In another mysterious arena also, the Christian must wrestle with the principalities and powers of darkness. And from this inner conflict he often longs to escape. There is a type of religion indeed which advocates withdrawal from the outward sphere of temptation as the only course which guarantees the safety of the soul. The life of cloistered seclusion is commended as the best, if not the sole condition of spiritual well-being. This attitude to the external world finds expression, for example, in the pages of Thomas à Kempis. "If thou attend wholly unto God and thyself," says this famous advocate of the ascetic life, "thou wilt be little moved by what thou seest abroad. . . . It is better for a man to live privately and to regard himself than to neglect his soul though he could work wonders in the world." The first comment to be made on these statements is that the alternatives which they suggest are not necessarily conflicting courses. When a man works for God in the world, it does not follow that he is neglecting his own soul. The second is that the escape which they commend is both selfish and cowardly.

The enmity of wicked men, too, has often caused the saints of God to long for "a lodge in some vast wilderness," where they might find rest from the strife of tongues and shelter from the designs of violence. The

Psalmist, for example, had a long experience of this kind of warfare. He had enemies who pursued and waylaid him with a fierce intensity of hatred. In one of the most plaintive of his songs he describes the "fearfulness and trembling" which came upon him as a result of their malice. Is there any wonder if in the midst of these heart-breaking experiences we find the royal sufferer giving utterance to his longing for peace and tranquillity? "Oh that I had wings like a dove," he cries, "for then would I fly away, and be at rest. Lo, then would I wander far off, and remain in the wilderness. I would hasten my escape from the windy storm and tempest." It is an exact parallel to the yearning of Jeremiah. Of the Psalmist, too, it may be said, in the words of an old writer, that he "rather longed than hoped to escape."

There is another form of conflict in which the children of God must engage, as a result of their efforts to promote the extension of His Kingdom in the world. If they do their part faithfully, they must identify themselves with those great public causes which are bound up with the progress of the Gospel in every department of human life—the cause of righteousness as opposed to every form of injustice and oppression, of truth as opposed to every variety of error, of purity as opposed to every kind of social and national corruption. And this is a long and strenuous warfare. For the forces of evil are strongly entrenched in the world, and their overthrow is not easily accomplished. The conflict involves a collision with many vested interests, the guardians of which have at their command a great variety of defensive instruments. Misrepresentation, abuse, intimidation, persecution—none the less effective because in civilised communities to-day it may not take the form of open violence—these are among the weapons with which their armoury is stocked.

It is under the strain of this kind of warfare that strong, true-hearted men have most frequently found themselves echoing Jeremiah's desire to escape to some secluded resting-place in the wilderness. But even when such a longing finds an outlet in words, it is straightway repressed at the demand of conscience. Here, for example, is what Mr John Buchan says regarding Oliver Cromwell: "Oliver had long thoughts of a little ease at last, of an old age like a Lapland night, when he could return to a simple life of family joys and country peace. But he resolutely put them aside, for he knew that he had entered upon a war in which there was no discharge, and that ease was not for him on this side the grave. . . . He must be up and doing, for he was called upon to assist in the building of the city of God. There was no security, no hope of laying aside the task."

A similar yearning for rest from the strife of many turbulent years was manifested by the dauntless Scottish Reformer, John Knox. In the preface to his last book, written after the cause of the Reformation had virtually triumphed in his native land, Knox states that he had already "taken good-night at the world and at all the fasherie of the same," and henceforth wished his brethren only to pray that God would "put an end to my long and painful battle." It was an attitude that came to light again and again in the utterances of his latter days. The veteran had fought a good fight, and longed for his discharge.

And if we come down to our own time we find this same wistful longing to escape from the turmoil of public life expressed in memorable words in one of the Addresses which make up Mr Stanley Baldwin's recently published volume, *The Torch of Freedom*. "One would not be a true son of the soil," declares the Prime Minister, "if one did not carry at the back of one's mind a hope that the day might come, some time, when one might be spared for a few peaceful years of life once more in that country in which one was brought up, to look out once more upon those hills, and ultimately to lay one's bones in that red soil from which one was made, in full confidence that whatever may happen to England, whatever defilements of her country-side may take place, . . . at any rate, in that one corner of England the apple blossom will always blow in the spring; and that there whatsoever is lovely and of good report will be born and will flourish to the world's end."

II. THERE IS ALSO A LONGING FOR ESCAPE FROM THE SUFFERING OF LIFE.—Suffering, which may be distinguished from conflict, inasmuch as it is passive rather than active, approaches human life by many avenues. Sometimes it takes the form of personal grief. The loss of a loved friend, for example, may pierce the heart like a sword, and the wound is so deep that life is never the same again. Or it may take the form of vicarious sorrow. We may be called upon to share the grief of others, or to bear the burden of their wrongdoing and shame; and when suffering of this kind is endured on behalf of those who are dear to us, it is often more bitter than death itself. Sometimes, again, it assumes the form of mental affliction. Among all the ills that flesh is heir to, this is, beyond question, the most overwhelming and the most mysterious. From one cause or another the mind itself becomes sick, its delicate adjustments are impaired, so that it cannot adequately fulfil its ordinary functions. And as a result of that disablement, the soul goes down into the depths, and is crushed beneath a great horror of darkness. There is surely no more difficult task in the world than to "minister to a mind diseased."

The most familiar form of suffering, however, is physical pain. It is true that bodily sickness may be relieved through the resources of medical science, but there is a limit to such alleviations. A man is laid low with some form of malignant disease, and his frame is racked in every nerve and limb with excruciating pain. Nowhere, perhaps, outside the Book of Job, can a more vivid and realistic account of this kind of suffering be found than in Ugo Bassi's "Sermon in the Hospital." Here is a characteristic passage:

> Such long weakness and such wearing pain
> As has no end in view, that makes of life
> One weary avenue of darkened days;

> The bitter darkness growing darker still,
> Which none can share or soothe, which sunders us
> From all desire, or hope, or stir of change,
> Or service of our Master in the world.
> Or fellowship with all the faces round
> Of passing pains and pleasures—while our pain
> Passeth not, nor will pass ; and only this
> Remains for us to look for—more of pain,
> And doubt if we can bear it to the end.

Little wonder if in such hours of anguish there should be a yearning for release. The cup is so bitter that the sufferer cannot but pray that it may pass ; and in itself, of course, this longing for escape is a natural human instinct. It is just here, however, that certain dangers beset the afflicted soul. It is hard to be courageous in the midst of the fiery furnace, and sometimes harder still to be submissive. A long-continued experience of mental and physical torture, accordingly, may beget a spirit of resentment and rebellion, and in such a mood a man may regard himself as a special mark for the arrows of the Almighty, and may challenge the righteousness of the Divine government. Nothing less than the sustaining power of the grace of God can make it possible under such conditions for patience to carry out her perfect work. But when this result is achieved, it will be found that an accepted Cross is among those treasures of darkness with which God is wont to guerdon His afflicted children. When faith, with however trembling a voice, is enabled to utter its "Nevertheless not my will but Thine be done," the Cross is already transmuted into a crown.

Here again we may listen for our profit to the searching words of Ugo Bassi. It is only in this present world, the preacher reminds us, that it is possible for a Christian to *suffer* for God's sake ; if, accordingly, he lets slip his Cross in impatience, he will never find it on earth again. Therefore when Christ presents to him the holy Cup of affliction, "with all its wreathen stems of passion-flowers and quivering sparkles of the ruby stars," he dare not and cannot refuse to accept it. Rather let him drink, and thereby enter into the fellowship of the sufferings of his Lord.

> Hold fast His hand,
> Though the nails pierce thine too! take only care
> Lest one drop of the sacramental wine
> Be spilled, of that which ever shall unite
> Thee, soul and body, to thy living Lord.

The mood of bitterness, however, may be followed by a feeling of despair, and it is when a man is held in the fell clutch of hopelessness that he is tempted to seek a short-cut to freedom. But no such method of release is permitted within the rule of God, and, recognising this, the believing heart firmly sets the temptation aside. In Sir James Barrie's inspiring Rectorial Address on "Courage"—the lovely virtue, as he describes it—there is nothing that more deeply touches the heart than the passage in which he tells of the letter which had been written to him by Captain Scott of the Antarctic, when the brave explorer and his companions were confronted with death among the eternal snows. "We are in a desperate state," it read, "feet frozen . . . no fuel, and a long way from food. . . . Later, we are very near the end. . . . We did intend to finish ourselves when things proved like this, but we have decided to die naturally without." The temptation to take the quick way out must have been great in the midst of those desolate immensities, but the unlawful method of escape was resolutely fought down by those very gallant gentlemen.

III. There is, further, a longing for escape from the Monotony of Life.—For a great many people life is a dreary round of commonplace happenings. They are cramped within a narrow environment, and chained, it may be, to some form of endless drudgery. "Fixed in a vegetable rooted lot," they have no colour in their experiences, and no variety in their contacts. Day after day they look on the same faces and listen to the same voices, are subjected to the same petty annoyances, and endure the same galling frustrations. In the evening they lie down in weariness, in the morning they rise up with little expectation of change. To-day has been the same as yesterday, to-morrow will be the same as to-day. Memory gives them no roses in December, and hope brings no breath of spring into the winter of their discontent. Life is always the same—one "endless vista of repellent monotony."

It is not surprising that there should be a longing to escape from all this tedium and bondage; a yearning for wider horizons; a thirst for the new wine of a richer experience; for romance that will warm the heart; for adventure that will stir the blood and bring a new interest into life. Nor should it be considered strange if, in the absence of healthy outlets, this longing should sometimes seek to realise itself in illegitimate ways. There are multitudes, for example, who try to escape from the drabness of life into a new world through indulgence in strong drink. Closely akin to those pathetic fugitives from reality are the men and women who attempt to escape from poverty by means of the gambler's throw. There are also, of course, people who shirk the common duties that lie to their hand because they consider themselves fitted for some loftier sphere of action. And there are others, of still meaner breed, who do their best to escape from the danger-zones of life to some safe retreat behind the firing-line. By far the commoner methods of escape from monotony, however, take the form of unhealthy excitement, sought through the medium of questionable associations and mean distractions.

There is, however, a more excellent way of deliverance from the monotony of existence. It is the way of escape *to* Jesus Christ. He is that Man who is "as rivers of waters in a dry place, and as the shadow of a great rock in a weary land." The Christian life should never be monotonous. It is full of surprises and exhilarations. It means romance and adventure on the highest plane of experience. It holds the key to lofty satisfactions, and provides the inspiration of splendid hopes. The life that is lived in Christ, and with Christ, and for Christ, is "life indeed."

IV. ONCE MORE, THERE IS A LONGING FOR ESCAPE FROM THE DISAPPOINTMENTS OF LIFE.—There must be few people in the world who have not experienced in one form or another the failure of their hopes. And there is scarcely anything that is more difficult to bear than the overthrow of cherished expectations. Even " hope deferred maketh the heart sick." But when hope is finally laid in the dust, nipped at the root by some " killing frost," the resulting sense of desolation is sometimes peculiarly bitter.

Disappointment comes in a hundred forms. Sometimes it happens in the ordinary affairs of life. A young man is filled with the desire to win the blue ribbon of academic distinction, and lives laborious nights and days to reach his goal. But in the struggle for supremacy he is surpassed by a rival competitor, and the coveted honour passes into other hands. A professional man sets his heart on some vacant post which will mean for him an increase of opportunity as well as social and financial advancement. But just when he thinks that " full surely his greatness is a-ripening," he is told that another has been preferred before him, and so his hopes are dashed to the ground. A business man has launched an enterprise which he has planned with enthusiasm, and to which he devotes all his strength. But for some reason —perhaps the emergence of some incalculable factor, or perhaps the folly of beginning to build without sufficiently counting the cost—it fails to achieve success, and he finds himself confronted with ruin.

These undoubtedly are disheartening experiences, but there are other forms of disappointment that are more desolating still. The disloyalty of a trusted friend, for example, or the pain of unrequited love—these are things that cause many a day to become dark with night. " One beautiful May morning when the lilac was in bloom "—the literary artistry is, of course, unconscious, for a great sorrow, in seeking to express itself, has no desire and no need to resort to the embroidery of fine language—" there was put in her hand a letter in which that was written which made a goblin of the sun": so Mildred Cable describes the supreme disappointment which, for a season, laid its blight on her own life. To that poignant record no word need be added here.

There are disappointments which are peculiar to the Christian life. The young believer enters on his course with high hopes of achievement in the service of his Lord. He is surprised at the lack of success which has marked the efforts of those labourers who have been before him on the field, and perhaps is secretly doubtful of their fitness for the work. Things are going to be different when he gets into action. He will scale the ramparts of wickedness, and demolish the strongholds of Satan. But after a time he finds that things are not turning out altogether as he had anticipated. The vision splendid is not being translated into actual achievement. The princes and potentates of the realm of darkness are refusing to capitulate. Old Adam once more is proving too strong for young Melanchthon. And the recognition of this fact often causes him to give way to dejection of soul. Weary and sick at heart he is oppressed with a sense of futility, and crushed with the consciousness of defeat. The struggle naught availeth, he is ready to exclaim, the labour and the wounds are vain. And in that mood of depression it may well be that there springs up in his heart a longing for escape. It was one of the greatest of the prophets of God who once cried, "I have laboured in vain, I have spent my strength in vain and for naught."

The life of Elijah provides a striking illustration of this kind of disappointment, with its consequent longing for escape. He had supposed that on Mount Carmel he had put an end to idolatry in Israel by one sweeping stroke, but Jezebel's furious communication showed him that he had only broken off some branches from the Upas tree which he had hoped to tear up by the roots—convincing proof, as he was to learn more fully later on, that physical force can never be an effective remedy for spiritual disease. So he concluded that all his efforts had been in vain, and in the soreness of his disillusionment longed to escape from the field of strife.

V. Finally, there is a longing for escape from the Loneliness of Life.—There are people who are more or less lonely all their days. It may be that in a literal sense they pass their life in isolation from their fellows, and are therefore strangers to the comforts and satisfactions of human companionship. But there is a loneliness which may be more keenly felt than any physical separation. It is a commonplace observation that one may be lonely in a crowd—possibly because to be in a crowd and to be *of* it are two different things.

Social ostracism, again, is sometimes hard to endure, although under modern conditions of life it seldom happens that every door is closed against those who offend against the accepted codes ; on the contrary a motor-car—especially if it happens to be of the Rolls-Royce variety—can be driven without penalty through all the conventions. But there are many who for other reasons are conscious of loneliness in the midst of their acquaintances. They have no gift for making friends. Perhaps they possess certain qualities which repel the advances of friendship—such deterrents, for example, as a sour temper or a biting tongue. Or it may be that they are encased within a proud reserve which makes intimacy impossible. They may long for fellowship but they are unable to create it. They neither give nor receive confidences, and they show little " kindness in another's trouble," whatever courage they may exhibit in their own. In a word, they do not " mix " well with their neighbours, and the result is that, like Goldsmith's Traveller, they are, to a great extent, " remote, unfriended, melancholy, slow." More earnestly than they might care to confess, men and women such as these must long for escape, not to the solitudes of the wilderness, but from the isolations of their everyday life.

But it is when the day has turned toward evening and the shadows of the end are closing in, that the sense of loneliness usually becomes most oppressive. The consciousness of failing powers becomes too real to be ignored. The earthly house of this tabernacle has begun to dissolve, the energies of the body are yielding to decay, and the mind is losing its clearness and vigour. Under such circumstances the Christian often desires to depart in peace. He fears that he has outlived his usefulness, and he knows that he has survived the friends of his early years. They have all been taken away from "the evil days" of mental and physical decrepitude, and he often wonders why he is left behind to groan under the burden of accumulating infirmities. He longs to follow them into the world of light, and in hours of loneliness he listens wistfully for the sound of Christ's chariot wheels.

We have all heard of the patience of Job, and have often marvelled at the deep wisdom and courageous faith displayed by that good man in the midst of sorrows and temptations which fell upon him in battalions. It is generally held that the loftiest utterances which fell from his lips in that season of trial were the familiar words, "I know that my Redeemer liveth . . .," and, "Though He slay me, yet will I trust in Him." These doubtless are amazing affirmations—even when they have suffered their worst at the hands of an eviscerating criticism—but I have often thought that there is another saying of Job's which is not less worthy of being graven on the rock forever. Let us recall the circumstances of his many-sided affliction. Stripped of his possessions, bereaved of his children, smitten with a loathsome disease, goaded by the reproaches of a trio of foolish friends, and tempted with the suggestions of an impatient wife—who urged him to yield to the promptings of the Devil and be done with it—Job is writhing in such an agony of mind and body that he curses the day on which he was born. But this short, bitter cry was only the reflection of a passing mood. Job's settled attitude to life and to God is set forth in words of a very different quality. "*All the days of my appointed time will I wait, till my change come*"—that is Job's final answer to the voice of temptation, and no braver words ever fell from the lips of a tortured man. For it is in that *waiting* for God's appointed time of release that the loftiest heroism of the soul comes to light.

The same high courage is revealed by the Apostle Paul in the closing scene of his crowded life. A prisoner in Rome, he too sometimes longed for escape from the restrictions and the loneliness of his outward condition. In his heart there was "a desire to depart and to be with Christ; which is far better." But this personal feeling was promptly set aside in the interests of the Church of Christ on earth. "Nevertheless," he adds, in writing to the Philippians, "to abide in the flesh is more needful for you." That was the unselfish desire of Christian love, and it found an abundant recompense. Paul's gracious Lord transformed the Roman prison into a kind of vast cathedral from which there sounded forth words that have been echoing through the world for wellnigh two thousand years. Paul's written word in the Epistles of the Imprisonment have exercised a far mightier influence on human life than the spoken message which he delivered in the days of his freedom.

This provides us with one reason why God allows His children to linger on in the world when their usefulness appears to have ended. It is He alone who is able to determine when their work is done. In the weakness and loneliness of their latter end they can still be witnesses to the power of His grace. Apart from any other kind of ministry, they can show how a Christian can grow old with resignation, and, better still, how a Christian can die in hope.

XI

FALSE AND TRUE GLORYING

THERE were many outward possessions in which the Jewish people boasted after they had ceased to glory in their God. They were proud, for example, of the wisdom which directed their foreign policy, that calculating shrewdness which led them to form alliances with their stronger neighbours, so that when danger threatened them from one quarter of the outer world they were justified in looking for protection from another. For this reason they also prided themselves on the security which rested, as they supposed, on those seasonable augmentations of their internal resources. And of course, as the Psalmist has expressed it, they "trusted in their wealth, and boasted themselves in the multitude of their riches." They had a natural aptitude for finance, and their skill in driving a bargain would not only have deepened their love of gain for its own sake, but would also have strengthened their appreciation of wealth as a source of power. It is against this deep-seated tendency of men to glory in themselves rather than in the living God that Jeremiah utters a protest in the remarkable passage to which our attention is now to be directed. "*Thus saith the Lord,*" he declares, "*Let not the wise man glory in his wisdom, neither let the mighty man glory in his might, let not the rich man glory in his riches; but let him that glorieth glory in this, that he understandeth and knoweth Me, that I am the Lord which exercise loving-kindness, judgment, and righteousness, in the earth: for in these things I delight, saith the Lord.*"[1]

It is natural for the human heart to indulge in some form of boasting. Few of the children of men are so

[1] ix. 23, 24.

emptied of self as not to have their own particular kind of vanity. However poorly endowed they may be in most respects, there is always *something* of which they are openly or secretly proud. A woman may frankly recognise that her face is lacking in nearly every attribute of beauty, but then has she not a handsome figure to make up for this obvious handicap ? Even Royalty has been known to regard a pair of shapely hands as a more or less adequate compensation for a regrettable lack of inches. A man will freely admit that he is deficient in book-learning, but he is equally ready to claim that he has a fund of common sense which is of more practical value than the best University Degree. And in moments of expansion the most modest of human beings will lift up their voice and chant the praises of that special attainment which helps them to live on good terms with themselves. Now it is only fitting that a man should cherish a thankful spirit for those talents, of whatever kind, which he may happen to possess ; but to glory in them, to make them the main preoccupation of his mind and the chief delight of his heart—that is an attitude which is not only hurtful to himself but dishonouring to God.

I

There are three familiar forms of pride against which Jeremiah directs his warning.

1. There is first of all *the pride of wisdom.* It is not, of course, the wisdom which is "from above," and which is therefore a gift of grace, that the prophet has in view, but the wisdom which is "of this world." Neither is it the wisdom that is derived from an enriching experience of life, in which the heart has given many a "useful lesson to the head," as opposed to the mere knowledge of external things. The distinction between wisdom and knowledge, so understood, is embodied in Cowper's familiar couplet :

> Knowledge is proud because he knows so much,
> Wisdom is humble that he knows no more.

As used by Jeremiah, the word must be understood in its more general sense as a term which embraces all the powers of the mind, its comprehensiveness of grasp, its keenness of penetration and clearness of discernment, expanded and strengthened by its acquired attainments. There are few things in which men are more ready to glory than in this kind of wisdom; and indeed if ever it were legitimate for them to boast at all in the presence of God, the readiest excuse would be furnished by the capacities and achievements of the human mind. It is a mere commonplace to say that the faculty of thought is the supreme endowment which raises man above the level of the brute creation, and proclaims him to be "the fallen kinsman of God." Just because he is a rational being, he is greater, in all his feebleness, than the whole material universe. "By space," says Pascal, "the universe encompasses and swallows me; by thought I encompass it. Man is but a reed, weakest in nature, but a reed which thinks. . . . Were the universe to crush him, man would still be nobler than that which has slain him, for he *knows* that he dies." The discoveries of science, which have not only revolutionised our conception of the universe, but in their practical applications to our industrial and social life have wellnigh surrounded us with a new world—these, and, to mention no more, the creations of literary and artistic genius throughout the ages, bear witness to the marvellous powers with which God has endowed His rational creatures. To enlarge on these achievements here, however, even if one were able to do so with adequate knowledge, would be to travel beyond the purpose of the present chapter; this only may be said, they are achievements which bring closer to reality the high-sounding tribute of Hamlet: "What a piece of work is a man! How noble in reason, how infinite in faculties, . . . in action how like an angel, in apprehension how like a god!"

All this being recognised, however, there is a great deal more that has to be said, and said with still greater emphasis, on the other side. Man may be God-like in apprehension, but he certainly has not the apprehension of God. The powers of his mind are definitely limited. There is a boundary beyond which thought cannot travel in its own strength. Neither science nor philosophy is able to solve the riddle of the universe, and reason with all its searching cannot find out God.

It is just here, however, that Jeremiah's word of admonition is particularly relevant. The wise man *is* prone to glory in his wisdom. It is indeed not too much to say that there is scarcely any form of arrogance so overbearing as the pride of intellect. If a man thinks he knows more than his neighbours in any department of knowledge, he is ready to assume an attitude of contempt for their ignorance, and to assail them with derisive epithets when they dare to challenge his judgments. It is right to say, however, that it is never those who know most that are inclined to give way to such exhibitions of vanity. It is " a little learning " that, in this respect is a dangerous thing to the man who possesses it. The real scholar is a humble man, because he realises that it is only a tiny section of the far-stretching kingdom of Truth that, as yet, he has been able to explore. Here, for example, are the closing sentences of Sir James Jeans's remarkable work on *The Mysterious Universe*: " We cannot claim to have discerned more than a very faint glimmer of light at the best; perhaps it was wholly illusory, for certainly we had to strain our eyes very hard to see anything at all. So that our main contention can hardly be that the science of to-day has a pronouncement to make, perhaps it ought rather to be that science should leave off making pronouncements: the river of knowledge has too often turned back on itself."

These are the words of one of the foremost scientists of this generation, and they present a refreshing contrast to the dogmatic pronouncements of half a century ago. All along the line of its operations modern scholarship is becoming less sure of itself, and the note of finality which used to mark its utterances on the great issues of life has largely disappeared. Largely, but by no means completely. In its relation to God and the Gospel of Jesus Christ the wisdom of this world still reveals its pride and maintains its age-long antagonisms. Sometimes, indeed, the antagonism flames with a new intensity. "For the first time in the human story," says Professor Daniel Lamont in his masterly work on *Christ and the World of Thought*, "God has been removed from the unique place which He held in the mind of the race, and has been relegated to a place among matters of opinion. . . . Man as never before has constituted himself the measure of God." This fact is only too clearly revealed in the glorification of atheism in Russia and the resurgence of paganism in Germany, to say nothing of less conspicuous developments of a similar character in our own and other lands. Human reason has always revealed a tendency to deify itself, and in many quarters to-day it is ready to contend that, if there should be regions which it cannot explore, they are desert places which are not worth the trouble of investigation.

It is against the Christian Revelation that human wisdom more especially lifts up itself in scornful pride. For the Gospel proclaims for the acceptance of men a series of supernatural facts, and reason is unwilling to include within its beliefs anything which it regards as incapable of scientific proof. The philosophers of Athens who stood before Paul on Mars Hill listened to his views on Creation, and Providence, and Natural Theology in general, with more or less respectful attention ; but when he began to speak about One who had been raised from the dead, his message was brought to a sudden close, for some of his hearers were unable to conceal their scorn, others evaded the moral issue which he associated with the fact of the Resurrection, and only a handful remained to inquire and pray. The Gospel also presents to sinners a salvation which is all of grace, and the natural man desires to stand before God in his own right, rather than as a debtor to the merits of Another.

In his Second Epistle to the Corinthians Paul declares that his aim in carrying on the warfare of the Gospel was to cast down "every high thing that exalteth itself against the knowledge of God," and foremost among those high things is the pride of human wisdom. The true knowledge of God demands from men a surrender of personality which has ethical as well as intellectual implications. And the pride of man revolts against such a subjection of the will to the authority of the Crucified, and resents the moral challenge for the same reason as moved Lord Melbourne on one occasion to protest indignantly that "things had come to a pretty pass when religion was allowed to invade the sphere of private life." As opposed to all this arrogance of spirit the true wisdom is child-like in its humility and teachableness. It rejoices in Christ Jesus, and has learned to have "no confidence in the flesh."

It is in Paul's First Epistle to the Corinthians, however, that we find the strongest and most searching indictment of this "high thing" of intellectual pride which exalts itself against the Gospel of the grace of God. That indictment occupies the greater part of the first chapter, but the sum of it is set forth in one pregnant sentence: "*After that in the wisdom of God, the world by wisdom knew not God, it pleased God by the foolishness of preaching to save them that believe.*" Several distinct elements come to light in this affirmation.

First of all, Paul declares that the wisdom of this world was provided with a full opportunity of exercising its strength in the highest interests of the human race. This appears to be the natural implication of the phrase, "in the wisdom of God." The wisdom of man was allowed a clear field, and an adequate time, in which to discover God, in order, on the one hand, that in the event of failure, it might never be able to plead that it had not been given a fair chance, and, on the other, that when its bankruptcy should be disclosed, the stage might be set for the revelation of the Divine resources. All this was done "in the wisdom of God," which not only conceived the plan, but foresaw the end of the experiment from the beginning.

In the second place Paul declares that the wisdom of this world had failed to achieve the end which ought to be the crowning glory of intellectual achievement. In other words, it "knew not God." The Greeks sought after wisdom with a greater keenness of perception and persistency of investigation than any other people in the ancient world, but on their acropolis in Athens there stood that altar "to the unknown god" which bore pathetic witness to the failure of all their philosophies. This also is a fact of universal experience. The knowledge of God in which there is eternal life, the knowledge which enriches and sanctifies while at the same time it humbles the soul, is not a matter of human discovery but of Divine revelation. It is an attainment, as our Lord assured Peter, to which flesh and blood cannot reach, but which is communicated through the renewing of the Holy Ghost.

In the third place Paul declares that when the supreme manifestation of the wisdom of God was given to the world in the Cross of His Son, the wisdom of men not only failed to recognise it, but derided it as foolishness. In other words, its blindness to the truth which lay unveiled before its eyes furnished an additional proof of its futility. "The foolishness of preaching" is simply the Gospel, described from the viewpoint of human pride. That same Gospel is the masterpiece of Divine wisdom, regarded from the viewpoint of spiritual discernment. To quote another deep saying of Paul, it is the mystery which from the beginning of the world had been hid in God, but has now been brought to light in such wise that it is the medium through which His "manifold wisdom" is being made known, not only to men on earth, but to the principalities and powers of the heavenly places.

The foolishness of preaching is the preaching of Christ crucified, and it was on the hill of Calvary that wisdom's eternal secret was at length completely unveiled. It is there alone that we can learn of that Way in which a holy God is glorified in the salvation of a guilty sinner; in which Righteousness and Love receive alike their clearest manifestation and their deepest satisfaction; in which weakness and omnipotence combine to secure an end which neither could accomplish without the other; in which death is compelled to become its own executioner, and a Cross of shame is made the pathway to a Throne of glory. And God exalts His wisdom still further by making the proclamation of the simple story of His redeeming love the channel through which His power is exercised in bringing men to repentance and faith in His Name. But human wisdom is so blinded by its own pride that it scorns as "foolishness" this splendour of revelation and achievement.

Finally, Paul declares that the wisdom of this world, in so far as it exalts itself against the Gospel of Christ, lies under the contumely and condemnation of Heaven. It is perhaps not too much to say that there is no sin of the human heart against which the face of God is more sternly set, and which He is more unchangingly resolved to lay low, than the sin of pride in relation to His own Son. The spirit which animated the conspirators whose actings are described in the Second Psalm—they are un-named in the prophetic oracle, but are identified in New Testament history—is not essentially different from the proud unbelief which in all ages judges and rejects the Christ of God. And wherever this spirit manifests itself, God's attitude to the rebels is always the same: "The Lord shall have them in derision." It is in accordance with this principle of the Divine procedure that Paul affirms that "God hath made foolish the wisdom of this world." Some of the ways in which this result is achieved have already been indicated. God gave the wisdom of man an opportunity of demonstrating its strength in the loftiest sphere of intellectual activity, and the result was absolute failure. He has also demonstrated that *His* wisdom—which the world regards as foolishness—has reached its goal, inasmuch as it has secured salvation for them that believe. But Paul's words convey more than this; they are charged with the note of judgment. "God," he reminds us, "hath chosen the foolish things of the world to confound the wise"—a statement which recalls the even more definite pronouncement of a Greater than Paul: "Thou hast *hid* these things from the wise and prudent, and hast revealed them unto babes." All this leads up to the Apostle's most sweeping utterance with regard to the wisdom of men. "It is written," he says, "I will destroy the wisdom of the wise, and will bring to nothing the understanding of the prudent." The final reason, therefore, why the wise man should not glory in his wisdom is that the wisdom of this world is lying under sentence of death.

The other two forms of arrogance against which Jeremiah utters his warning must be discussed more briefly.

2. The second is *the pride of power*. "Let not the mighty man," he says, "glory in his might." The word "might" is also a comprehensive term, including every form of strength in which men are wont to make their boast.

The young man, for example, glories in his bodily strength. His blood is warm, and his heart sings with the sheer joy of physical well-being. And this is as it should be, so long as he does not make physical fitness the chief end of man. But the strength of youth is a transient possession, which gradually diminishes before the pressure of advancing years. The wind passeth over it, and it is gone, and in the absence of more enduring satisfactions it becomes at last only a saddening memory.

There are others again who glory in the might which is derived from social position. They have either been born into the purple or have climbed into the appearance of it. They enjoy the prestige of rank, and are ready to hold at arm's length, so far at least as social intercourse is concerned, those who do not belong to the circle in which they themselves are privileged to move. It is indeed true that to-day these distinctions are gradually disappearing through the spread of democratic ideas; but the pride of long descent dies hard, even when blue blood may have lost its native hue through successive waterings. Let not the man who is pinnacled in this sphere of eminence boast in his might. It is well for him to remember, as often as possible, that "the glories of our blood and state are shadows, not substantial things," and that the crest of a lordling is not always a pledge of true nobility.

Then there is the man who glories in some form of authority with which he may be rightly or wrongly invested —the political leader whose judgment and sagacity have won for him the confidence of his party; the demagogue who sways the unthinking multitude with promises which he can never fulfil; the patron who holds at his disposal the gifts of place and preferment; the commander of victorious armies whose prowess has made him a national hero; the dictator who struts about like a demigod and speaks great swelling words of vanity, whose caprice may affect the destiny of a nation, and whose ambition may disturb the peace of a world. Let not these mighty men glory in their authority, saith the Lord. It is at the best a precarious endowment, for in a little while even the monarch's sceptre will be reduced to the level of "the poor crooked scythe and spade."

> Authority forgets a dying king,
> Laid widow'd of the power in his eye
> That bowed the will.

And if this is true of the highest earthly dignity, it applies with still greater force to men of less noble degree.

3. Last of all, there is *the pride of riches*. This is one of the most familiar forms of self-exaltation among men. It may, of course, be wealth which its owner has never earned, either by the sweat of his brow or the travail of his brain. It has simply been handed on to him by others, and even they may have secured it by methods that will not bear strict investigation. In any case the man who possesses stately houses and spacious lands, who is "an incarnation of fat dividends," and is therefore in a position to indulge himself in every form of luxury, is ready, on that ground alone, to regard his poorer neighbour as a

representative of the lower orders. Of all forms of human arrogance this is the one which it is hardest to suffer with Christian patience. Christ Himself has written the epitaph of the man who glories in his material possessions, but is destitute of the true riches. It is a brief but pregnant estimate, expressed in two shattering words—"Thou fool." Money can fill our barns with "much goods," but it cannot fill our hearts with true peace; it cannot buy off the last enemy, nor can it provide our souls with a good hope.

Wisdom, power, wealth—it is on these three objects of human glorying that Jeremiah lays the interdict of Heaven. The wise man, after all, is ignorant if he lacks the knowledge of God; the mighty man is a weakling if he is not equipped with the armour of God; and the rich man is a bankrupt if his soul is empty of the grace of God.

II

Having uttered his word of warning against these false grounds of confidence, Jeremiah directs our thoughts to the supreme fact in which men ought to glory. That is the knowledge of God which is the fruit of a direct personal experience of His grace. There is a certain knowledge of God as Creator and Ruler of the universe which is derived from observation. There is a clearer knowledge of Him which is based on revelation. But the knowledge of which the prophet here speaks is more than an intellectual apprehension of revealed truth; it is a knowledge which has its roots in an understanding of His character and purposes, arrived at through the illumination of His Spirit: "Let him that glorieth glory in this, that he understandeth and knoweth Me." This surely is a high and holy attainment—to *understand* God. It means that we are endowed with a spiritual discernment in the light of which false conceptions of His character are removed, and the secrets of His working in the realms of law and grace, and particularly with reference to our own souls, are to some extent made plain. To understand God in this sense is to love Him as our own Saviour and Lord, and to trust Him as the Judge of all the earth.

There are three manifestations of the Divine character which are embraced within the knowledge to which Jeremiah refers.

The first is the *Loving-kindness* of the Lord. Our English word, formed through the union of love and kindness, is filled with grace and beauty. Among men we sometimes meet with a love which is strangely divorced from kindness, and therefore seldom rises above the level of barren sentiment. On the other hand there is a kindness which somehow lacks the bloom of love, and whose actions, accordingly, fail to warm our heart even when they relieve our need. But when the two are found in combination—love supplying the motive, and kindness providing the helpful word or generous deed—they represent one of the finest things in human life. And what shall we say of the loving-kindness of the Lord? When the Psalmist attempts to describe it, he can only utter an exclamation of adoring wonder. "How excellent," he cries, "is Thy loving-kindness, O God!" Like the pure water of the river of life which John saw, it flows out from the Throne of God and the Lamb, and so has its springs in eternity. And it manifests itself in the innumerable kindnesses of God's redemptive activity. It looks out on us from the Manger in Bethlehem, and irradiates the darkness of the Cross. It transfigures the empty Tomb in the garden, and encircles with benignant grace the Throne within the veil. It pursues the sinner with "deliberate speed, majestic instancy" in his flight into the far country, and attends the believer with its healing and protective ministries on his pilgrimage to the Father's House. The measure of God's loving-kindness is the unsearchable riches of Christ. We begin to understand it when we have tasted that the Lord is gracious. We shall arrive at fulness of understanding when we know even as we are known.

The second is His exercise of *Judgment*. This aspect of God's character is by no means inconsistent with His loving-kindness, as many would have us believe. On the contrary it is essential to the glory of His Name in the government of a world in which moral evil is a reality. He Himself bears witness that He is a God of Judgment, and the testimony of His Word finds ample confirmation in the history of the world. From the great bulk of current religious teaching one might suppose that Jesus revealed nothing about God but His Fatherly benevolence. That, however, is an absolute misrepresentation of the facts. As surely as Jesus spoke about the love of God He also revealed His wrath. Those who attempt to get rid of this element in His eschatological teaching, by affirming that it has been superimposed on His authentic words by the evangelists, are merely substituting what they think He ought to have said for what He actually did say. Christ's own Cross was not a manifestation of love only, it was also in a mysterious way a revelation of judgment. And His Resurrection is a pledge of that final day of reckoning in which God will judge the world. This is a conception of the Divine character to which the modern mind offers scant hospitality. "The world," says Professor Daniel Lamont in the volume to which reference has already been made in this chapter, "prefers a God who will not judge, a God whose love includes no wrath. But there is no such God. The God who has revealed Himself is One whose Love has provided a way of escape from His Wrath. If that is not the teaching of the New Testament from beginning to end, one must despair of knowing the meaning of anything at all."

The third element in the glory of God is His *Righteousness*. This is an attribute which is revealed in all His dealings with the children of men. There is a sense even in which it underlies the exercise of His loving-kindness. This is no doubt what Carlyle had in view when he declared that there is nothing in the world but Justice. It is certainly what the Apostle John means when He assures us that "if we confess our sins, He is faithful and *just* to forgive us our sins, and to cleanse us from all unrighteousness."[1] God's forgiveness is based on the Righteousness

[1] 1 John i. 9.

which He Himself has provided in His Son, and which is revealed in the Gospel.[1]

And righteousness certainly underlies the exercise of God's judgment. The retributions which overtake men in this world may be overwhelming in their severity, but the Judge of all the earth can do nothing but what is right. That is a fact on which faith must take hold in hours when the heart is crushed and the mind is benumbed. And in the last Judgment of all, "to which the whole creation moves," He will deal justly with every individual of the human race. It would indeed be a fearful thing to fall into the hands of an unrighteous God, but the whiteness of the Judge's Throne[2] is a symbol of the righteousness of His Judgment.

Loving-kindness, Judgment, and Righteousness — in these things let men glory, for in these things God takes delight.

[1] Rom. i. 16, 17. [2] Rev. xx. 11.

XII

THE LESSON OF THE EASIER TEST

It was a striking answer that the Lord gave to the complaining of Jeremiah during a season of special trial and perplexity in the prophet's history. The men of Anathoth—Jeremiah's native place—had conspired against his life, and had proved themselves to be the enemies of the Lord as well as of His servant. But notwithstanding the enormity of their wickedness these malignants were not only left unpunished, but enjoyed a large measure of outward prosperity. It was this latter fact that specially distressed the prophet. The hostility of his own kinsfolk was no doubt painful enough to a man of his sensitive nature, but it was the far more serious question of the righteousness of the Divine government—that age-long problem which has so frequently offered a challenge to believing hearts—that particularly troubled his spirit and gave rise to his despondent questionings. "Wherefore," he asks, "doth the way of the wicked prosper? Wherefore are all they happy that deal very treacherously?" The answer given to these appeals is of a somewhat unexpected character. The Lord does not seek—in the first instance at least—to "assert eternal Providence" to Jeremiah. On the contrary, He admonishes him not to be unduly cast down by his present troubles, in view of the severer trials that are yet in store for him. "*If thou hast run,*" He says, "*with the footmen and they have wearied thee, then how canst thou contend with horses? and though in a land of peace thou art secure, yet how wilt thou do in the swellings of Jordan?*" [1]

In the first of those questions the prophet is represented

[1] xii. 5 (R.V.).

as a competitor in a race, striving against "footmen," that is, against rivals with whom he is competing more or less on terms of equality, and with whom, accordingly, he might justly be expected to hold his own. But if, in so manifestly reasonable a contest as that, he is hopelessly outdistanced, and finds himself unable to continue through lack of breath or spirit, how will he fare when he has to match his powers with the far greater swiftness and endurance of horses? The second question points to the same conclusion under a different figure. "The swellings" of Jordan may possibly refer to the tumultuous rush of its waters when in flood, but more probably the reference is to the thickets which grew on the river's banks and were infested with beasts of prey. If Jeremiah was disquieted in a land of comparative security, how could he expect to face the risks of a dark and trackless jungle where danger lurked at every step? And, translated into simple language, the message of these two questions was a warning to the prophet against failure in the less exacting tests of life.

For the easier test is meant to be a preparation for trials of a severer kind. That is why the Lord appears to show so little sympathy with His servant's trouble. His design was to brace the prophet's soul for the bitter sorrows and conflicts which were to be his lot in the coming days. Jeremiah, indeed, was but entering on his *via dolorosa*, and the discipline of this early experience was meant to strengthen his shoulders for the burden of his cross. Psychologists tell us that there is great moral benefit to be derived from subjecting ourselves every day to some form of effort that will keep the sinews of the soul in exercise. "Keep the faculty of effort alive in you," says William James, "by a little gratuitous effort every day. Be systematically ascetic or heroic in little unnecessary points, for no other reason than that you would rather not do it. So that when the hour of dire need draws nigh, it may find you not unnerved and untrained to stand the test."

This was, no doubt, the principle according to which

James Taylor, father of the famous founder of the China Inland Mission, trained up his family. "See if you can do without" was one of the family maxims, and it applied to "the simple pleasures of the table." As a rule the parents allowed to their children a share in whatever provision they permitted to themselves. But they took special pains to develop in the young people the power of self-control, and for this end the practice of "doing without" was encouraged from the very first. Sometimes, accordingly, when a favourite dish appeared on the table, the father would say, "Who will see if they can do without to-day?" It was beyond question a Spartan code, and it may be that it was not without a slight quivering of the young lips that the desire to taste of some special dainty was set aside. But judged by its effect on the life of Hudson Taylor, it was a healthy discipline.

This, then, was the meaning of God's unexpected answer to Jeremiah's complaining. It taught him the lesson of the easier test. It conveys the same message to ourselves to-day.

I

If we fail in the minor tasks of life, how can we face its larger responsibilities?—There is perhaps no surer test of a man's character than the way in which he discharges the common tasks which lie to his hand. There are some people who put their whole strength into the lowliest duty, applying themselves to it as conscientiously as if it were the supreme business of life. In the recent history of our own country there have been instances of Cabinet ministers who were at the same time Sabbath School teachers, and we may be quite sure that they aimed at being as efficient in imparting religious instruction to the children under their care as in guiding the affairs of the British Empire. There are others, however, who are careless in the discharge of these ordinary duties. Perhaps they consider themselves fitted for a wider sphere and a loftier responsibility, and regard the performance of commonplace tasks as something unworthy of their powers. In any case the performance is half-hearted and perfunctory. In the race with the footmen they do not make a very creditable show. Now in such a case as that, the question addressed to the prophet is surely pertinent. If we fail in the humbler tasks of life how can we be trusted with its more responsible duties ? The principle embodied in that question is constantly applied in the affairs of the Kingdom of God. We find Paul, for example, using it as a test of fitness for office in the Christian Church. " If a man," he declares, " know not how to rule his own house, how shall he take care of the Church of God ? " Our Lord Himself also in one of His parables makes faithfulness in the performance of " a few things " a condition on which His servants are advanced to the oversight of " many things." Let us ever remember that the surest road to promotion, whether it be in the service of God or of man, is to apply ourselves with all our might to the task that lies nearest our hand.

II

IF WE SINK UNDER THE LIGHTER TROUBLES OF LIFE, HOW SHALL WE ENDURE ITS SORER TRIALS ?—There are people who do not bear up well under affliction. It may not be a specially testing ordeal, but it brings to light the weaknesses of their character. Perhaps they are ready to faint in the day of trial, magnifying ordinary losses into disasters, taking a doleful view of their own plight, and losing heart before they have run far in the race. Or perhaps their spirit is embittered through loss or disappointment. They fret and complain, and speak as if they were a special target for the slings and arrows of adversity. There are people, again, who react in a disagreeable way to the petty vexations and frictions of life. There is nothing big or fine in the way they face those inevitable experiences. In the home, perhaps, where men and women have to live together day by day in intimate contact, and where, because of their common human imperfections and individual idiosyncrasies, there must always be a certain amount of give and take, they reveal no special gift of adaptability. They have no reserves of forbearance or good-humour on which to draw in moments of strain or collision. On the contrary, their temper gets on edge, they become cross and irritable, and are ready to magnify pin-pricks into gaping wounds. In running with the footmen they fail to give a good account of themselves. And the result is that when they have to contend with horses, or, to drop the figure, when they have to bear more desolating afflictions, they find themselves ill prepared for these heavier demands on their strength.

It is indeed the case—and it is one of the many anomalies of our human nature—that there are men and women not a few who fail badly in the minor trials of life and yet emerge with conspicuous credit from the severer tests, comporting themselves with resignation and courage under the most overwhelming calamities. But as a general rule the principle we are considering holds good. The lighter ordeal should be a preparation for the heavier. Submission to the yoke in the days of youth should mean a certain training for the approach of age with its increasing burdens and its failing strength. And especially the discipline that is undergone on the battlefield of life should stand men in good stead when they are face to face with the last enemy. The swellings of Jordan—whatever the specific meaning of the figure—represent a reality from which no man can escape. He must

> Feel the fog in his throat,
> The mist in his face.
> When the snows begin, and the blasts denote
> He is nearing the place,
> The power of the night, the press of the storm,
> The post of the foe;
> Where he stands, the Arch Fear in a visible form,
> Yet the strong man must go.

Well it is for those whose running with the footmen has in some degree prepared them for the final contest with that "pale horse" whose rider is called Death.

III

IF OUR RELIGION IS FOUND WANTING WHEN COMPARED WITH THE ATTAINMENTS OF OUR FELLOW-MEN, HOW WILL IT ABIDE THE SCRUTINY OF THE HIGHER STANDARDS OF GOD?—In the Christian race we are often weary enough when running with the footmen. We cannot keep pace with the godliness of the saints. They are men of like passions with ourselves, travelling on foot along the journey of life, exposed to the same trials and engaged in the same conflicts; but they press so eagerly toward the mark that they soon leave us far behind. They are so ardent in their love to God and so consecrated to His service, so pure of life and so generous of hand, so prayerful and unselfish and courageous, that when we compare their attainments with our own, we feel that we are unworthy to bear the Christian name. But if we are so deeply conscious of unworthiness in the presence of God's people, how shall we stand before God Himself? At the best "they are but broken lights" of that beauty of holiness in which there is no darkness at all. And before the awful purity which convicts the saints of uncleanness, and causes the very seraphim to veil their faces with their wings, how can we hope to stand? But it is here that the consciousness of failure as a result of the lower test may serve a useful purpose. If we cannot keep up with the footmen, it is surely our wisdom to flee for refuge to lay hold on the hope set before us in the Gospel. After all there *is* a Gospel for sinful men, even for those who are spiritual bankrupts and unable to help themselves. Let the experience of the easier test, then, be our schoolmaster to lead us to Christ.

IV

IF WE YIELD TO TEMPTATION IN THE QUIET AND SHELTERED PLACE, HOW SHALL WE FARE WHEN EXPOSED TO THE STORM ?—Our early life may be passed in surroundings that are wholly favourable to the religious life. Careful instruction, a good example, the ordinances of the House of God—all those helpful ministries that tend to strengthen the defences of the soul and to allure it into the ways of holy living—these surround us on every side. But if we fail to benefit by those inspiring influences, if we break through all the protecting fences and take furtive excursions into the paths of sin, how shall we withstand the fiercer assaults of temptation when we go out into a new environment in which the early restraints and supports are entirely lacking ? Here again the experience of success in the earlier conflicts should prepare the way for future victories, just as David's triumph over the lion and the bear nerved his heart for the battle with Goliath. But if we are defeated in the easier encounters, the recollection of our failure will be a serious handicap when we have to wrestle with stronger and more terrible foes.

And this leads us to an application of the words, which may be stated in one or two sentences. If we fail to seek the Lord in the day of health and opportunity, how can we expect to find Him in the swellings of Jordan ? In that last experience of all, when the mind may be clouded and the body racked with pain, a man often has enough to do in the struggle with death. It may be too late for him to make his peace with God.

The sum of what has been said in this chapter is that the easier test is a preparation for the harder task. And let us not forget that a call to the harder task means promotion in Christ's service. The most difficult place in the work of God's Kingdom is the place of highest honour. A striking illustration of this fact comes, naturally enough, from the mission field. In the Life of

"Coillard of the Zambesi," there is a letter which was received by Mme. Coillard from the Rev. W. G. Lawes, of the London Missionary Society in New Guinea. Mr Lawes had been transferred from Savage Island, where he had been working for many years, to another place of service. He tells of the result of his labours in the earlier sphere—he had had the happiness to baptise upwards of a thousand converts, had trained a band of young men who were now at work as pastors in their native island and as pioneers in other islands, and had translated into their own language the whole of the New Testament and part of the Old. He felt sorry, he said, to leave the work on Savage Island. "But," he adds, "the call to harder work, more self-denying work, is an honour from the Master's hands. Does He not in this way deal with His servants? *Is not the reward of service in His Kingdom, more service, harder service, and (measured by human standards) less successful service?*"

Are there any readers of these lines who are conscious of the strain of a more difficult enterprise which they have been called to undertake for God? Let them seek to realise that it is in recognition of their faithfulness "over a few things" that they have been entrusted with this exacting task, and that continued loyalty in the discharge of the heavier responsibility is the way that leads to the crowning "Well done" of their Lord.

XIII

A PROBLEM IN BLACK AND WHITE

When Christiana and her fellow-pilgrims came to the Delectable Mountains, the shepherds showed them a number of wonderful sights. Among these were two strikingly contrasted scenes. In the first they saw a man all in white, and two other men continually casting dirt upon him. But in a little time the dirt would fall off again, and his garment would look as clean as if it had never been soiled. In the second they saw two other men "washing an Ethiopian with an intention to make him white, but the more they washed him the blacker he was." In the one case there was an attempt to make white black; in the other, an attempt to make black white. In each case the effort proved utterly futile; both the white and the black were too deeply ingrained in the constitution of the men to yield to external treatment. Bunyan's little parables carry their interpretation with them. They remind us on the one hand that the innocence of a good man is too deep to be defiled by the assaults of prejudice and ill-will, and on the other that the corruption of a bad man is too radical to be removed by any outward cleansing. The latter of those representations is based on a familiar passage in the Book of Jeremiah. The prophet had his own problem of converting black into white. He was engaged in the work of effecting a reformation in the life of his countrymen, and was oppressed with the hopelessness of his task. "*Can the Ethiopian change his skin,*" he cried, "*or the leopard his spots? then may ye also do good, that are accustomed to do evil.*" [1]

[1] xiii. 23.

I

The answer to Jeremiah's questions is, of course, a decided negative. We can easily understand that the Ethiopian might wish to change his colour. In the days of Jeremiah, as in our own time, he was no doubt exposed to bitter humiliations on account of the blackness of his skin, and would many a time have envied the apparent superiority of the white man. But if ever he considered the question of improving his complexion, he found that it involved not merely a change of colour, but a change of skin. The blackness of the Ethiopian, indeed, is no mere surface discolouration that can be removed by the application of soap and water. It is an inherent quality of his physical constitution which cannot be changed by any process known to men. The same difficulty must attend every attempt to transform the appearance of the leopard, for although in this case the task seems easier because the leopard is not completely black, the spots of the leopard are as deeply imbedded in his bodily structure as the blackness of the Ethiopian is in his. And Jeremiah affirms that it is as difficult for men to transform their own evil character as it is for the Ethiopian to change his skin or the leopard his spots.

This difficulty is sometimes understood to be entirely due to the moral impotence caused by evil habit, and the prophet's description of his countrymen as a people who were " accustomed to do evil " appears to lend colour to this restricting interpretation. It is clear, however, that he is thinking of something more radical than that kind of disability. The analogies of the Ethiopian and the leopard imply not merely difficulty, but—so far as human resources are concerned—impossibility of change. Now, while the self-reformation of men who have become " accustomed to do evil," is without doubt so difficult as to be rarely achieved, it is by no means impossible. The tyranny of habit can be broken, and has been broken, without the miracle of saving grace. The confirmed drunkard sometimes becomes sober, the thief becomes honest, and the slave of lust renounces his uncleanness, without giving any evidence that they have undergone an inward spiritual change. But Jeremiah is speaking of something which men *cannot* accomplish by their own efforts. His problem is a problem not merely of weakness, but of helplessness. Beyond question he has the paralysing effect of evil custom before his mind. But behind the enslavement of habit there is the corruption of the unregenerate heart.

This, then, is the initial factor that must be taken into account in considering whether those who have become "accustomed to do evil" can learn to do good. The bias of a sinful nature is a fact to be reckoned with, even before the influence of sinful habit makes itself felt. And it is a fact which is no mere dogma of an antiquated theology. Modern psychology freely recognises that man is not merely "a bundle of habits," but "a bundle of inherited tendencies," a conclusion which is in agreement with the old-fashioned Scripture doctrine of original sin. The thing, then, that the prophet declares to be impossible for men in their own strength is first of all to change the bias of a sinful nature. Not that sin is so bound up with human nature that it is inseparable from it. That would indeed be a doctrine of despair, for it would mean that evil is a natural necessity from which there can be no escape. Sin is a tremendous fact of human nature, but it is an abnormal fact, and it can be completely removed from the heart and life of men.

II

A second element in Jeremiah's problem, however, arises from the tyranny of evil habit. It is impossible for men to plead excuse for a sinful life on the ground of any inherited predisposition to wickedness. It is not long until their natural tendencies are strengthened by the fact that they become "accustomed to do evil." The growth of habit is one of the most familiar, and in some respects one of the most terrible facts of human experience. Our actions have a tendency to reproduce themselves, and through repetition to weave themselves into the texture of our character. In feats of physical skill practice gives us a certain facility in doing difficult things, for it is a matter of scientific observation that "our organs grow into the way in which they have been exercised." The same thing holds true of moral actions. It is a fatally easy thing to become "accustomed to do evil." There is, no doubt, some difficulty at first. At that stage "an act of vice requires effort and a contest with moral principles." Conscience condemns the evil thing, and the influences of early training are cast on the same side. But ere long this early difficulty passes away. Successive acts of transgression lead to a hardening of the heart. The reproofs of conscience are stifled, and the transgressor takes pleasure in his wrong-doing, and may even sink so low in moral debasement as to glory in his shame.

To a man who is "accustomed to do evil" vicious practices become easy and natural. There are men, for example, who acquire the habit of swearing, and become at length so steeped in profanity that they can scarcely utter a sentence that is not punctuated with some kind of oath. In many cases they lose all sense of the meaning of the expletives they use ; blasphemy, as some one has said, is their idiom, a turn in their way of speaking. The same remark applies to the habit of lying. There are people who become so accustomed to pervert the truth that they are scarcely conscious of doing it ; the language of falsehood is so natural to them that it would seem to be their mother tongue. And how easy it is for men to acquire the habit of living without God. They leave Him out of their reckoning so completely that they can lie down and rise up, can weep and rejoice, can form their plans and discharge their tasks day after day, year after year, without as much as a thought about Him. The result is a gradual atrophy of their religious instincts. How soon, too, men get into the way of absenting themselves from the House of God. Let them but fail in this duty even for a few weeks, and the urge of heart and conscience in the direction of the sanctuary becomes perceptibly weaker, while after a more prolonged absence it requires no small effort of will to resume the habit of regular attendance.

And when habit becomes strong through persistent indulgence, it exercises an appalling tyranny over the hearts and lives of men. Habit, we often say, is second nature. The Duke of Wellington, as might be expected from a man who had a lifelong experience of the effects of military discipline, went further, and declared that "habit is ten times nature." It becomes almost as much a part of our character as the Ethiopian's skin is part of himself. The ascendency which evil sometimes obtains over the man who has become "accustomed to do" it is indeed terrible beyond words. The victim's moral defences are gradually broken down, and in the end he sinks into a degradation so complete that he loses his self-respect, and ceases even to wish for recovery. The drunkard would sell his soul for a glass of liquor when his thirst is on him, and the drug addict suffers indescribable torments when he is unable to gratify his craving.

It is a significant fact that the word "habit" originally meant a garment, and it is undeniably true that there is no garment that clings to a human being so tenaciously as the evil he is "accustomed to do." When a man, who has fallen into the grip of some degrading lust tries to divest himself of his besetting sin, he finds that, like the poisoned shirt which proved the undoing of Hercules, it has so eaten its way into the fibres of his being that the removal of it is a process so painful that it may be fitly compared to the tearing away of his very flesh. Professor William James, in his famous chapter on "Habit," speaks of "the hell we make for ourselves in this world by habitually fashioning our characters in the wrong way." That final stage of ruin is not, of course, reached in a single day. But every concession to evil habit helps the downward course. The man who tries to impose upon himself by saying that he " will not count " his latest indulgence in sin, is all the while playing into the hand of his enemy. " Down among his nerve-cells and fibres," says Professor James, " the molecules are counting it, registering and storing it up, to be used against him when the next temptation comes."

III

We are not to conclude, however, that Jeremiah took an absolutely despairing view of the problem which confronted him. He certainly despaired of the self-converting power of human nature, but he had unlimited confidence in the regenerating power of the grace of God. The Ethiopian cannot change his skin by scrubbing it, and the efforts of men to wash away their own sin and to improve the quality of their depraved nature are equally doomed to failure. The Gospel of Psychology is poor comfort for a man who is struggling in the toils of his corruptions and lusts. You may exhort him to shake himself free by a resolute effort of his will, but the chief part of his trouble is that his will itself is enslaved. But Jeremiah has a message of hope for the victims alike of heredity and of habit. That message is enshrined in his doctrine of the New Covenant with its " better promises " of forgiveness and spiritual quickening. Through the washing of regeneration and the renewing of the Holy Ghost, the soul that had been black as the Ethiopian's skin in guilt and defilement becomes " whiter than snow." The reign of death is over, and the tyranny of habit is ended. For, on the new heart which He bestows, God writes His own law, and that means a new inward disposition " to do good," a new hunger and thirst after righteousness, and a new impulse to render obedience to the good and perfect will of God.

When this radical change has been effected, however, it must not be forgotten that habit still has an important part to play in the life of men. It is possible to become accustomed to do good as well as to do evil, and good habits become a powerful ally of the Christian soul, reinforcing the will in its resistance to the assaults of evil and in its strivings after purity of life. The maxims of the moralist are now in place, and the lessons of psychology may prove of practical value. These lessons may be said to be summed up in the duty of seeking to "make automatic and habitual as many useful actions as we can," so that, as it has been tersely put, our nervous system may become our ally, and not our enemy, in the battle of life. To say this is only to affirm with a different accent the principles of Christian conduct that are set forth in the Word of God.

How important it is, for example, to form the habit of moderation in all things, to acquire the poise and balance of self-control in our feelings and appetites, our temper and our speech. And in order to attain to this desirable condition it is necessary also to learn the habit of watchfulness. So long as we are in an evil world we are always in the zone of moral danger, and must be on our guard against surprise attacks. Especially must we resist the beginnings of temptation, and see to it that every resolution "to do good" is followed by its appropriate course of action. The habit of joining in the corporate worship of the Christian Church is also of incalculable benefit. "Accumulate," says the philosopher, "all the possible circumstances which shall reinforce the right motives. . . . Put yourself assiduously in conditions that encourage the new way." And where shall we find conditions that are more favourable to the new way than in the worship of the sanctuary and in the atmosphere of Christian fellowship? It has nowadays become fashionable in certain quarters to speak slightingly of the value of church-going as a means of fostering the spiritual life, but it is an undoubted fact that there is "something added to the individual as he worships, not by himself, but in a fellowship with others."

The best habits, however, may degenerate in course of time into a lifeless routine, and so may prove to be hindrances rather than helps to the Christian life. In order, therefore, that the observances we have been considering may be as living springs to the soul, and not simply as wells without water, it is necessary, above all, that we should form the habit of prayer. And the habit of prayer means, among other things, that we have set times for prayer, and that as far as possible we bind ourselves to these occasions with steadfastness of purpose. The more we cultivate this habit, the easier and more delightful it will become ; the more we neglect it, the less disposed we shall be to repair to the secret place. Here is a passage from the Diary of David Brainerd, that great saint and servant of God, which bears striking testimony to this vital fact : "It is good, I find, to persevere in attempts to pray if I cannot pray with perseverance, that is, continue long in my addresses to the Divine Being. I have generally found that the more I do in secret prayer, the more I have delighted to do, and have enjoyed more of a spirit of prayer : *and frequently have found the contrary when with journeying or otherwise I have been much deprived of retirement.* A reasonable, steady performance of secret duties, and a careful improvement of all time, filling up every hour with some profitable labour, either of heart, head, or hands, are excellent means of spiritual peace and boldness before God."

The prayer of faith opens the hand of the God of salvation, and brings fresh supplies of His grace into our souls. That means an endowment of power that will enable us not only to persevere in religious duties, but to persevere in them with a warmth and liveliness of heart that will cause every good habit to yield its full return of spiritual helpfulness.

XIV

WHEAT AND CHAFF

In the tempestuous life of Jeremiah there were few elements that more severely tested his character than the opposition of the false prophets. This is, of course, an experience that was by no means peculiar to Jeremiah: the true messenger of God always finds his bitterest enemies among the degenerate members of his own official class. The men who contended with Jeremiah claimed to speak in the name of the Lord and to know His secret purposes. They alleged that the Divine Will was revealed to them through the medium of dreams, and they were never tired of boasting about the communications which came to them by this mysterious channel. Jeremiah does not take up the position that God never speaks to men through dreams; the recorded experience of the saints in former days afforded him convincing evidence that the Lord does sometimes use this method of making known His mind to men. The prophet's attitude to the dream as a medium of revelation is one of caution. The dream must always stand in its own name and be judged on its own merits; it must never be placed on the same plane of authority as the Word of the Lord. "The prophet that hath a dream, let him tell a dream; and he that hath my word let him speak my word faithfully"—that, he declares, is the Divine rule of procedure in the matter. For the dream may be an authentic message from God, or it may be a lying invention on the part of a charlatan. To this latter category, it would seem, belonged the dreams of the false prophets of Judah. They stole the words they spoke every one from his neighbour. And in one pregnant question Jeremiah contrasts the vain imaginations of those men with the authoritative intimations of His mind which the Lord makes to His servants—" *What is the chaff to the wheat?*" saith the Lord.[1]

I

Here, first of all, we have a figure which sets forth in a striking way the difference between the Word of the Lord and every kind of false doctrine. It is the difference between wheat and chaff. In no censorious spirit, but in simple recognition of obvious facts, one feels constrained to say that there is a great body of religious teaching in our own time which may rightly be described as chaff. For one thing, it is as *light* as chaff, without spiritual weight or moral seriousness. Sometimes it is merely entertaining, with scarcely the semblance of an elevating or edifying purpose. Sometimes it is merely eloquent, and surely there can be few things more deserving of the name of chaff than fine language without intellectual or spiritual substance. Or again, it may be merely topical, the theme being some current event that is occupying the minds of men, or some book that is widely talked about, or some other fleeting interest of time that has little bearing on the concerns of eternity. And even when religious subjects are under discussion the treatment they receive is often so superficial that one rarely catches a glimpse of the majesty of Divine Truth. Too often also the affirmations of God are displaced by the speculations of men.

For another thing it is as *deceptive* as chaff. On a hasty view chaff may easily impose upon us. It stands in intimate relation to the wheat; it has the appearance of pure grain; and accordingly it offers us the promise of sustenance. But it flatters but to deceive. Between the chaff and the wheat there is a vital difference, the difference between the empty husk and the real staff of life. And there is a type of religious teaching which in that sinister sense is nothing better than chaff. It has the

[1] xxiii. 28.

appearance of truth without the reality. One or two instances of the kind of doctrine which finds favour in many quarters to-day will serve to illustrate this fact. Modernism admits the divinity of Jesus of Nazareth, but with the same breath it proclaims the divinity of man, the difference between Christ and us being one of degree and not of kind. It represents the Death of Christ as being mainly a revelation of the compassion of God, a moving exhibition of the Father's wounded love, without any redemptive significance. Christ is alive from the dead in the sense that His spiritual influence abides as a more or less powerful dynamic in the hearts and lives of men, but as for His body, it is still sleeping in Joseph's tomb beneath the Syrian stars. And as regards the way of salvation, all that is required of us is that we should believe in God as Jesus did, that we should adopt His ideals of conduct, and walk with Him as our Leader and Comrade on the pilgrimage of life. In each case the language of evangelical Christianity is retained, but the vital content of the terms is denied. This is surely to substitute the empty chaff for the wheat.

And, finally, the kind of teaching we are considering is as *unsatisfying* as chaff. It contains no nourishment for our spiritual being, and, however attractively it may be presented, and however plentifully it may be supplied, our hungry souls look up and are not fed. It is a kind of fare that will never build us up in holiness and comfort through faith unto salvation. It imparts no strength, inspires no devotion, and begets no living hope. This is the final count in the indictment which must be framed against a great deal of present-day religious doctrine. It does not convey the bread of life to famishing souls. It lacks the solidity and permanence of truth, and moves to a great extent on the plane of triviality. For that reason it does not breed saints. It is empty of inspiration, and fails to satisfy the deepest cravings of the human spirit.

In contrast with this unsubstantial fare is the teaching of the Word of the Lord, which is compared to wheat. It is like wheat because of its weight and solidity. It possesses the dignity and loftiness of a message from Heaven. Whatever its particular theme may be, whether it be designed for reproof, for correction, for doctrine, or for instruction in righteousness, it has a moral elevation which bears witness to its divine origin. There is no part of it that is not worthy of God. And as it possesses the attribute of dignity, so also it bears the stamp of truth. Unlike the chaff which is tossed about by every wind that blows, it abides in unchanging steadfastness, with the seal of eternity on all its parts. It is a "sure word of prophecy," whose every utterance is divinely guaranteed. The changes and transitions of this mortal life can never invalidate the authority of its precepts or wither the grace of its promises. And because of all this it provides sustenance for the souls of men. In this sense, specifically, it is the wheat of God which nourishes and satisfies our spiritual nature. It meets the needs of our understanding because it is a word of truth, the demands of our conscience because it is a word of life, and the hunger of our heart because it is a word of love. As we ponder the difference between these two forms of doctrine we may well reiterate the prophet's exclamation, "What is the chaff to the wheat?"

II

But the Word of the Lord may also be distinguished from every kind of counterfeit message by its effects in human life. This is the further test of genuineness with which Jeremiah supplies us. God's Word authenticates itself by the results which it produces in the hearts of men. For one thing, it is "like a hammer that breaketh the rock in pieces." A hammer that is wielded by an arm sufficiently strong will shatter the hardest rock, and the divine message has a similar effect on the obduracy of the unregenerate heart. In the hand of the Spirit of God it will break down the most obstinate resistance, and lay low the most boastful pride. However securely entrenched a man may be in spiritual insensateness and defiance of God, it needs but a touch of the divine hammer to shatter his self-complacency and bring his arrogance to the dust. It is the judicial function of the Word of God that is specially indicated by this figure of the hammer.

But the Divine Word is also compared to fire. This is a particularly appropriate symbol. Fire, for example, has an enlightening effect. In the darkness of night it makes its presence known by dispelling to a great extent the surrounding gloom. And the sure word of prophecy is like " a light that shineth in a dark place." It brings to us illumination in the night of our ignorance and uncertainty. It sets forth great guiding principles which may cover a wider area than our particular difficulty, but in the application of which to our own circumstances we find the solution of our problem. And fire also burns. The touch of its flames will soon awaken the soundest sleeper and cause him to writhe with pain. Similarly the Word of God is sometimes like fire in a man's conscience. It arouses him from the slumber of spiritual indifference, and convicts him of guilt and ill-desert. To not a few this experience has been so painful that it seemed to them as if a spark from the fire of the Divine wrath had entered their soul. " Day and night," said the Psalmist in describing his own distress in such circumstances, " Thy hand was heavy upon me ; my moisture is turned into the drought of summer." Jeremiah himself could bear a similar testimony under somewhat different conditions. In the travail of soul produced by the difficulties of his mission as a prophet of judgment, he resolved to withhold for a season his message of doom ; but the Word of the Lord was in his heart as a burning fire shut up in his bones, so that it was impossible for him to remain silent.

Once more it has to be noticed that fire has a melting effect. We do not always think of it as a fierce devouring flame. More often we are conscious of its genial warmth as it banishes the chill of the wintry air from our bodies and infuses a glow of comfort and good cheer into our hearts. And the Word of the Lord has a gracious and winsome quality. The Gospel is a message of good cheer, bringing into our hearts the warmth of the love of God, and conveying the assurance of forgiveness and peace. And when it speaks to us with this gracious voice it has a melting effect. The hammer of the Law may crush our spirit, but the fire of the Gospel will melt our hardness, and bring us to the feet of God in lowly penitence and submission of soul. As a final consideration it may be remarked that fire has a cleansing property. As a disinfectant it has no rival, for it makes an end of impurity by consuming it. And the Word of God has a matchless cleansing efficacy. "Sanctify them," said Jesus in His great intercessory prayer, "through Thy truth: Thy word is truth." For the Divine Word is the vehicle which conveys into the soul all the cleansing potencies of Christ's redemption, and all the transforming energies of the Holy Ghost. It is a holy word itself, and it makes for holiness in the heart in which it dwells. Its pure flame burns up the dross of unclean thoughts and unhallowed desires. This is the final test of prophetic inspiration which Jeremiah lays down. The message of the man who stands in the counsel of the Lord will have a sanctifying effect on human life; with the blessing of God it will turn men "from the evil of their way and from the evil of their doings."

III

In view of all he has spoken regarding the oracles of God, Jeremiah has a closing message for those who are engaged in the ministry of the Word. Their duty, he declares, is to speak the Word "faithfully." Let it have free course to do its work. If it is like a hammer, then let it smite. If it is like a fire, let it flame and burn. The duty of the messenger is to speak faithfully. There must be no mingling of the chaff with the wheat, no silencing of the voice of God in favour of the dreams of men. And there must be no toning down of the message. Let no man dare to handle the Word of God deceitfully by refusing to declare any part of the divine counsel, or by attempting to bring what the Lord has actually said into harmony with his own conception of what the Lord ought to have said. There is perhaps nothing that the servants of God have greater need of keeping constantly before their minds to-day than the duty of letting the Word of God deliver its own message and thereby produce its own effects. We have so many words of our own to speak that we fail to give the Divine Word its opportunity.

Let us not forget that our attitude to the Word of the Lord will have reactions on our own heart and life which, broadly regarded, will place us in categories corresponding to the chaff and the wheat. There are men who are compared to chaff because they are unstable in principle and worthless in character, slaves of wickedness who are driven before the winds of temptation and passion. There are others who are likened unto wheat; they are the fruit of the soul-travail of Jesus Christ, that solitary "grain of wheat" that on the hill of Calvary fell into the ground and died, and through death yielded an abundant harvest. And let us also remember that of that Just One it is written that His "fan is in His hand, and He will throughly purge His floor, and gather the wheat into His garner; but the chaff He will burn with fire unquenchable."

XV

THE TWO VOICES

THE thirty-first chapter of the Book of Jeremiah is one of those oracles in which the soul of the prophet soars to its loftiest height of predictive vision. Its opening portion contains a glowing picture of the Return of the Jews from Babylon. This is a passage which is charged with tender feeling and coloured with poetic imagery. The Lord who loved His people with an everlasting love, and who describes Himself as "the Father of Ephraim," is to gather His scattered flock from "the coast of the north," and to place them again in their own land. This will be for them a time of jubilant rejoicing, as well as of restored material and spiritual prosperity. "They shall come," the Lord declares, "and sing in the height of Zion . . . and their soul shall be as a watered garden, and they shall not sorrow any more at all." "My people," He adds—and this puts the finishing touch to an incomparable tale of happiness—"My people shall be satisfied with my goodness."

But this vivid picture of the Restoration recalls the sadness of the departure into the land of captivity seventy years before. And so, at this point, Jeremiah introduces into the story an episode which reveals a remarkable power of imaginative conception. We now see the captive Jews on the road to Babylon, and as the procession moves along its sorrowful way, it is represented as passing Rachel's tomb in Ramah. And then the prophet hears the voice of the mother of Ephraim's race lamenting over the unhappy plight of her children. She gives vent to her sorrow in bitter weeping, and refuses to be comforted. Her travail, she supposes, has been wholly in vain, and her labour of love has been for naught, for the children whom she had nourished and brought up are now, as it appears to her, under sentence of perpetual banishment. So she grieves with the bitterness of a hopeless sorrow. But in the midst of this disconsolate wailing the prophet hears another voice—the voice of the Father of Ephraim, speaking words of hope and cheer to the heart of the stricken mother. "Refrain thy voice from weeping, and thine eyes from tears," says the Divine Comforter, "for thy work shall be rewarded . . . and there is hope in thine end . . . that thy children shall come again to their own border." This, beyond any doubt, is a passage of singular beauty. It shows us that even under the sorrow and humiliation of the Exile, the prophet saw "the bright light" of hope shining through the clouds.

But the Return from Babylon, with its marvellous rebirth of gladness and song, gives rise to another closely related train of thought. The banishment of Israel and Judah into captivity was the outcome of no arbitrary decree. It was the judgment which their own stubborn and persistent rebellion had wrung at length from the hand of a patient but righteous God. They had refused to yield to persuasion, and their disease, accordingly, demanded a more drastic remedy. So they were sent into exile for their sins.

But, this being the case, they could not be brought back except on a certain condition, and that was that their chastisement should manifestly bear the fruit of repentance. The stroke of judgment was not merely intended to inflict punishment; it was designed to serve a remedial purpose. Restoration therefore must be contingent on penitence. So, to complete his picture of the Return, the prophet proceeds to describe the contrition and humility of soul in which the exiles sought the way to Zion when the Lord turned again their captivity. Here again he strikes the note of dramatic impressiveness. In direct succession we hear two pairs of voices: the first, dealing with the Exile; the second, bearing upon the Return. Formerly he had spoken of the inconsolable grief of Rachel and of the Lord's comforting response. Now he makes us hear the voice of Ephraim's godly sorrow and of the Divine promise of mercy in reply. Once more we listen to the sound of weeping, but once more there falls upon our ear an answer from the lips of God which turns the moaning of the penitent into the song of the forgiven. "*I have surely heard Ephraim bemoaning himself thus; Thou hast chastised me, and I was chastised, as a bullock unaccustomed to the yoke: turn Thou me, and I shall be turned; for Thou art the Lord my God. Surely after I was turned, I repented; and after that I was instructed, I smote upon my thigh: I was ashamed, yea, even confounded, because I did bear the reproach of my youth.*" That is the voice of a penitent soul. And here is the answering voice of the God of salvation: "*Is Ephraim My dear son? is he a pleasant child? For since I spake against him, I do earnestly remember him still; therefore My bowels are troubled for him: I will surely have mercy upon him, saith the Lord.*" [1]

Let us listen to the message which is conveyed to ourselves by those two voices.

I

First, we have the Voice of Sincere Repentance.—It describes various elements in the normal experience of a soul that is turning unto God. It is necessary to emphasise the word "normal," for not every believer has travelled by this road to the Divine Mercy-seat. And even when there is a definite experience of the kind here described, it is not in the same degree that any one of its constituent elements enters into the consciousness of the penitent heart. But the words we are considering certainly do set forth the general character of a true repentance.

The first fact which emerges from the record of Ephraim's experience is that "Repentance unto life is *a saving grace*," which is wrought in the heart by the Spirit of God. It is, of course, the act of the sinner, but it is God who takes the initiative in securing the return of the soul to Himself.

[1] xxxi. 18-20.

So we find Ephraim not only declaring that it was after he "was turned" that he repented, but also beseeching God to "turn" him, so that contrition might be generated within him as the result of the Divine action upon his soul. Real repentance is no mere superficial emotion; it is an experience that affects the whole man—mind, conscience, heart, and life. It does not merely consist in being sorry when we do wrong; that may be a purely natural feeling, which soon passes away and leaves no abiding trace upon our conduct. Nor is it simply a matter of giving up certain habits which we know to be hurtful to soul or body; renunciation of this kind may be prompted by considerations which leave God entirely out of account. Repentance has both an inward and an outward side. It goes as deep as the hidden man of the heart, and it comes to light in the outward man of our daily walk and conversation. But always it is God who first lays His quickening touch on the inner springs of life, and brings the sinner to a sincere and fruitful repentance.

The second thing to be observed is that *God sometimes uses outward means for bringing men to repentance.* "Thou hast chastised me," cries Ephraim, "and I was chastised." The sorrow and the reproach of Babylon were instrumental in bringing the captive Jews to a penitent frame of mind. Not always, indeed, does God employ such visible means of achieving His purpose of mercy. Sometimes He reaches the impenitent heart by ways that are secret and much more direct. By interjecting a thought into the mind, for example, which leads to reflection and then to conviction; or by arresting the soul by some passage of His "living and powerful" Word which pierces the conscience like a keen-edged sword; or, again, by conquering the heart by the glory of Christ's Face revealed in the preaching of the Gospel; or, once more, by the silent appeal of some saintly life, which draws as a magnet to the Christian hope.

But He often does use the dispensations of His Providence to reinforce the message of His Word. Many a man has been impelled to seek God's face by some disabling sickness. He is laid aside from his usual pursuits, and feels his strength ebbing away. Then comes the thought of the world to come, and with it the consciousness that he is not prepared to die. So, like Manasseh, he humbles himself before God in the day of his affliction, and turns from the old life of indifference and sin. Many others have been brought to repentance through the experience of sorrow. Some well-loved friend—parent or wife, child or lover—is removed from their side, and through the blessing of God the natural loss becomes a medium of spiritual gain. And so it happens that

> Precious things of everlasting grace
> And secret glory, are revealed to eyes
> That mourn the death of every earthly joy.

Another fact which comes to light in Ephraim's confession is that *repentance involves a new conception of sin.* "When I was instructed," he says, "I smote upon my thigh." The opening clause of this sentence may be rendered, "when I came to know myself." It points to an awakening of soul which brings with it a self-knowledge that is not far removed from a recovered sanity. The word most frequently used in the New Testament to express the fact of repentance literally means a change of mind. The man who comes to know himself through the instruction of the Spirit of God sees his past life in a new light, which discloses not only its guilt, but its barrenness and futility. It may not, indeed, always happen that "sudden in a moment all is accomplished," and self-revelation yields the fruit of practical repentance. Very significant in this connection are the words in which Ephraim describes himself as "a bullock unaccustomed to the yoke." They are words which suggest that a period of stubborn resistance, of more or less violent plunging and kicking against the authority of God's will, often precedes an unqualified submission to the truth. But the process of instruction continues, until at last the Divine verdict on the unregenerate life is accepted in its completeness and finality. In the experience of Ephraim this acceptance took place in the hour when, in lowly self-condemnation, he smote upon his thigh. When that result is achieved, sin is no longer regarded as a trivial irregularity. It is seen as an act of rebellion against the Divine will, the wages of which is nothing less than death.

Ephraim's history also reminds us that *repentance is marked by sorrow for sin.* This is perhaps its most characteristic feature. The change of mind is followed by a change of heart in which contrition occupies a prominent place. So we find Ephraim "bemoaning himself" in bitter self-reproach. This is the "godly sorrow" of which Paul speaks in the classic passage [1] which provides the fullest analysis of the psychology of repentance contained in the whole Bible—that cleansing grief which produces in men's lives a "carefulness" and a "clearing" of themselves, and a moral "indignation," and a "fear," and a "vehement desire" and a "zeal," and—to crown all—a "revenge" which is the echo in a human conscience of God's righteous judgment upon sin. The man who passes through such a tumult of soul realises, and is not slow to confess, the ill-desert of his transgressions. "I have sinned against heaven and in Thy sight," he cries to God, "and am no more worthy to be called Thy son." This is no mere antiquated type of experience, unknown on the wider horizons of our modern religious world. "I can say," declared one of the foremost preachers of this generation only the other day, "I can say—and many will say with me—that the most unhappy moments I have known were those in which I felt the scourge of conscience. In the course of my cure of souls I have seen no agony like that which is felt when a man is summoned to the bar of conscience."

But we also learn from the language of Ephraim that *repentance has in it an element of shame as well as of sorrow.* "I was ashamed," exlaims the penitent exile, "yea, even confounded, because I did bear the reproach of my youth."

[1] 2 Cor. vii. 10, 11.

When a man whose conscience has been awakened reviews his past life, he finds many things that cause him to bow his head in shame. The self-indulgence that at one time appeared to be no more than harmless pleasure; the grosser excesses to which he may have given way in secret, and which it required deception to conceal; the pride and waywardness which rejected admonition and resented reproof; the selfishness which insisted on taking its own way, regardless of the pain which it inflicted on others—all this unhappy "remembrance of things past" gives rise to profound self-loathing. Sin is recognised to be an unclean disease, an unsavoury and degrading thing, the one shameful fact in human life. That man or woman has fallen low indeed from whose heart the sense of shame has completely disappeared. There is indeed much truth in the old saying that "the sense of shame is the basis of all the virtues."

One final thing, however, must be added before this description of Repentance is complete. There can be no genuine repentance which does not include *a turning unto God*. This is the crowning element in the experience. That transformation of life to which we give the name of conversion is the outward and visible sign of the grace of repentance. So we find Ephraim declaring that it was only when he was "turned" that his repentance became an accomplished fact. Repentance, too, is inseparable from faith in God. It is not alone the consciousness of guilt, with its accompanying sense of danger, that constrains a man to break with his sinful past; the fetters are finally broken only when he cherishes the hope of mercy inherent in Ephraim's appropriating words, "For Thou art the Lord my God." So it was with the erring son in the most moving of all our Lord's parables. The misery and the destitution of the far country served but to overwhelm him with a voiceless despair; it was only when the thought of his early home, with its ordered security, its warmth of love, and its "bread enough and to spare," came into his mind in piercing anguish of remembrance, that "he arose," and entered on the journey which led him from the swine-trough to his Father's welcoming arms. This homeward attitude of the contrite heart—and particularly of a heart that has wandered into the ways of disobedience after having tasted that the Lord is gracious—is well described in the familiar words of Henry Vaughan:

> O how I long to travel back,
> And tread again that ancient track!
> That I might once more reach that plain
> Where first I left my glorious train;
> From whence th' enlightened spirit sees
> That shady City of Palm trees.

It is when we have begun to "travel back" that our repentance becomes a reality.

II

In the second place, we have the Voice of Divine Mercy.—This part of the oracle sets forth, in words that go straight to the heart—so "full of grace and truth" are they in every syllable—the attitude of God to the penitent soul. To begin with, He hears Ephraim's moaning cry. Even when the sorrow of the heart does not become articulate, and is only a dumb, dry-eyed grief, the God of all grace is conscious of its unuttered supplication. He hears, because He is ever listening for "this self-same thing." The moan of the penitent is music in His ear. The language of the contrite heart finds access to His secret pavilion. "I have surely heard Ephraim bemoaning Himself," He declares; and the adverb brings into the affirmation a note of satisfaction as well as of certainty. And when God hears, there are certain results which follow, according to the words which the prophet here puts into His mouth.

First of all, there is the moving of His Compassion. "Since I spake against him I do earnestly remember him still," He exclaims; "therefore my heart is troubled for him." This "trouble" represents the depth, as well as the reality, of the Divine compassion for sinful men.

There are few things, surely, that are more encouraging to the penitent sinner than the fact that the heart of God is full of pity. The righteousness of God is both humbling and encouraging ; His power is inspiring, even when its " thunder " produces a sense of awe ; His goodness is attractive in its every manifestation ; but His compassion is irresistible to the soul that is convicted of sin. The God of infinite majesty " remembereth that we are dust." His tender pity received its fullest revelation in the character and work of Jesus Christ. He who was " moved with compassion " when He beheld the shepherdless multitude, and when He looked on the ghastly whiteness of the leper ; who mingled His tears with those of Martha and Mary in Bethany, and wept over the city that, a little while later, was to clamour for His blood, was disclosing through these human emotions the fathomless depths of the pity of God. The Voice which answers the moaning of Ephraim is beyond question a Voice of Compassion.

Then there is the outflowing of His Love. " Is not Ephraim My dear son ? Is he not a pleasant child ? " These are words of tenderest affection, all the more moving because we seem to catch in their accents a very human ring. Sometimes an earthly father and his son are estranged from each other. The son perhaps has been disobedient and rebellious, and has brought grief and shame to his father's heart. Under such conditions real fellowship between them is impossible. The father's love has in no wise changed, but it cannot find expression in the former intimacies until an honourable reconciliation has been effected. In course of time, however, the son repents of his wrongdoing, and makes a frank and contrite acknowledgment of his offence. And no sooner does the confession which gives evidence of his change of attitude fall from his lips than a wave of tenderness breaks over the father's heart, and his love flows out in an enveloping warmth of manifestation which is all the fuller because of the repression that went before. So it is that God welcomes His penitent child with words of endearment, and rejoices over him with singing. "Let us eat," He exclaims, "and be merry: for this My son was dead, and is alive again; he was lost and is found."

It is this gracious reception which lifts the last shadow of doubt and fear from the returning wanderer's soul. "The son forlorn forgetteth half his prayer," says Archbishop Trench, in reference to the fact that the prodigal omitted to use the petition which follows the confession that he had rehearsed on his way from the far country. The comment scarcely does justice to the significance of this delicate touch in the picture. No, the son forlorn did not forget his prayer, but he was unable to utter it. It may be that as he was about to frame the words, a gentle hand was laid on his mouth, and the reference to the "hired servants," never found expression. Or, as seems to me more likely, he saw something in his Father's eyes, as he looked up to the well-remembered face, which caused the self-depreciating appeal to die on his lips. Then he *knew* that any request for a servile position in the old home would be dishonouring to a love so divinely generous. In any case it is nothing less than the honour and glory of sonship that is bestowed by this "manner of love" upon the sinner who turns in sincerity of repentance to the God and Father of our Lord Jesus Christ.

It is the personal experience of this love, too, that, as has already been indicated, finally conquers a sinner's will, and melts his heart in a contrition which, for that reason, is not only bitter but sweet. The thought of sin as transgression of the Divine Law—a law which, in the sternness of its condemnation, may appear to be "coldly sublime, intolerably just"—may only have the effect of hardening the transgressor in his rebellion against God; but the thought of sin as something that wounds the heart of infinite Love—a love that yearns over the guilty wanderer, and waylays him with gracious stratagems, and pursues him down the ways of folly and pride with a persistency that will not let him go—it is this that overcomes the last strugglings of resistance, and brings the soul to the point of unconditional surrender. Dr J. H.

Jowett tells that one of the most vivid memories of his childhood, a memory "which never lost its colour or its strength," was the recollection of his mother reproving him with tears. "Punishment," he says, "might have been bearable, and I could have faced it. But tears, they vanquished me. A mother's suffering for a son's disloyalty to truth—that was something that made my act repulsive, and at the same time revealed to me a heart of love and reconciliation and peace." Which thing is an allegory of the spiritual experience we have been considering.

Finally, there is the assurance of His Mercy. This is of course implied in the words of love which He has already uttered; but the forgiveness of God is not merely an inference which we are warranted to draw from His love. The promise is set forth in explicit terms, with a "surely" added to put an end to all doubt. Our guilt, like that of Ephraim, may be intensified by many aggravations, but when we turn to the Lord our God with contrite hearts, He forgives all our iniquities, and heals all our diseases, and crowns us with loving-kindness and tender mercy. In other words, mercy lifts the curse from the sinner's head, and puts on a crown of loving-kindness in its place. Well might Hosea exclaim, "Who is a God like unto Thee? . . . He retaineth not His anger for ever, because He delighteth in mercy."

Two brief observations of a general kind may perhaps be regarded as a relevant close to this discussion. The first is that Repentance is a human duty; the second is that Repentance is a divine gift.

Repentance is essential to salvation for every sinful man. That is the concurrent testimony of every Book of the Bible in which the question of deliverance from sin is discussed. In the Word of reconciliation down through the ages God is calling men everywhere to repent. Both Law and Gospel proclaim it to be an indispensable condition of eternal life—*the fact*, that is, without stipulation as to degree. It is the part of all who hear the message of salvation, therefore, to give heed to this, its opening call.

But Repentance is also a gift of God. Christ is exalted as a Prince and a Saviour to *give* to guilty men, not only remission of sins, but also that very Repentance which is a condition of forgiveness. So amazingly true is it that salvation is all of grace. A soul that is conscious of personal ill-desert often anxiously ponders the question, How can I bring myself to a contrite frame of mind? To any one in that condition the old simple words of admonition are specially appropriate:

> Let not conscience make you linger;
> Nor of fitness fondly dream.
> All the fitness He requireth
> Is, to feel your need of Him.

Wherever there is this consciousness of need, an unhesitating appropriation of God's gift of life should follow.

XVI

THE NEW COVENANT

JEREMIAH'S doctrine of the New Covenant has been discussed with some fulness in the Introduction to this volume, and it is not proposed to repeat in the present chapter what has been written there. It is instructive, however, to notice the central place which is given in the New Testament writings to the teaching of the Old Testament prophet with regard to the way of salvation. The Apostles of Christ have really nothing to add to Jeremiah's presentation of this great theme. They not only appropriate his general idea of the New Covenant, but, in one instance at least, make use of the very words in which he unfolds its content, as the final expression of the Gospel way of reconciliation. This literal reproduction takes place in the Epistle to the Hebrews,[1] and Jeremiah's doctrine of "the grace of God which bringeth salvation" runs broadly through the whole of the Pauline Epistles. In particular we find that his reference to the contrast between the New Covenant and the Old is expanded in considerable detail in the Second Epistle to the Corinthians.[2] In the striking passage devoted to this subject Paul declares that God had made his fellow-workers and himself competent ministers of the New Covenant; that the Old Dispensation undeniably possessed a glory of its own; but that this splendour fades into insignificance when viewed in the light of "the glory that excelleth."

This is a profoundly significant fact. It not only bears witness to the clearness of Jeremiah's spiritual perception in an age of almost universal religious darkness, but also provides a striking illustration of the unity of the

[1] viii. 8-12. [2] iii. 5-18.

Scriptures in their presentation of God's way of life for sinful men. It may be interesting for us, therefore, to consider for a little what a New Testament Apostle has to say in elucidation of the teaching of an Old Testament Prophet with regard to one of the fundamental doctrines of revealed religion.

No man ever had a nobler conception of the ministerial office than the Apostle Paul. He had a profound sense of the loftiness of his vocation because there flamed continually before his eyes the glory of the Gospel of Jesus Christ. The freedom and spirituality and abounding grace of the evangel moved his soul to rapture, and filled his lips with praise. The contrast between the New Covenant, of which he was made a minister, and the Old Dispensation under which the Church of God lived before the coming of Christ, was often forced upon his attention because of the efforts of those false teachers in Corinth, Galatia, and elsewhere, who were continually dogging his steps and endangering his work by striving to lead the people back into the bondage of the old economy. Paul accordingly was constrained to set forth repeatedly, and with all the clearness and vigour of which he was capable, the difference between the law which was given by Moses and the grace and truth which came by Jesus Christ. In the great passage in Second Corinthians, to which reference has just been made, he proclaims the transcendent glory of the Gospel dispensation. When we examine his argument we find that there are three main facts on which he bases the superiority of the New Covenant.

I

To begin with, there is the excelling glory of its Mediator.—The Law was given by Moses, and the Mediator of the New Covenant is Jesus Christ. So the contrast between the two dispensations is represented by the difference between Moses and Christ. Now Moses undoubtedly possessed a singular glory. The shining of his face when he descended with the Law from Mount

Sinai was a symbol of that fact. The leader of the Exodus and the law-giver of Israel, Moses was one of the great figures of all time, a majestic personality, who throughout all his days moved on a lofty plane of speech and action, a man of outstanding purity of soul, of strong faith, and magnificent courage. He was favoured with a remarkable fellowship with God: "there was not a prophet in Israel like unto Moses whom the Lord knew face to face." He manifested, too, a spirit of unique self-sacrificing devotion in his leadership of Israel. In entering upon his task he esteemed "the reproach of Christ greater riches than all the treasures of Egypt," and at a later stage in his career he was willing that his name should be blotted out of God's book for the sake of the people with whose destinies he had linked his life. These are all qualities which have a certain kinship with the character of Jesus, but they have "no glory in this respect by reason of the glory that excelleth."

For both in His personal qualities and in His official work Christ occupies a position of immeasurable pre-eminence. The glory of Moses was the glory of a faithful servant in the house; the glory of Christ is the glory of the eternal Son to whom the house belongs. He is the effulgence of the Father's glory and the very image of His substance, and so stands on an infinitely higher plane than any created being, whether angel or man. He is the Leader of the spiritual Exodus and the true Law-giver of His Church. The moral elevation of Moses was but a faint reflection of His stainless purity, and the devotion of Moses but a dim foreshadowing of His substitutionary love.

II

In the second place, there is the excelling glory of its provisions.—From this point of view, again, the Law had an undoubted glory. It was holy and just and good. It revealed the purity of the character of God, and the majestic splendour of His righteousness. But it was a glory that on the whole had a terrifying effect on men. This fact is symbolised, Paul reminds us, by the circumstance that "the children of Israel could not steadfastly behold the face of Moses for the glory of his countenance." In this respect there is a twofold contrast between the two dispensations.

The Old Covenant was a "ministry of condemnation." It had no pardon for the guilty. The Law had nothing for sinful men but a curse. It had no compassion for the ignorant and those who were out of the way. Its keen eye was never moistened with any gleam of pity. Its stern voice was never softened with any note of tenderness. It could not be entreated. The Law was austerely and inexorably just. But the glory that excelleth is pre-eminently the glory of grace. It is "the ministration of righteousness"; and when we inquire what that righteousness is, we find ourselves at the Cross of Christ. Through His work of expiation on Calvary Jesus brought in an everlasting righteousness, and it is through this righteousness that the Gospel is the power of God unto salvation to every one that believeth. It is the glory of the Gospel that it has pardon for the guilty. "This cup," said Jesus, in instituting the memorial of His death, "is the New Covenant in My blood which is shed for many for the remission of sins." Christ is full of compassion, and rich in mercy and grace. Unlike the Law, He is

> Not as though blind and deaf to our beseeching,
> Neither forgetful that we are but dust;
> Not as, from heavens too high for our up-reaching,
> Coldly sublime, intolerably just.

And the old economy was a "ministration of death" as well as of condemnation. In addition to the fact that death was the penalty with which it visited sin, it had no regenerating power, and, therefore, had no remedy for the spiritual impotence of men. Its authority was external, and it could not secure obedience to its own demands. That was why it failed; it was "weak through the flesh." Against the corruption and rebellion of the unregenerate heart its commands were unavailing. But it is part of the more excellent glory of the New Covenant that it provides life for the dead. It is "the ministration of the Spirit," and so is the channel of a quickening and transforming energy. The Gospel provides a remedy for "the flesh" in all its impotence and corruption. The regenerating power of the Spirit of Christ creates a new heart within men, and on the fleshy tables of that heart, as distinct from the unresponsive tables of stone which represented the external authority of the Old Covenant, the law of God is written. The result is that the impulse to obedience comes from within. Under the constraints of love and gratitude the believing soul walks before God in newness of life. Here then is a further ground for the claim to superiority. "If the ministration of death was glorious . . . how shall not the ministration of the Spirit be rather glorious?"

III

FINALLY, THERE IS THE EXCELLING GLORY OF ITS PERMANENCE.—The Old Covenant was not meant to endure. Like the shining of Moses' face, its glory was a fading splendour. Sometimes, indeed, there is a peculiar glory in transient things. There are many things of beauty that are lying under the sentence of death. The lily and the rose have a surpassing loveliness, but their root is ever in its grave. The beauty of the autumn woods and fields makes a special appeal to us, but it is like "a gilded halo hovering round decay." The heavens themselves, with all their solemn and varied grandeurs—there is one glory of the sun, and another glory of the moon, and another glory of the stars—shall at length wax old and vanish out of sight. And so it was with the Old Covenant. It belonged to the order of things that could be shaken; and at length it yielded place to that new dispensation which bears the seal of everlastingness. The Gospel represents a kingdom which cannot be moved.

Christ is a priest for ever. His one sacrifice possesses eternal validity, and His intercession endures throughout the endless years. All the blessings of salvation possess the crowning glory of permanence. God's forgiveness of sins is complete and final; the life which He bestows is imperishable; the inheritance of His saints is incorruptible, undefiled, and unfading. And so the Apostle puts the cope-stone on his argument by exclaiming, "If that which is done away was glorious, much more that which remaineth is glorious."

Its behoves us all to give thanks to God for the privileges of the New Covenant. Let us fill our minds with the thought of the glory of its Mediator, the grace of its provisions, and the stability of its foundations. Above all, let us give more diligence to attain to the assurance of a personal interest in its blessings, so that throughout all the changing experiences of this mortal life our hearts may be sustained with the comforts of the old promise, "The mountains shall depart and the hills be removed, but My kindness shall not depart from thee, neither shall the Covenant of My Peace be removed, saith the Lord that hath mercy on thee."

XVII

THE MEDIATOR OF THE NEW COVENANT

We have already seen that Jeremiah's doctrine of the New Covenant runs through the New Testament writings; and, indeed, this is inevitable, seeing that it is a doctrine which embodies with singular fulness the grace of the Christian dispensation. In the Epistle to the Hebrews, which adopts not only the prophet's teaching on this subject but also his very words, we are told that the Mediator of this New Covenant is Jesus Christ;[1] that is to say, it is through His redemptive agency that its stability is established, and its benefits are made over and guaranteed to sinful men. It would be surprising if Jeremiah—the man who saw so clearly into the heart of the Gospel—should have nothing to say about the Person by whom, in a day to come, this mediatorial function was to be discharged. As a matter of fact his prophecies do contain references, which are by no means obscure, to the promised Messiah. The fullest of these is contained in the twenty-third chapter: *Behold, the days come, saith the Lord, that I will raise unto David a righteous Branch, and a King shall reign and prosper, and shall execute judgment and justice in the earth. In His days Judah shall be saved, and Israel shall dwell safely, and this is His name whereby He shall be called, The Lord our Righteousness.*[2] This promise is repeated, in almost identical terms, in a subsequent oracle,[3] in which the work of the King is expressly related to the perpetuity of the Covenant.[4]

It is more particularly in His kingly character that Jeremiah describes the work of the Mediator, but His priestly function is implicit in the great name, Jehovah-

[1] Heb. viii. 6; ix. 15; xii. 24.
[2] xxiii. 5, 6.
[3] xxxiii. 15, 16.
[4] xxxiii. 20-26.

Tsidkenu, which represents both His Person and His office.

We shall consider the prophet's words, then, as referring to Jesus Christ, "the Mediator of the New Covenant." There are three great facts concerning Him which they set forth.

I. The Mystery of His Origin.—The mystery is indicated by the fact that terms are applied to Him so widely divergent in their connotation as to yield the presumption of a unique personality.

On the one hand He is spoken of as a "Branch" of the line of David which the Lord was to "raise up." That designation points to *an element of lowliness* in His origin. The same figure is used by Isaiah,[1] and the same word by Zechariah,[2] with unmistakable reference to the Messiah.[3] It is a word which means, not so much a branch in the usual sense of that term, as a sprout or shoot, springing up from the roots of a tree which once had flourished in stately pride, but now is laid low. The goodly boughs that once waved in the breeze in varied grace of form and colour, or yielded their store of fruit in its season, are all gone. No longer do they provide a lodging for the birds of the air, or a covert from the heat for the beasts of the field. Nothing is left but the stock, scarcely rising above the level of the ground. Perhaps not even that; only the roots hidden beneath the surface. But in the roots there still remains life. "There is hope of a tree," says Job, "if it be cut down, that it will sprout again, and that the tender branch thereof will not cease. Though the root thereof wax old in the earth, and the stock thereof die in the ground; yet through the scent of water it will bud, and bring forth boughs like a plant."

That is Jeremiah's figure. The royal house of David had become like a fallen tree. Its early glory had in every sense decayed. Its dominion was wellnigh gone, for the sceptre was departing from Judah. But from that lowly stock there came forth in the fulness of time a tiny shoot, feeble and inconspicuous at first, but gradually

[1] xi. 1. [2] vi. 12. [3] Cf. Rom. xv. 12.

spreading forth its branches and increasing in strength, until at length it became a mighty tree. This is a fitting representation of the lowly human origin of Jesus Christ. How slender and unpromising the shoot from the stem of Jesse at first appeared. The Virgin of Nazareth had a queenly soul, but of the outward trappings of royalty she had none. It was in no stately palace that she brought forth her Child ; it was not even in the inn of Bethlehem. There was no room for her in any dwelling of men when her hour was come. It was in a stable, " amidst the squalor and musty odours spread by the night wind, and the noisy rattle of rings, and the movements of restless animals, that in the long dark watches of the night Mary bore her travail." By the hands of some nameless woman —nameless, that is, in the records of men, but surely preserved in God's book of remembrance—the Babe was wrapped in swaddling clothes and laid in a manger. In keeping with the circumstances of His birth was the manner of His after life. From childhood to manhood He grew up in Nazareth, an obscure village of Galilee, with a reputation for evil that seems to have passed into a proverb.[1] There He toiled for years in Joseph's workshop, and was known as " the carpenter." He had no wealth or social influence. During the term of His public ministry He had not " where to lay His head," and His only followers were a handful of Galilean peasants. So literally true was it that He grew up " as a tender plant, and as a root out of a dry ground."

On the other hand, however, He is described in terms which indicate a *loftier origin.* The Branch is not only referred to as a King, but He is called by a name—Jehovah-Tsidkenu, the Lord our Righteousness—which speaks of infinite majesty. As has already been said, it is in this combination of diverse titles, each of them appropriate within the range of its particular application, that the mystery of Christ's Person is set forth in Jeremiah's oracle. Let us return to Bethlehem and look again at the infant cradled in " the little curb of clay on

[1] John i. 46.

the floor in which the provender of the beasts used to be placed for their faring." Who is this helpless child that needs to be fed and clothed, and lifted up and laid down, and that has no language but a cry? Be still, and know that His name is—Jehovah. This is the mystery of the Incarnation. The eternal Son of God came into the world

> A little baby thing
> That made a woman cry.

The Word that was in the beginning with God, and that was God, tabernacled in human flesh among the sons of men. The little child that was fondly clasped to Mary's breast was in the bosom of the Father, in the embrace of a Diviner love, from all eternity. At the appointed hour He came forth from the decayed stock of Jesse in Bethlehem Ephratah, but in the volume of the Book it is written of Him that "His goings forth were from of old, from everlasting." The hand that measured the boards with unfailing care in Joseph's workshop was the hand that in the morning of creation meted out heaven with the span, and weighed the mountains in scales and the hills in a balance. "In Jesus Christ, Son of God, and Son of Mary 'of the house and lineage of David,' monarchy in Israel found at length the actualisation of the ideal. In Him the dualism of a divine and human sovereignty over the people of God was resolved into a higher unity. In Him the provisions of the Deuteronomic Law, the brighter hopes of Samuel, the King-maker, the promises through Nathan to the House of David, and all the glories predicted of 'the Branch' by prophet and psalmist, paradoxical as they seemed when given, found their justification, their interpretation, and, in the strictest sense of that word, their 'fulfilment.'"[1] The Mediator of the New Covenant is well qualified for His office, for He is that "second Man" who is "the Lord from Heaven."

II. The Loftiness of His Character.—Jeremiah's description of the Messiah is brief but comprehensive. "A king," he declares, "shall reign and deal wisely"—this is

[1] Dr James Oscar Boyd in *The Princeton Theological Review*, Jan. 1928.

an alternative and preferable rendering of the word "prosper"—"and shall execute judgment and justice in the earth." Two outstanding qualities of His character are here emphasised.

The first is *Righteousness.* Long years before, at the close of his own eventful reign, David had described the ideal of kingship to which he himself had aspired but had not fully attained: "He that ruleth over man must be just, ruling in the fear of God. And he shall be as the light of the morning, when the sun riseth, even a morning without clouds; as the tender grass springing out of the earth by clearing shining after rain." Few of his successors on the throne had conformed in any degree to that lofty standard. The rule of most of them had been neither just nor beneficent. Jeremiah's own contact with royalty was not an inspiring experience. An acquaintance with a proud and unscrupulous oppressor like Jehoiakim, and, later, with a selfish and vacillating weakling like Zedekiah, was scarcely fitted to increase his respect for kings.

But in direct contrast with these mean representatives of sovereignty is the King whose glory flamed, in the far distance, before the eyes of the prophet. He is a just king: righteousness indeed is imbedded in the name by which He is to be called. This description applies first of all to His personal character. Jesus Christ has a pre-eminent claim to be designated "that Just One" because of the purity of His life. He loved righteousness with a love that never abated, and hated iniquity with a hatred that never relented. If it is true that "no heart is pure that is not passionate," then the heart of Jesus was a burning flame in its love for holiness. When He came into the world He is represented, in another prophetic utterance, as exclaiming, "I delight to do Thy will, O my God: yea, Thy law is within my heart." Not one unguarded word, not one unrighteous deed, not even one unlawful desire, ever dimmed the white radiance of His soul. In His personal life this King walked in the paths of righteousness throughout all the days.

The description applies with equal accuracy to His

official work. He came down from heaven to execute judgment and justice in the earth. The world into which He came was full of unrighteousness, for it was a world that, for the most part, was in revolt against the Divine rule. His task was to restore the moral order that had been set aside through the iniquity of men, and to establish the Kingdom of God on the basis of an everlasting righteousness. Like Melchizedek, therefore, He is "first King of Righteousness, and after that King of Peace." And that means that He must also, like Melchizedek, be a Priest of the most high God. It was deep down in the merits of His oblation on the Cross that He laid the foundations of His kingly dominion. He loved righteousness so vehemently, and hated iniquity so intensely, that He laid down His life on Calvary to vindicate the one and to make an end of the other. It was only by satisfying the claims of justice through His death that He could establish the reign of grace in a sinful world.

The second outstanding quality which Jeremiah assigns to the Messianic rule is *Wisdom*. The King, he declares, shall "deal wisely." This witness also is in accordance with other prophetic oracles concerning the Messiah. Isaiah, for example, in speaking of the Branch which was to grow out of the roots of Jesse, testifies that "the Spirit of the Lord shall rest on Him, the Spirit of wisdom and understanding, the Spirit of counsel and might, the Spirit of knowledge and of the fear of the Lord."[1] The fruit of this anointing, he adds, was to be a spiritual insight which would enable Him to form His judgments with unerring discernment, and not according to outward appearances, which are often misleading, or to current opinions, which are often mistaken. The fulfilment of this prophecy is seen in its completeness in Jesus Christ. During His life on earth the Spirit of wisdom shone so clearly within His soul that it revealed in its true character everything on which He turned His eye.

He dealt wisely, for example, with the various classes

[1] xi. 1, 2.

of men with whom He came in contact. Certainly He needed a more than human keenness of discernment to recognise and defeat the confederacies of evil which assailed Him on every side. But He knew what was in man. Because He did not judge after the sight of His eyes, He was able to detect the most cunning devices of malice, and to see through the most skilful artifices of hypocrisy. Behind the religious pretensions of the Pharisees, for example—their rigid adherence to ceremonial, their ostentatious exhibitions of devotion—He saw the hatred and pride, the covetousness and corruption, which warranted Him in denouncing them as "whited sepulchres." And on the other hand He discerned with equal clearness the most slender indications of spiritual life in men's souls. Was it but the feeblest groping of faith, or the faintest awakening of love, or the slightest dawning of hope—He nourished them all unto fuller growth and more vigorous activity. The bruised reed He did not break, and the smoking flax He did not quench.

But it was in His redemptive work that His wisdom was most conspicuously revealed. Some observations on this subject were made in an earlier chapter,[1] and these need not be repeated here. But we cannot too often remind ourselves that Christ crucified is "the wisdom of God;" that is to say, the redeeming cross of His Son is God's complete and final word of wisdom to the human race. Even the omniscience of Heaven could not devise a better way of salvation for guilty men. Human wisdom is most frequently seen in the adaptation of means to ends. The means may not always be obvious; to the undiscerning eye, indeed, they may appear to be hopelessly inadequate for the purpose in view; but they achieve the desired result at last, even "though a wide compass round be fetched." And when the goal is reached by such an unlikely path, wisdom is the more completely justified of her children. Christ was a king who had to establish His dominion through conquest. He achieved His purpose by dying on a cross. He overcame death by

[1] P. 160 f.

subjecting Himself to its power, and conquered the grave by becoming its Tenant. He obeyed that He might rule, and humbled Himself that He might be exalted. No one has ever looked on God's Redemption with anointed eyes who has not read on the Cross—in letters that flame through its enveloping darkness—this superscription: "O the depth of the riches both of the wisdom and knowledge of God! How unsearchable are His judgments, and His ways past finding out!"

III. THE GREATNESS OF HIS WORK.—That work is described as salvation. "In His days," says Jeremiah, "Judah shall be saved, and Israel shall dwell safely." The immediate reference is to the deliverance from Babylon, but Messianic prophecy as a whole is clothed in imagery derived from events in Jewish history which—of course on a lower plane and within a narrower range—are so essentially akin to the work of Jesus Christ as to foreshadow the culminating Deliverance which was to be achieved through Him. In the present instance the words used by the prophet have a latent, expansive significance which extends beyond the local and temporary restoration to which they directly apply, and includes salvation in its fullest sense. And even in their primary reference they are words which suggest a triumph of surpassing greatness. The release from Babylon, we are told, is to possess a more excellent glory, and to win a more enduring fame, than the deliverance from Egypt.[1]

In any case we are warranted in filling Jeremiah's description of the work of the ideal King with its complete New Testament meaning. The mediator of the New Covenant is called Jesus because He saves His people from their sins. His deliverance of banished men implies salvation in the fulness of its redemptive and moral content. He sets them free from their guilt and corruption and spiritual impotence, as well as from the tyranny of material things, the oppression of fear, and the bondage of selfishness. On the other hand, He

[1] xxiii. 7, 8.

mediates to them the blessings of the New Covenant—that everlasting Covenant through the grace of which they are made partakers of "the sure mercies of David."

And if inquiry be made as to the method by which this salvation is secured, the answer is to be found in the word "Righteousness" which is enshrined in the name given to the Messianic King of Jeremiah's vision. The central theme of the Gospel is righteousness. It may be said, of course, that its dominant note is grace, and from one point of view that is undoubtedly true. But it must not be forgotten that it is because of righteousness that grace occupies its regnant position in the Good News, and is therefore able to address its authoritative assurances to the guilty conscience, and its moving appeals to the fearful heart. Grace reigns through righteousness, both in the message of salvation and in the souls of the saved. Nowhere is this fact more emphatically proclaimed than in the Epistle to the Romans. Paul tells us that he was not ashamed of the Gospel of Christ for the simple reason that it is the power of God unto salvation to every one that believeth; and he adds that it possesses this resistless potency because "therein is revealed the righteousness of God from faith to faith."[1]

The meaning of this arresting utterance Paul proceeds to unfold. The necessity for a Gospel of Righteousness—this is the sum of his teaching—lies in the fact of human sin. In his vivid exposition of this theme we see the whole world summoned before the bar of God. Jews and Gentiles, with no essential difference in their condition, are charged with a common unrighteousness. It is a terrible indictment which is brought against them by the Divine Law—terrible on the one hand because of the nature of the offences which it records, and on the other because of the severity of the penalties which it demands. As to the one, it affirms that all have sinned and come short of the glory of God; as to the other, it declares that the wrath of God is revealed from Heaven against

[1] Rom. i. 16.

all ungodliness and unrighteousness of men. And the result of the trial is a verdict of guilty: there is none righteous, no not one. To this tremendous charge no defence is offered. Every mouth is stopped, and there is a great silence, unbroken on the part of the accused by any word of denial or any attempt at evasion. The reason is that the condemnation of the law has been endorsed by the judgment of conscience.

How, then, is that oppressive stillness broken? Surely by the voice of the Judge of all flesh pronouncing the dread sentence of death upon the guilty. But no, it is not a word of doom that Paul causes us to hear in that hour of dramatic silence, but a word of life—a word that conveys to the accusing conscience the hope of a righteous acquittal, and that is sweeter to the contrite spirit than the music of "harpers harping with their harps." "But now," says the Apostle, "*the righteousness of God* without the law is manifested, being witnessed by the law and the prophets; even the righteousness of God which is by faith of Jesus Christ unto all and upon all them that believe."[1] A message of grace, we immediately exclaim. Yes, certainly, a message of grace abounding to the chief of sinners; but it is a message of grace because, first of all, it is a message of righteousness.

At this point it may be mentioned in passing that the course which Paul's teaching follows in the chapters which have been briefly summarised in the foregoing paragraphs is also the usual order of religious experience. The lips of the transgressor are closed in self-condemnation in the hour when he comes to himself in the far country. They are opened again in the gladness of the new song in the day when God reveals to him His way of salvation through the righteousness of Christ. William Cowper, for example, was first delivered from the depths of gloom into which, like a "stricken deer," he had sunk, by reading that great verse in the third chapter of Romans which speaks of Christ as set forth by God to be "a propitiation through faith in His blood, to declare

[1] Rom. iii. 21, 22.

His righteousness for the remission of sins. . . ." This is how he describes his release from the bondage of conscious ill-desert: "Immediately I received strength to believe it, and the full beams of the Sun of Righteousness shone upon me. I saw the sufficiency of the atonement He had made, my pardon sealed in His blood, and all the fulness and completeness of His justification. Unless the Almighty arm had been under me I think I should have died with gratitude and joy."

It was through these same words that the peace of God flowed into the soul of Colonel James Gardiner, whose *Life* by Dr Doddridge is one of the classics of Christian biography. He too—arrested suddenly in the midst of a dissolute career—immediately gave judgment against himself that he deserved to die, and so acquiesced in the justness of the Divine sentence. But one day his eyes were opened to see Christ as the propitiation for his sins, and his soul passed into the light of the Gospel. And whereas formerly he had thought that the justice of God required his destruction, now he was convinced that that same justice was not only vindicated but glorified in his salvation through Jesus Christ. This man experienced so much of the joy of God's salvation that for the space of seven years he enjoyed a heaven on earth; and till the end of his days he lived one of the most consecrated Christian lives ever witnessed in this land.

It is the Gospel of Righteousness alone which provides a satisfying peace and an abiding joy. It is because of the absence of this element in the presentation of the evangel—the affirmation is made in all charitableness and humility—that a great deal of modern preaching is so sterile, and a great deal of modern religion is so ill-conditioned. A Gospel which sees nothing in God but Fatherhood, and nothing in the Cross but Love, can scarcely fail to produce a race of anæmic Christians. It cannot meet the demands of an enlightened conscience, or beget an adequate sense of the wonder of God's forgiveness. These ends are achieved only when we realise that Christ, the Lord from Heaven, is our Righteousness.

When Paul speaks of the righteousness which is revealed in the Gospel, he is not referring to the attribute of righteousness which is essential to the perfection of the Divine character. What he has in view is the righteousness which Christ has provided for sinful men through His redemptive work. When He made reconciliation for iniquity He brought in—"through the door of the Cross"—an everlasting righteousness. That, as Dr Hugh Martin has finely described it, is "the righteousness which God's own righteousness requires Him to require." It constitutes the one adequate basis of our acceptance with God. And the name, "the Lord our Righteousness," implies more than the mere fact that it is through Christ that we receive the forgiveness of sins. It points to the completeness of the salvation which becomes ours through faith in His Name. He Himself, in all the wealth of His Divine glory and all the merit of His atoning sacrifice, is made unto us of God wisdom and righteousness and sanctification and redemption. All that He is, and all that He has done as the Redeemer of men is put down to our account. He is our answer to every charge and our title to every privilege, the guarantee of every promise and the warrant of every hope.

It is worthy of notice that in the second passage in which this Messianic title is used by Jeremiah there is a significant change in its application. "This," we read, "is the name wherewith *she* shall be called, The Lord our righteousness."[1] The change of gender in the pronoun is advanced by a number of critics as a reason for denying the authenticity of the passage, and regarding it as an insertion by some later hand. But does this minute difference in the text constitute any real justification for so drastic an excision? What if, on the contrary, it is an alteration which bears the seal of Heaven, because it proclaims so clearly the riches of Gospel grace? The reference of the feminine pronoun is to Jerusalem, and Jerusalem represents the Church of God. And the fact which is thereby indicated is that the union between

[1] xxxiii. 16.

Christ and His people is so complete that He bestows on them His own Name, with all the rights and privileges which that implies. He identified Himself with them in His sufferings and death, and in the day of their espousal to Him He makes them heirs of all the benefits which His death procured. It is because of this spiritual oneness that, in Jeremiah's prophecy, Jerusalem is given the name, which represents the reality, of Righteousness. That also is the fact which is set forth in one of the profoundest utterances of the New Testament on this theme: "He hath made Him to be sin for us who knew no sin, *that we might be made the righteousness of God in Him.*"[1] Is not this also the meaning of those striking words which describe the final glory of the redeemed, "His Name shall be in their foreheads?"[2]

When John Bunyan realised that his Righteousness was in Heaven, where Christ is, he had a great deliverance which saved him from the worst of his fears. He saw that it was not his good frame that made his Righteousness better or his bad frame that made his Righteousness worse, for his Righteousness was Jesus Christ Himself, the same yesterday, to-day, and forever. "Now," he exultingly declares, "I could look from myself to Him, and should reckon that all those graces of God that now were green on me, were yet like those cracked-groats and fourpence-halfpennies that rich men carry in their purses when their gold is in their trunks at home! O, I saw that my gold was in my trunk at home! In Christ, my Lord and Saviour! Now Christ was all; all my wisdom, all my righteousness, all my sanctification, and all my redemption. Further the Lord did also lead me into the mystery of union with the Son of God. . . . By this also was my faith in Him as my Righteousness the more confirmed to me; for if He and I were one, His Righteousness was mine, His merits mine, His victory also mine." In this striking testimony John Bunyan is speaking for the whole family of God.

I am well aware that the view of Christ's death which

[1] 2 Cor. v. 21. [2] Rev. xxii. 4.

is set forth in this chapter is not the doctrine which finds favour in a great deal of modern theology, but I am persuaded, nevertheless, that, if words mean anything, it is the interpretation of the Cross which is written on every page of the New Testament that is concerned with this vital theme.

XVIII

THE SIGN OF THE PURCHASED FIELD

THE incident which took place during Jeremiah's confinement in the court of the prison in Jerusalem, when his cousin, Hanameel, paid him a visit, and offered him, as next-of-kin, a field in Anathoth for the comparatively small sum of seventeen shekels, has already been considered in the Introduction to this book. It will be remembered that the prophet agreed to the purchase without demur, and that the transaction was carried through with impressive legal formality. The immediate significance of this procedure has also been discussed already. The readiness of the landowner of Anathoth to dispossess himself of a family inheritance for a mere trifle, and the equal readiness of the captive prophet to make himself a landed proprietor, are alike suggestive. Hanameel's benevolence, at least, is easily understood. The Chaldean army were at the gates of Jerusalem, and had already secured possession of the surrounding territory. There was, therefore, if one may borrow a familiar American phrase, a slump in real estate at Anathoth. And the astute son of Shallum would have reckoned that seventeen shekels in his own hand were better than a field in the hand of the enemy.

Jeremiah's part in the incident is not less intelligible. The willingness with which he consented to become the owner of an apparently valueless piece of land was a sign of his faith in his own predictions, and—underlying that confidence—of his trust in the faithfulness of his God. The whole transaction was, at the same time, a severe test of his faith. On the one hand he was inspired by the hope of future prosperity for the nation, based on the prophetic word which, a little while before, he had been commissioned to speak. On the other, he was conscious of the present fact which to the eye of sense was so directly opposed to that glowing prospect that it seemed to leave no star of hope in the sky. But Jeremiah's faith survived this searching ordeal, and the sign of its triumph was the purchased field. It was not without earnest prayer, however, that his soul was able to maintain its confidence. "There is nothing too hard for Thee," was the final plea which he advanced in the urgency of his cry for strength. The omnipotence of God, as that was revealed in the deliverances vouchsafed to His people in the past, was the unchanging fact which inspired his hope for their future restoration.

This apparently trivial episode in the life of Jeremiah is full of instruction for the children of God in all ages. It is particularly illuminating in its bearing on those experiences in which "sense is at war with soul," and faith has to contend with unbelief for the mastery. Faith derives its warrant from the promises of God's Word, and unbelief is often fed from the darker dispensations of His Providence. Belief in the Divine testimony gives rise to many bright hopes, but these hopes appear to be flatly contradicted by the present fact. The outward eye sees only the invading army and the ravaged land. The eye of faith pierces the enveloping gloom, and realises that "God is on the field when He is most invisible," fulfilling His purposes in conquering power and restoring mercy. In these moments of spiritual vision the believer purchases his field in Anathoth. In other words, he is enabled to rise above his outward adversities, and to act as if the hope enshrined in God's promise were a present reality. And in that hour of victory there is one thought that sustains the courage of his soul: "There is nothing too hard for Thee."

Let us think of some of the circumstances in which Faith is so energetic in its exercise that it purchases a field at the time when the enemy has overrun the land.

I. There is, first of all, the Day of Trial in Providence.—The Christian hope with regard to every kind of affliction rests on God's promise of complete and final deliverance. The Lord will bring back the captivity of His people from every land of bondage in which they have been oppressed. They shall come to Zion at last with songs and everlasting joy on their heads, and sorrow and sighing shall flee away. In that day the redeemed shall enter into full possession of their inheritance, and shall be "made perfectly blessed in the full enjoying of God to all eternity." They shall hunger no more, neither thirst any more; neither shall the sun light on them, nor any heat. For the Lamb which is in the midst of the Throne shall feed them, and shall lead them unto living fountains of waters: and God shall wipe away all tears from their eyes. That is the hope that is set before us in the Gospel.

The present fact, however, is a reality of a very different character. The afflictions of the righteous in this life have constituted a problem for faith in every age. Saintliness is no guarantee of immunity from the common ills of life.

> Streams will not curb their pride
> The just man not to entomb,
> Nor lightnings go aside
> To give his virtues room.

Sometimes indeed it would seem as if the children of God received more than their equal share of suffering. This is one of the main themes that are discussed in the Book of Job. It is the mystery which caused the steps of the Psalmist to slip, until he entered the sanctuary, and found illumination in the oracles of God.[1] It is a cause of perplexity, and sometimes of stumbling, to reflecting minds in our own time, and for that reason it still challenges the Christian apologist to "assert eternal Providence and justify the ways of God to men." There are sorrows that come upon the believer like an invading army, and lay waste his most pleasant things. Disappointments, too, contribute their own share to his experience, when confidence is betrayed, and love is wounded, and hope is

[1] Ps. lxxiii.

crushed. And who among the family of God does not know the pain of some bereavement which leaves behind it empty places that once were filled with life and love and song?

In such circumstances the faith of the Christian may be sorely tried. His soul is cast down within him, and he forms hasty judgments and even gives way to bitterness of spirit. My way is hid from the Lord, he sadly cries, and my judgment is passed over from my God.

This, however, is only his first reaction to the stroke of adversity. Sooner or later his soul recovers its poise, and not only bows in quiet submission to the will of God, but sometimes even is enabled to rejoice in tribulation. "Blessed be the name of the Lord," said Job, in the midst of an experience of apparently irretrievable loss. "Most gladly therefore will I rather glory in my infirmities," cried Paul, in an hour of intense personal distress. One of the most remarkable instances of this triumph of faith over outward circumstances is recorded in the Book of Habakkuk. The prophet represents himself as standing in the midst of a ruined homestead, after a series of calamities had stripped him of all his possessions. There was no fruit on the trees; some killing frost had nipped their early promise. There was no grain in the fields; they had somehow been smitten with barrenness. There was no flock in the folds, and no herd in the stalls; they too had been cut off by some mysterious disease. It was a scene of utter desolation. The disaster had been so complete that we might expect to see the man sitting down in the midst of his shattered hopes, and bewailing the hardness of his lot. But Habakkuk also had his Anathoth in which he redeemed his inheritance. He is not weeping; he is singing. He is not desponding; he is exulting. Instead of grieving over his loss, he is rejoicing in his everlasting portion. The storm of adversity had not deprived him of everything. One thing remained, and that was—God; and the fact of God stood out all the more clearly against the sombre background of his loss. So it is a song that we find on his lips, and not a lament. "Yet I will rejoice in the Lord," he says, "I will joy in the God of my salvation. . . ."

This is a high attainment, and it is reached only in the measure in which we understand the purpose of God's afflictive dealings with His children. "He for our profit," is the final explanation of the mystery of pain. The cross is remunerative. It does not exclude us from communion with God; on the contrary, it admits us into the fellowship of Christ's sufferings. It is when the believer realises this fact, that his faith exhibits to the world the sign of the purchased field.

II. Then there is the Day of conscious Short-coming in the Spiritual Life.—The Christian hope with respect to spiritual attainment is glorious beyond all aspiration or conception; for God is able to do—and therefore will do—"exceeding abundantly above all that we ask or think." It is nothing less than perfect conformity to the likeness of Christ. When the believer is presented before the Throne of God at last, he will not only be "holy," but "unblameable and unreprovable." No tongue can condemn, because no eye can detect a flaw in that radiant beauty.

The present fact, however, is far removed from this hope of ultimate perfection. The Christian has, indeed, perfection of standing in this life, for already, through faith, he has been "made the righteousness of God" in Christ; but perfection of attainment is another matter, and exists only in the imagination of men and women who have an inadequate conception of the holiness of God and a superficial acquaintance with the plagues of their own heart. The beauty of the saints in this present world is beyond question a fact which forms one of the weightiest evidences of the power of the Gospel, but it is those children of God who have advanced farthest in the life of godliness that are most painfully conscious of their personal short-coming. It is indeed true that the life of the Christian is a life of victory. Sin does not have dominion over him; the grace that is in him has dominion over sin. But victory presupposes conflict, and the believer is engaged in a warfare from which there is no discharge in this world. It is true that in a forensic sense he was once for all crucified with Christ, but there is a process of crucifixion which goes on within his soul to the end—a crucifying of the old man with his affections and lusts. And sometimes the consciousness that there *is* an old man that needs to be crucified gives rise to a feeling of discouragement and depression. In the stress and "confused noise" of the conflict, the Christian soldier may conclude that the forces of evil are gaining the ascendency, and that he is being led into captivity, instead of entering more fully into the freedom that is in Christ.

No man ever lived a fuller or more triumphant Christian life than the Apostle Paul, but even from this "man in Christ" the intensity of the struggle drew the cry, "O wretched man that I am! who shall deliver me from the body of this death?" Why do so many expositors insist on maintaining that the whole of the seventh chapter of Romans is the record of a pre-Christian experience? Even a writer of such insight and well-balanced judgment as the Rev. James S. Stewart affirms that there is "a clear indication that it is the experience of a life still needing to be born again which is here being described,"[1] and that such phrases as the yearning for deliverance just quoted "are not the normal notes of a life that Christ has changed." But this pronouncement—which is no doubt prompted by the laudable desire to rescue the Christian life from the reproach of failure and misery—is too hasty, and is based on a faulty interpretation of Paul's words as well as on a too narrow survey of the facts of Christian experience. This assertion obviously demands some evidence in its support, and, accordingly, a brief discussion of the Apostle's teaching in the seventh chapter of Romans will be found in the appended footnote.[2] It may here be pointed out, how-

[1] *A Man in Christ*, p. 99.

[2] To begin with, we must constantly bear in mind that, as has already been indicated, Paul's theme in this much-discussed passage, as well as

ever, that Paul's main object in that chapter is to proclaim the impotence of the Law to secure the sanctification of a believing soul. The Law cannot release a man from the power of indwelling sin; rather does it reveal to him more clearly his abounding corruption. And so at length there breaks from the Apostle's heart the moving cry, "Who shall deliver me?" It is not the utterance of despair, but of passionate longing for emancipation from the evil thing of which he was so bitterly conscious within him.

And to that cry he himself provides a ready answer. "I thank God," he exclaims, "through Jesus Christ our

in the preceding part of the Epistle, is the insufficiency of the Law to liberate men either from the guilt or the power of sin. In chapters i.-v. he is affirming that the Law cannot justify a guilty sinner: we are justified by faith alone. In chapter vi. he is contending that this doctrine is not subversive of morality, but, on the contrary, is a potent instrument of holiness. In chapter vii. he is demonstrating, with a poignant emphasis derived from his own experience, that the Law is equally powerless to sanctify a justified believer. It is plainly true that vv. 1-5 of this chapter set forth the condition of unregenerate men; in them Paul does not yet use the present tense, nor does he write in the first person. Verse 6—introduced by the significant words, "But now"—is a comprehensive description of a state of grace, and vv. 7-11 recount the experience of conviction of sin through the Law which in Paul's own case formed the pathway to this happy condition. He still writes in the past tense, but now, and from this point onwards, he uses the first person.

It is impossible, with any regard to the meaning of words, to deny that in the remaining part of the chapter, Paul is describing his personal experience as a man who is not under the Law but under grace. He uses a number of expressions which cannot possibly be applied to an unregenerate man. To quote but a single instance, no unregenerate man could ever honestly say, "I delight in the Law of God after the inward man." Even Bishop H. C. G. Moule, who was one of the most fervent exponents, as he certainly was one of the worthiest representatives, of the victorious life, is constrained by his exegetical conscience to acknowledge that the passage under discussion is neither a description of the collision between will and conscience which often takes place in the natural man, nor yet a picture of a half-renewed man, "stumbling across a border zone between the power of Satan and the Kingdom of God." His considered judgment is that "he who can truly speak thus of an inward sympathy, a sympathy of delight, with the most holy Law of God is no half-Christian." [1]

It is indeed the case that there are expressions used by Paul in this chapter which, when isolated from their context, would lead to the conclusion that he is writing of his pre-Christian life. But every statement

[1] *Romans* pp. 190, 192.

Lord." These are the words of a man whose heart leaps up in glad adoration as he turns away from the Law and from self to that all-sufficient Saviour who of God is made unto him "wisdom, and righteousness, and sanctification, and redemption." Faith triumphs over the consciousness of personal shortcoming, and buys its field even when the enemy may appear to have won the day. The eighth chapter of Romans, and especially the exultant confidence which flames in its closing section, is simply an evidence of the purchased inheritance. Faith, indeed, never manifests a more heroic courage than when it

must be interpreted in the light of its setting. When he says, for example, that he is "carnal, sold under sin," or that he is being brought into "captivity to the law of sin" which was in his members, he is not to be understood as declaring that he is the helpless slave of sin, and that he knows of no escape from its toils. Viewed in the light of the sentences among which they stand, his words must be regarded as no more than an acknowledgment that, while he is under the dominion of grace, he is still influenced by the flesh, and that his spiritual attainments, accordingly, come far short of his aspirations. We must not forget that the presence of sin in the heart of a child of God is a fact of universal experience. But neither, on the other hand, should we fill the Apostle's words with a content which they are not designed to express. As has already been stated, the further a Christian advances in the life of holiness the more vividly is he aware of the distance he has still to travel before he attains to perfect conformity to the likeness of Christ; the more acute also is his consciousness of every deviation in thought or in deed from the demands of God's Law; and the more severe therefore will be the judgment which he passes on himself for his every failure to achieve the ideal which it is the deepest desire of his heart to attain. "The resultant failure," says Bishop Moule —"though it be but a thought of vanity, a flush of unexpressed anger, a microscopic flaw in the practice of truthfulness, an unhallowed imagination darting in a moment through the soul—is to him sorrow, burthen, shame." [1]

When Paul, therefore, says of himself that he is "carnal, sold under sin," he is using the language of a spiritual man whose conscience is so sensitive that it not only records, but condemns with a vehemence which is an echo of the Divine Law, every transgression, and every want of conformity to the will of Christ which his life reveals. He is not representing the Christian life as a constant experience of bondage, of frustrated desire, and of humiliating defeat, in the conflict with iniquity. "A prisoner of war," said Rabbi Duncan once, "is not a deserter." And Bishop Moule emphasises this distinction when, in commenting on Paul's reference to his "captivity" in the spiritual warfare, he says, "Observe the present tense, which indicates not necessarily the full success of the strategy, but its aim."

[1] *Romans* p. 195.

stretches its hand across the neck of conscious unworthiness and appropriates the blessings of God's salvation. I am poor and needy, the believer says at such a time, but the Son of God loved me and gave Himself for me. Therefore shall I live as a ransomed soul, and rejoice as becomes an heir of God and a joint heir with Christ.

III. Further, there is "the day of small things" in connection with the Lord's Cause in the World.—Here again the promises of God warrant us to look forward to a golden age of spiritual prosperity. Ezekiel's vision of the river which had its rise in the Temple in Jerusalem—small in its beginnings, but increasing in depth and volume as it flowed—and whose living waters transformed the barren deserts through which it ran into places of fruitfulness and beauty, and brought healing at length into the very sea of death, is a figure of the progress and final triumph of the Gospel in the earth. There is a day coming when the kingdoms of this world shall become the Kingdoms of our Lord and of His Christ, and He shall reign forever and ever. In that day the mountain of the Lord's House shall be exalted above the mountains—which is a figurative way of saying that religion shall place its crown of glory upon every form of human activity. Jesus must reign till His enemies be made His footstool.

But the present fact often reveals a dismal contrast to this bright hope. It will scarcely be affirmed by any serious observer that in our own time the Church of Christ is in a flourishing condition throughout the world. The modern equivalents of the Chaldean army are in possession of vast tracts of territory, and, in one form or another, are menacing the Christian faith. Both atheism and paganism are arrogant in their challenges, and other anti-Christian systems are claiming many devotees. Worldliness and pleasure are the only gods to which multitudes of people render allegiance, and the authority of Christ is ignored in various spheres of life in which lip homage is offered to His Name. And in the midst of so much disloyalty the believer is sometimes tempted to surrender to a despondent mood. Like Jeremiah, amid the desolations of his own day, he is ready to cry, "O, the Hope of Israel, the Saviour thereof in time of trouble, why shouldest Thou be as a stranger in our midst, and as a wayfaring man that turneth aside to tarry for a night?"

But faith lifts up its head even in the day of small things, and buys the field which is in the hand of the enemy. It turns to the enduring word of God, and finds comfort and strength in its assurances. "There is nothing too hard for Thee," it pleads, and ere long supplication passes over into praise. Thou shalt arise and have mercy upon Zion: for the time to favour her, yea, the set time, is come. His Name shall endure for ever: His name shall be continued as long as the sun.

There is an incident in the life of Robert and Mary Moffat which furnishes a striking parallel to the event in Jeremiah's history which we are now considering. They had laboured for a long time among the Bechuanas of South Africa before their efforts yielded any signs of fruit. On every side of them there stretched—in a spiritual as well as a physical sense—a vast barren wilderness in which a not unfriendly people were living in ignorance and corruption. This state of matters continued for ten years, and then an awakening took place. But before this happy result was achieved, and when darkness still prevailed, Mary Moffat received a letter from a friend in Sheffield asking if there was anything that she desired to be sent to her as a help in her work. And the brave-hearted missionary wrote back and said, "Yes; send us a set of Communion vessels; we shall need them yet." Communion vessels before there was a single communicant or the least indication of conversions! But across that desolation of winter, faith saw the autumn sheaves in their golden splendour, and made ready for the harvest. Mary Moffat bought her field in Bechuanaland when it was still in the hands of the enemy. The box containing the communion vessels was duly despatched, but a year elapsed before it reached its destination. It was delivered at the missionaries' house on the day before the first little company of converts sat down at the sacramental table.

IV. Finally, there is the day when Death comes to claim its prey, and the Grave is waiting for its Victory.—The Christian hope includes the final redemption of the body. It is movingly expressed in the familiar words of the Shorter Catechism : The bodies of believers, "being still united to Christ, do rest in their graves till the Resurrection." Sown in weakness and dishonour, they shall be raised in power and glory. "For this corruptible must put on incorruption, and this mortal must put on immortality. So when this corruptible shall have put on incorruption, and this mortal shall have put on immortality, then shall be brought to pass the saying that is written, Death is swallowed up in victory. . . . Thanks be to God who giveth us the victory through our Lord Jesus Christ."

The present fact, however, appears to furnish little warrant for this glorious expectation. Enclosed within "this muddy vesture of decay," our souls seldom catch an echo of the song with which the glorified body greets the dawn of the Resurrection morning. There is a phrase used by Paul with reference to our physical existence on earth, the meaning of which is obscured in the English of our Authorised Version. He speaks not of "our vile body," but of "the body of our humiliation." It is a profound and suggestive expression. The sons of God are in a state of humiliation in this world, and that humiliation is, to a great extent, revealed in the experiences of the body. A well-developed frame, radiating the energy of healthy life, is a thing of beauty and a marvel of creative wisdom. But it is not long until the humiliations begin to appear. The humiliation of weakness, when the once strong man is laid low, and other hands must raise the cup to his white lips ; the humiliation of disease which is sometimes loathsome as well as painful ; the humiliation of an old age which has sunk into "second childishness and mere oblivion." And the last humiliation of all, when the body is consigned to the tomb and becomes the prey of corruption.

But faith has its confidence, and hope has its song, even in this hour of extremity. Faith remembers that there was One whose "returning footsteps broke the eternal calm" of the tomb, and who has become the first-fruits of them that slept. The believer clings to the Divine promise, and lives "a life which dares send a challenge to its end," thereby regarding death as only an incident on the Christian pilgrimage. "Death," says George Herbert, "thou wast once an uncouth hideous thing . . .

> But since our Saviour's death did put some blood
> Into thy face;
> Thou art grown fair and full of grace,
> Much in request, much sought for, as a good."

Ruth Bryan was a saintly woman who died in Nottingham more than seventy-five years ago. During the greater part of her life she suffered much affliction. She was many years in distress of soul before she entered into the peace of the Gospel. Then she was stricken with cancer, and suffered intense pain. But her faith triumphed over all those distressing circumstances. The day when she knew that the end of her troubles was at hand was "a high day of festival to her." A friend discovered her removing from her cap the black ribbons she had always worn since her mother's death, and putting in white ones instead, as if getting ready for her bridal day. "I am going to my wedding," she said, "and the Bridegroom must not find me in mourning." Ruth Bryan also bought her inheritance in the hour when the last enemy had arrived at the gate. In other words, her faith leaped across the present fact of death, and rejoiced in the hope of the glory of God .

XIX

THE TWO ROLLS

AMONG the many striking incidents recorded in the Book of Jeremiah there is scarcely any that is more suggestive than that which is described in the closing verses of the thirty-sixth chapter. King Jehoiakim, attended by his princes, is sitting in his winter palace in Jerusalem, and Jehudi is standing before him reading the Roll of Jeremiah's collected prophecies, which had been written by Baruch to the prophet's dictation. It soon becomes apparent that the reader is to have a stormy passage to the end of his task. He has not read more than three or four leaves of the book when the royal listener starts from his seat in uncontrollable anger, snatches up his penknife, cuts off the offending columns, and casts them into the fire. Again and again this explosive interruption is repeated, until at last the whole Roll is reduced to ashes.

I

The reason for Jehoiakim's wrath is of course not difficult to discover. The prophecies which he committed to the flames were charged for the most part with the note of doom, predicting especially the punishment of the nation at the hand of the King of Babylon, because of its unfaithfulness to God. And Jehoiakim, who was a frivolous and arrogant man, resented those messages of judgment, because they disturbed his complacency and wounded his pride. But his fury was really an exhibition of childish petulance, as futile as it was undignified. If the warnings of the prophet were well-founded, no outburst of royal fury could invalidate their truth; no dramatic burning of leaves in the fire could arrest the approach of the hordes of Babylon. And indeed it was not long until the futility of Jehoiakim's action was revealed. At the Lord's command Jeremiah, making use of the services of Baruch as before, produced another Roll, and not only did this new manuscript contain "all the words of the book" which had been destroyed, but "there were added besides unto them many like words." The old denunciations and warnings all reappeared, and they were reinforced with additional messages of a similar character. The Roll had become bigger. Its charges of guilt were extended, and its threatenings of judgment were multiplied. Jehoiakim's problem, in short, was not of a kind that could be solved by means of the penknife and the fire, and it soon presented itself again in an aggravated form.

The Bible has always had its assailants in the world, for in every generation the tribe of Jehoiakim has been more or less widely represented. And in most cases the hostility has been due to very much the same cause. The Bible bears witness against human sin. It is a holy Book, giving its verdict without fail for righteousness, and declaring that the wrath of God is revealed from heaven against every form of iniquity. And there are many who resent this very faithfulness of warning. They love darkness rather than light because their deeds are evil. The testimony of the Roll is convicting and alarming. So they produce some form of penknife and apply its edge to the offending passages, hoping in this way to silence the condemning witness and to regain their sense of security. This antagonism to the Bible reveals itself in various ways. Sometimes it has taken the form of actual violence. There were times in our own land when the reading of the Scriptures was prohibited by law upon pain of fine or imprisonment, and when the sacred volume was literally burned in the fire. At other times the method of attack, while less crude, was even more dangerous. Infidelity sharpened its penknife and kindled its fires. Gibbon and Hume, Voltaire and Tom Paine, applied to the Divine Word the resources of a disintegrating scepticism or of a biting ridicule, with a view to undermining its authority. But their efforts were in reality as futile as the blustering rage of Jehoiakim. When the knife and the fire had done their worst, the Bible reappeared in its integrity, and continued to assert its authority in the hearts and consciences of men.

II

In our own time the Bible is dissected by the knife of a destructive criticism, in the hand, not of its avowed enemies, but of its professed admirers. It is mutilated in the house of its friends, and its claim to be regarded as the very Word of God is dismissed as the survival of an antiquated doctrine of inspiration. The methods of Jehoiakim, indeed, are followed with a ruthlessness which appears to acknowledge no restraint. The excisions began with the Book of Genesis, and especially those opening pages which deal with the Creation and Fall of Man. The Biblical account of Creation is rejected because it is supposed to conflict with the pronouncements of science. Human life, it is affirmed, is the outcome of a process of evolution which has been going on through countless millenniums. Consequently there has been no Fall, and sin is a natural necessity arising in the course of man's gradual development into a moral being. But when the Bible record of origins is cut out, a more extended use of the critical penknife becomes inevitable. So the pages of the New Testament which speak of redemption through the atoning death of Jesus Christ are made to share the fate of Genesis, and the theology of Paul and Augustine is relegated to the limbo of discredited dogmas. Under the influence of the same view of human history there is an increasing tendency to cut out the supernatural elements in religion, and to account for miracles in ways that are supposed to satisfy the scientific mind. This rationalising principle is applied even to Jesus Christ, and the reality of His bodily Resurrection, as well as the fact of His virgin Birth, are denied by many who claim to represent the assured results of Christian scholarship.

Now it is characteristic of those who subject the Bible to this drastic handling that they are never tired of proclaiming that their excisions have resulted in incalculable gain. The use of the critical penknife, they tell us, has liberated the Church from the bondage of tradition; it has removed many stumbling-blocks from the path of the religious inquirer; and it has restored the Bible to the world, "shining with new moral and spiritual splendour." They are also in the habit of affirming that the results of modern criticism are "assured," and that those parts of the Scriptures which have been consumed in the fire of scholarly research have been destroyed for ever as authentic and trustworthy records. This was also, no doubt, the view of Jehoiakim when he burned the prophet's Roll in the fire. He too, in all probability, felt inclined to boast of his achievement. But, as we have already seen, his success as a destroyer of the Word of the Lord was soon proved to have been a barren victory, and his difficulties were accentuated instead of being solved. Similarly, it may be affirmed with the utmost emphasis that the "free handling" of the Bible by modern criticism not only fails to dispose of the old problems, but adds "besides unto them many like" difficulties, for which it provides no satisfactory answer.

III

It has to be acknowledged of course that if the Modernist position is accepted, there is a sense in which every difficulty presented by the Bible disappears. It is a position which, like the method of Jehoiakim, seems to bear the stamp of a magnificent finality. Everything that is mysterious or hard to be understood is simply cut out; there is nothing left that reason cannot explain; and the occupation of a humble and reverent faith is gone. But the trouble with this method of simplification is that when it has finished its work and made it completely easy for us to believe, there is not much left in the Bible that is really worth believing. It is not without significance that Jehoiakim's destructive zeal was not satisfied with cutting away the first few columns of Jeremiah's Roll; he continued his efforts until the whole Book was consumed. Modern criticism appears to be infected with the same lust of mutilation. "We hoped," said Dr Foulkes Jackson a few years ago, "we could accept the criticism of the Old Testament . . . and yet leave the New Testament untouched. We tried to expunge the miracle of the Virgin Birth from the Creed, and at the same time to accept the rest. We tried to sacrifice the Fourth Gospel, and at the same time not to question the historicity of the Marcan tradition. We are always wondering where to draw the line; our efforts are doomed to failure." Our modern critics have a short and easy way of removing difficulties from the Bible, but it is a way which reminds us forcibly of the method adopted by another race of destroyers long ago, of whom it is recorded that they made a desert and called it peace.

The real truth is that the modern view of the Scriptures gives rise to tremendous difficulties. The theory of Evolution, for example, produces a whole crop of problems for which we are offered no adequate explanation. Not only are its advocates not agreed among themselves on many important questions which it involves, but there are eminent men of science who reject the whole hypothesis. The evidence on which it rests is so slender that it would never gain a verdict in a court of law. The missing link between man and the brute creation has never been found; "the oldest specimens of men known to science are just as truly men as any of their successors"; and the evolutionist finds it necessary to postulate immeasurable time to allow for the development which he assumes. The theory of evolution indeed leaves us in the dark as regards both the origin of man and his gradual ascent from lower forms of life. It cannot tell us how the "little speck of jelly at the first dawn of life" began to be, nor can it explain to us how the gorilla remains a gorilla still, without any change throughout the passing of the ages, while man is everywhere, and at all times, so far as we are able to trace his history, an intellectual, moral, and religious being. "Of absolute origins," says Professor E. W. Hobson of Cambridge, himself one of the foremost scientists of our time, "science knows nothing"; may we not say that she is equally nescient with respect to *transitions* from animal to human life? Here, to begin with, then, the cutting of the Roll, instead of removing our difficulties, involves us far more deeply "in wandering mazes" of perplexity.

But that is not all. If we surrender the Biblical account of the Creation and Fall of man in deference to the supposed verdict of science, we are faced with overwhelming difficulties in relation to sin. The evolutionary theory involves a denial of the reality of guilt and therefore of human accountability. But the fact of sin and the disorder of the world remain, and the sense of guilt persists in the human conscience. In addition to this, the denial of the Fall, as has already been stated, rules out the necessity for redemption, and undermines the whole fabric of Christian theology. That this is no exaggeration is made plain by the fact that the frequent utterances of the Anglican Bishop of Birmingham on this subject have been allowed to pass with scarcely a murmur of dissent by the ecclesiastical authorities of his own communion. In an official letter addressed to his Archbishop a few years ago, this well-known prelate declared that "the whole theological scheme reared by Augustine on the Fall can be rejected without injury to the main fabric of Christian belief." In certain former utterances to the same effect he used the name of Paul instead of that of Augustine, and that, perhaps, enables us to understand the position even more clearly. The theological system of Paul and Augustine is nothing more or less than evangelical Christianity, having as its central fact the redeeming Cross of Christ. This being the case, it is simply trifling with language, and not only with language but with Christian truth, to declare that the rejection of the Pauline and Augustinian theology leaves " the main fabric of Christian belief " uninjured. By the main fabric of Christian belief the Bishop no doubt means the ethical teaching of Jesus, but the teaching of Jesus without His Cross is not Christianity.

The position is made still more plain by the Bishop's exposition of his doctrine of the Sacrament of the Lord's Supper. In the same official document he repudiated, rightly enough, the Anglo-Catholic dogma of Transubstantiation, and then proceeded to unfold his own theory of sacramental grace. " We understand sacramental grace in its fulness and power," he wrote, " not by foolishly speaking of bread as if it were God Himself, but when the heavens open for us, and for a moment we see the whole of creation as the expression of God's purpose, and He Himself in wisdom, might, and love, the goal to whom our striving leads, and the end where man's restless spirit has peace." So far as these fine-sounding words can be made to yield any sense, they can only be understood to mean that the Sacrament of the Lord's Supper is to be associated—in some mysterious way that is even more unintelligible than Transubstantiation itself—with the process of evolution, and not with the fact of Redemption. Thus does the pen of the prelate " deal falsely," for it becomes a knife which cuts out from the New Testament not only the theology of Paul, but the very words of our Lord Himself, when in instituting the Sacrament He said, " *This is my blood of the New Testament which is shed for many for the remission of sins.*" [1] The most significant fact revealed by the correspondence, however, has still to be mentioned. The Archbishop in his reply considered it necessary to administer a mild rebuke to his subordinate for his references to the Sacraments. With regard to the repudiation of Christian doctrine on the other hand he deemed it expedient to say no more than that it was not on what he had said " with regard to that branch of science or theology that the attention of thoughtful men has been centred. It is too

[1] Matt xxvi. 26.

familiar." Which, to the present writer at least, appears to fall little short of a surrender of the very citadel of the Faith.

But here again concession lands us in a morass of difficulties. If Christ did not die for our sins on Calvary, and did not rise again from the dead on the third day, there are a number of facts that simply clamour for explanation. How, for example, if that view be true, did His followers so completely misunderstand His mission as to give the central place to His death, and how were they able to invent the majestic Figure of the Gospel story if He was only a Jew of Palestine with essentially human limitations? It is not too much to say that if we evacuate the Cross of its redemptive meaning we are tearing the very heart out of the New Testament. And if Christ be not risen from the dead, there is no Gospel for humanity, no forgiveness of sins, no life everlasting, no hope that stretches across the darkness of the grave. But, beyond question, the need for the Gospel remains. The cry of the human conscience for peace with God still rises to heaven, and the hunger of the soul for the bread of life continues to make its appeal to the heart of the Eternal.

IV

It is on Jesus Christ, indeed—that steadfast Stone of stumbling and Rock of offence to all who reject the testimony of the Divine Word—that Modernist attacks on the Bible are broken and confounded. Christian people as a whole may not be able to speak with authority on questions of science, but they do know something about Jesus Christ and His salvation. And when they have to choose between Evolution and Redemption they will have little difficulty in making up their mind. It is a choice between an unconfirmed hypothesis and a fact of history and experience, established by a great cloud of witnesses. Christ set His seal to the truth of the Genesis account of Creation, and accepted, indeed, the whole of the Old Testament Scriptures as the inerrant Word of God. We cannot mutilate the Bible, therefore, without being guilty of treason to Him. But under the shield of His authority we can abide with confidence the issue of the present critical assault. The Word of God is an anvil on which many a hammer has been broken. It is charged with a living energy which no penknife can hurt and no fire can destroy. From the severest trials to which it may be subjected it will emerge not only in its original integrity and power, but with its authority confirmed by many additional proofs.

The action of Jehoiakim represents the attitude to the Word of God which is too frequently manifested by the unregenerate heart. Men who are living in sin do not like to be reminded of its guilt and punishment. Sometimes they are indifferent to the Divine warnings, and dismiss them as idle tales ; sometimes they become angry, and denounce those who refer to the Judgment to come as fanatical prophets of doom. The real reason why they are angry with the Bible is that they are afraid it is true.

But however vehemently a man may repudiate the witness of the Roll, and however contemptuously he may cast it from him, it has a way of coming back, and often it reappears at unexpected times. And always when it returns, it speaks with a more insistent voice. Not only are all the old affirmations there, with no softening of the condemnation and no lowering of the demand, but, as happened in Jehoiakim's experience, " many like words " are added. For now it has to speak of added transgressions, and therefore the scroll is more sternly " charged with punishment." The longer the warnings of the Divine Word are neglected, the more heavily does the soul become involved in guilt, and the more securely does it become ensnared in corruption. And whatever may happen in this life, this at least is one of the clearest facts of revelation, that there is a day coming on which the Roll will be finally opened, and " God will judge the world by that Man whom He hath ordained," according to the things which are written in the Book.

We must never forget, however, that the voice which urges men to flee from the wrath to come is the voice of Love. The message which warns them of present guilt and approaching doom is a message which comes straight from the heart of the God of mercy. The warnings which they scorn and the smitings which they resent are designed to awaken them from a fatal slumber, so that they may flee for refuge to the hope which is set before them.

In the early days of the year 1928 two young men were caught in a storm on the Cairngorm hills, and perished in the snow. A few days after the tragedy occurred a man wrote a letter to one of our daily newspapers giving an account of an experience through which he himself and a companion had passed in the same place some seventeen years before. Many of those who read that letter must have agreed that it was one of the most thrilling narratives that had ever come under their notice. It told how the two climbers were overtaken by a fierce storm, and made their way with difficulty to the hut near the foot—built to meet such an emergency—and under its shelter passed the night in tolerable comfort. Next morning they found themselves in complete darkness, for the snow had mounted up above the windows. On the second night came "the Great Fear." The storm continued with what seemed "a frenzy of hate"; their rations were running low; and they were suffering from cold and hunger. One night more they remained in the shelter, sleepless and afraid, and then, when morning came, they felt that there was nothing for it but to venture out into the blizzard and make a desperate attempt to fight their way to safety. With bleeding fingers they dug themselves out of the hut, inch by inch, and staggered silently through wreaths of snow that sometimes were breast deep. The storm came on again, fine powdered snow that blinded their eyes. Each man fought for himself, and they succeeded in advancing two miles in three hours. Then came the final crisis—and it is this part of the story that has led to the retelling of it here. "My companion," said the writer of the letter, "seized my arm and said, hoarsely and thickly like a drunken man, 'What about a snooze? I'm done.' The temptation was terrible, for rest seemed like heaven; but it was Death himself who stood near, and I felt his wings. I struggled with my friend, but he lay down in spite of me. There was only one thing to do, and I did it. *I struck him on the face with my iron-shod boot.*"

This drastic action produced its designed effect. The reeling senses of the exhausted man reacted to the stinging blow, and he rose in a fury and wanted to fight. His companion did not fight—except against the storm. Together the two pressed forward once more; ere long they emerged on clearer ground; and at last they staggered into the warmth and comfort of the nearest cottage.

It seemed a savage, ruthless thing, that blow on the face with an iron-shod boot, which the young man received, and it may well be that he bore the mark of it, or will bear if he is alive still, until his dying day. But it was a blow that saved his life; and one can believe that in after days, as often as he looked at it, he would say quietly in his heart, "Thank God that my friend, in the greatness of his love, struck me hard enough to revive my senses in that terrible hour of danger!"

And the bearing of all this on our present theme? Simply this: God sometimes not only speaks to us with a stern voice, but smites us sorely on the face, in order to rouse us from the sleep of death. And if the smiting achieves its design, we shall never cease to praise Him for a kindness which, when first it reached us, seemed to be utterly heartless in its cruelty.

XX

THE SNARE OF AMBITION

FULKE GREVILLE, who afterwards became Lord Brooke, left instructions that his tombstone should record the single fact that he had been " Friend to Sir Philip Sidney." *That* he regarded as the highest honour of his career, although he had won for himself considerable renown in literature and politics. It is the crowning distinction of Baruch, the son of Neriah, that he earned the right to be held in lasting remembrance as the friend of Jeremiah the prophet. He was a young man of high social standing, as is evident, among other things, from the fact that his brother was chief chamberlain to King Zedekiah, but it was not the favour of princes or the companionship of nobles that he coveted, but the fellowship of a prophet of God.

It was a choice that demanded no little courage, for the prophet was despised and rejected in his own country ; but, like Moses in an earlier day, Baruch chose rather to suffer affliction with the people of God than to enjoy the pleasures of earthly dignity and power. His friendship, too, was no mere empty attachment ; it gave as well as received. Throughout his whole recorded history, indeed, it reveals itself in helpful deeds. From the hour in which he first appears on the scene, in the fourth year of the reign of Jehoiakim, when on two separate occasions he acted as Jeremiah's amanuensis, he never seems to have been far from the prophet's side. Baruch was certainly " a friend that sticketh closer than a brother." When Jeremiah was shut up in prison, Baruch visited him, and as usual proved the quality of his friendship by rendering useful service. Again, when Jerusalem was captured, and Jeremiah, having been given his choice, elected to remain with the feeble remnant who were left to occupy the desolated land, Baruch stayed behind along with him. And last of all, when Johanan and his arrogant associates carried off Jeremiah to Egypt, along with the rest of the children of Judah, we find Baruch in that unhappy train. It is there that we get our last glimpse of this faithful companion. There are several notable examples of friendship recorded in the Scriptures —David and Jonathan, Paul and Timothy—but it may be claimed that the association of Jeremiah and Baruch stands as high as any that may be found in that illustrious fellowship.

I

For the present, however, we shall consider more particularly the message which on one occasion the prophet found it necessary to address to his young helper. The words were spoken after Baruch had written the first Roll of Jeremiah's prophecies at the time already mentioned. The contents of the book had a depressing effect on the writer's soul, and his grief found expression in an anguished cry. "Woe is me now," he wailed, "for the Lord hath added grief to my sorrow." His distress was manifestly occasioned by the nature of the oracles which he had just committed to writing, and which he had then possibly heard for the first time. They were, for the most part, prophecies of judgment, stern in their denunciation of the national ungodliness, and clear in their intimation of approaching doom. And to Baruch they seemed to proclaim the final extinction of the chosen people, together with the desolation of the land and the destruction of the city and the Temple. In his heaped-up sorrows the young patriot could see no ray of hope for his country. "I fainted in my sighing," he declares; "and I find no rest."

Jeremiah first of all replies to this utterance of despair. "The Lord saith thus," he declares; "Behold that which I have built will I break down, and that which I have planted I will pluck up, even this whole land."

This answer consists of two parts. The first is a definite affirmation that the threatened judgment, terrible in its thoroughness though it was to be, must be traced back, through all secondary causes, to the hand of God Himself, and must therefore be an infliction which would be in accordance with the demands of His righteousness. The second is an inference from this assertion, and that is that the breaking down and the plucking up of that which He had built and planted must be a greater grief to God Himself than it could possibly be to any of His servants. This would surely have been a salutary reminder to Baruch in the bitterness of his own disappointment.

But Jeremiah's message contains a further part which is addressed to an undisclosed condition of mind which lay behind Baruch's lamentation. "*And seekest thou great things for thyself? Seek them not*"[1]—these are the words which the prophet is commissioned to speak directly to the conscience of the younger man. What precisely were the expectations which Baruch had allowed himself to cherish we cannot tell. It may be that he had looked for a reviving of religion within his own time, and that in a purified kingdom he hoped to rise to a position of commanding influence in the service of God as Jeremiah's colleague, and possibly as his successor. This, however, is nothing more than conjecture. It is clear, at the same time, that the words contain an element of reproof, and whatever their particular application may have been to the circumstances of Baruch, they furnish, in their general sense, a warning against selfish ambition.

II

It is important for us, to begin with, to decide on the meaning which should be attached to the phrase "great things." For there are great things which, in accordance with many a New Testament exhortation, we are enjoined to covet earnestly. These are the things which

[1] xlv. 5.

belong to the realm of the spiritual, and which therefore possess enduring value. To deny this would be to ignore the place which aspiration occupies in the Christian life. Our Lord Himself exhorts His followers to seek the Kingdom of God, and to seek it "first," and to this appeal He adds the assurance that if we attune our desires to this royalty of attainment, all other "things" that are demanded by our earthly necessities shall be thrown in with that supreme gift. In this lofty region men of faith and vision seek great things because they know they have a bountiful God to deal with. Great promises warrant great expectations, and the promises of God are adjusted, not to the measure of our deserving, but to the riches of His own glory by Christ Jesus. It is a healthy thing for believers to forget the things that are behind, and to reach forth, in eagerness of desire and concentration of effort, toward those greater things of attainment which lie before them in their Christian life.

But the great things which men often covet are not great at all when judged by a spiritual discernment. On the contrary they are essentially petty and unsatisfying because they are of the earth earthy. The prizes of material success, for example, how sordid a struggle does the seeking of them frequently involve! What secrecy of scheming, what bitterness of rivalry, what days of feverish anxiety and nights of consuming fear are demanded as the price of getting on in the world! And after all the grinding toil, how little the satisfaction gained in the end. Even after the prize is won, how short a time is it enjoyed; at the best it is but a little while

> Till all things end in the long dust of death.

Or it may be the great things of social position on which the heart is set. This is certainly a quest which the royal Preacher would describe as vanity and vexation of spirit. For it is a climbing of which it is particularly true that it is performed in the same posture as creeping.

The devices to which many people resort in order to add even less than a cubit to their social stature are among the most humiliating revelations of human nature in the whole world. And the quest of political power lies under a like condemnation. "Men in great place," says Bacon, and he has a right to be heard on the subject, "are thrice servants—servants of the . . . state, servants of fame, and servants of business. . . . It is a strange thing to seek power and to lose liberty; or to seek power over others, and to lose power over a man's self." The scramble for preferment in this sphere of greatness is often undignified enough, and the disappointment which results from failure in the hunt has embittered many a man for life.

One of the most ambitious men in the political life of this country during recent years was the late Lord Curzon. The brilliant pages of Mr Harold Nicolson tell us of the various triumphs of his career, but also of the one final disappointment which appeared to blot out the glory of his former achievements. During the early months of 1923, we read, his day-dreams swirled persistently around a single formula, "Viceroy of India, Secretary of State for Foreign Affairs, Prime Minister of Great Britain." This formula, he once confessed, had echoed in his heart for fifty years. The first two of those glittering prizes he had already won, and in that year it seemed as if the copestone was to be placed on the edifice of his ambition. The Prime Minister of the day was compelled to resign his office through ill-health, and Lord Curzon, who had retired to the country for a few days to await the development of events, was summoned by telegram to return to London without delay. He travelled up from Somerset the following morning, and waited in his house for the expected message from the King. But when the messenger arrived in the afternoon, it was to tell him that another man had been summoned to Buckingham Palace, and was at that moment being invited to become head of the Government. The scene which followed may be told in the dramatic sentences of his biographer: "Curzon gasped. The dream of his lifetime lay shattered at his feet. Lord Stamfordham left him. In an agony of mortification he collapsed into a chair. Lady Curzon tried to console him. He wept like a child. He had forgotten Baldwin. Nobody had ever thought of Baldwin. . . ."

This is, perhaps, a cruelly realistic description of frustrated ambition. We can understand the bitterness of Lord Curzon's disappointment, especially in view of the fact that the cup of final success had been so near his lips; but, for all that, it is impossible to invest his grief with dignity. "My high-blown pride at length broke under me," Cardinal Wolsey is represented as exclaiming in the hour of his own downfall, nearly four hundred years before. It is often the cry of those who set their heart on "great things" of this kind.

The great things of intellectual achievement belong to a worthier order of desire, but the poet who described the thirst for fame as the "last infirmity of noble mind" also reminds us that often in the hour when we hope to find "the fair guerdon" of our toil, our life is cut short by "the blind fury with the abhorred shears," and so we miss the prize. And even when the prize is won, it often seems a reward which is scarcely worth the dust and heat of the contest. In the year 1801 an examination was being held in Cambridge to decide the order of merit among the mathematical students of that University. Among the competitors was a young man, not yet twenty years old, who had recently come under religious impressions. He had been somewhat perturbed in mind about his performance in the forthcoming test, for much was expected of him, and a good deal seemed to depend on his success. Nor was this anxiety diminished when he entered the Senate House and found before him an unusually large number of able young men who were to be his rivals in the academic contest. But his mind was calmed in that same hour by the recollection of a sermon which he had heard not long before on the text, "Seekest thou great things for thyself? Seek them not." This word in season banished his fears and enabled him to exert his powers without distraction. When the results were announced it was found that he had gained the coveted distinction of being Senior Wrangler in his year. That young man was Henry Martyn, the heroic soul who afterwards "burned out" for God as a missionary in India. Now mark the sequel to that intellectual achievement. This is how he describes his feelings in the hour of his triumph: "*I obtained my highest wishes, but was surprised to find I had grasped a shadow.*" Baruch's text had proved to be a faithful saying in the experience of Henry Martyn.

The vanity of human wishes in this region of desire was brought home, by somewhat different means, to the heart of another young student of a later generation who also became a notable missionary. The soul of Temple Gairdner passed through a crisis when during the Christmas vacation of 1892 he watched beside the death-bed of his younger brother Hugh. In a letter to his mother he describes the thoughts which coursed through his mind during that sorrowful vigil. "The nothing of 'successful life,' 'popularity,' 'influence,' and of many things I had before prized, was very plain to me when I knelt over him on Monday evening. I felt that unless I could get to a greater extent than ever before the one thing needful—search for it and get it—I would live in vain." Years afterwards he described to his son the crucial effect of this experience on his life. "I went back to Oxford," he said, "having tasted Eternity at first-hand."

III

It is important for us also to grasp the significance of the words "for thyself" in Jeremiah's message to his friend. And here again it is necessary to discriminate. There are regions in which it is legitimate for a man to seek great things for himself. Not all personal ambitions can be regarded as selfish. The trouble with most Christians is that their aspirations are pitched on too low a key. Their spiritual horizon is too narrow, and they are satisfied with meagre attainments. The great prayers of the Bible, for example, show us how spacious is the enrichment of soul which a believer is warranted in asking for himself. But the human heart is deceitful above all things, and self has a way of obtruding into the most sacred desires and the most spiritual performances. Jeremiah's warning therefore is two-fold : it has reference not only to the quality of the things desired, but also to the end for which they are sought.

It reminds us of the danger of seeking great things—great even in the sense of being good as well as extensive—for selfish ends. It is possible for a man to ask for spiritual favours in order that with them he may glorify himself—great gifts that he may win applause, great holiness that he may be venerated as a saint, great success that he may receive some share of personal credit. George Herbert has a little poem entitled *Submission*, in which he sets forth, with a force which is not lessened by the quaint simplicity of the lines, the subtlety with which self sometimes lurks in the most innocent-looking desires. The poet is communing with God, and suggests that it might be a good thing if he were exalted to " some place and power," for then, he argues, he would be in a better position to declare the praises of his Lord. But when he examines this proposal more closely he discovers that, for all the piety with which it seems to be prompted, it contains an insidious fallacy :

> How know I, if Thou shouldst me raise,
> That I should then raise Thee ?
> Perhaps great places and Thy praise
> Do not so well agree.

There is another danger of a similar kind which may be mentioned in a sentence. We may be so engrossed in the pursuit of great things that we neglect the little things of duty that lie beside our hand. The result often is that we fail, not only to realise our ambitions, but also to fulfil our ordinary obligations.

The words we are considering have come home to many a man's heart with light and guidance in the decisive hours of life. The recently published biography of Dr John R. Mott, whose name has for many years been so closely identified with Christian work in every part of the world, provides us with a striking illustration of this fact. When Mott was a young student in Cornell University, he was undecided as to his future career. On the one hand, there was the opportunity of entering his father's business, which offered the prospect of wealth and comfort; on the other, there was the call of law and politics, which made a strong appeal to an able and ambitious youth. One day he heard that a religious meeting was to be held in the University, and resolved to attend. The speaker was Mr J. E. K. Studd, one of three famous brothers. No sooner had Mott taken his seat in the rear of the lecture-room, where the address was being delivered, than he heard the speaker utter three short sentences: "Seekest thou great things for thyself? Seek them not. Seek . . . first the Kingdom of God." That moment proved to be the turning-point in his career. "These words," he afterwards declared, "went straight to the springs of my motive life. I have forgotten all else that the speaker said, but on these few words hinged my life-investment decision."

Sometimes, too, Jeremiah's message to Baruch has proved a word of consolation to men in times of discouragement caused by the failure of cherished expectations. Let a single example of such an effect of the prophet's exhortation suffice. Soon after young Spurgeon began to preach in the village of Waterbeach, he was strongly advised to enter Stepney College, London, in order to prepare himself more fully for the work of the ministry. This proposal was in agreement with his own inclination, because he believed that a college training would increase his usefulness in the service of Christ. It was accordingly arranged that an interview should take place in a friend's house in Cambridge between the youthful preacher and Dr Angus, the tutor of the College. Through the mistake of a maid, however, who showed Spurgeon into one room and Dr Angus into another, without letting anyone know that either of them had arrived, the meeting never took place. Spurgeon was naturally disappointed at this miscarriage of his plans, and thought of sending at once a written application for admission to the College. That same afternoon, however, as he was making his way to a neighbouring village in order to fulfil a preaching engagement, he " was startled "— to use his own words—" by what seemed a loud voice, but what may have been a singular illusion." He seemed very distinctly to hear the words, " Seekest thou great things for thyself ? Seek them not." This led him to look at the College project from another point of view, and to challenge his motives and intentions. The result was that, there and then, being convinced that he had received a definite intimation of the mind of God on the way of duty, he solemnly renounced the idea of a college *curriculum*. This decision he never found cause to regret in after life.

Not long ago, in discussing this incident with a clerical friend, I put to him the question whether after all Mr Spurgeon might not have been a more able minister of the New Testament if he had had the advantages of a fuller scholastic equipment. " Of course not," he emphatically replied ; " can you conceive of any college education making Spurgeon a better preacher than he was ? " This answer seemed to me to close the discussion. It must be borne in mind, however, that not every candidate for the Christian ministry is endowed with the natural or spiritual genius of a Charles Haddon Spurgeon.

XXI

ON THE WAY TO ZION

THE fiftieth and fifty-first chapters of Jeremiah consist of a lengthy passage which is described as "the word that the Lord spake against Babylon and against the land of the Chaldeans by Jeremiah the prophet." The claims of the prophecy to be regarded as an authentic utterance of Jeremiah and not, as is usually maintained by modern scholars, a post-exilic accretion, have been discussed in the Introduction to this work, and need not be reconsidered here. With far-stretching vision the prophet foretells the downfall of the great kingdom in which his countrymen were to spend the appointed time of their captivity, and describes, in a spirit of righteous exultation, the completeness of its overthrow. The destroyers of God's heritage were themselves to be made desolate by a still mightier nation from the north. "The hammer of the whole earth" by which Israel had been broken was in turn to be cut asunder in the day of the Lord's vengeance. The Persians were to carry out their work of judgment with unsparing thoroughness.

But the hour of Babylon's destruction was to be the hour of Israel's deliverance. So we find that Jeremiah has a message of hope for the children of the captivity. Before his eye there rises up, not only a vision of slaughter and desolation through the clash of contending armies, but also a more peaceful and inspiring scene. He sees the tribes of Israel, released at length from the bondage of more than three generations, moving out from the land of their exile, and setting their faces—stained indeed with tears but also radiant with hope—once more towards the home of their fathers. "*In those days and at that time, saith the Lord, the children of Israel shall come, they and the children of Judah together, going and weeping: they shall go and seek the Lord their God. They shall ask the way to Zion with their faces thitherward, saying, Come and let us join ourselves to the Lord in a perpetual covenant that shall not be forgotten.*"[1]

This description of the Return from Babylon represents in its general character the abiding experience of believing men. Especially does it set forth some of the normal features of a genuine revival of religion in a community. When men's consciences are awakened to a sense of the reality of sin in its guilt and its power, and when, as a result of that, they become conscious of their spiritual homelessness, there arises within their hearts a real seeking after God. In that greatest of all quests there are reproduced in varying degrees of definiteness those elements of inward consciousness and outward conduct which marked the attitude of the returning exiles in Jeremiah's vision. Let us turn our thoughts to this permanent application of the prophet's words. We find:

I. A Contrition which is accompanied by Action.—On their way to Zion the liberated tribes are represented as "going and weeping." It is not weeping without going. Grief in itself can be paralysing in its effect; it may absorb the mind to such an extent as to leave the mourner incapable of action. The sense of danger too can sometimes be so acute as to benumb a man's faculties and leave him the helpless prey of circumstances. Nor should it be forgotten that grief—so inexplicable sometimes are the workings of the human heart—may sometimes be so generously entertained that it becomes a form of self-indulgence. "In reading his life," says Walter Pater, writing of Michelangelo in his *Renaissance*, "the thought again and again arises that he is one of those who incur the judgment of Dante, as having 'wilfully lived in sadness.'" It is possible that a goodly number of repining souls lie under this strange condemnation. The man who has to eat the bread of

[1] l. 4, 5.

sorrows may linger over the repast, and he who is doomed, for a season, to go in company with pain may derive a morbid satisfaction from that cruel friendship. There are people who take a kind of mournful pride in their afflictions, and say, with Shakespeare's Lady Constance, "Here I and sorrow sit." But sitting is seldom the most helpful posture in any time of sorrow. We need not wholly accept Dr Johnson's sweeping assertion that "grief is a species of idleness," to recognise that it is better to be up and doing than to give way to unavailing regret. Many an afflicted soul has thanked God for the blessing of work, with its power "to ease the hollow heart from paining."

For the present, however, we are mainly concerned with sorrow for sin. And here too it is possible to have weeping without going. Regret for past transgressions may terminate in itself and fail to produce any lasting change of life. Real contrition, however, does not make tears a substitute for deeds, but is accompanied by appropriate action. The pilgrims whom Jeremiah saw not only wept but walked. "Godly sorrow *worketh* . . .," and in the repentance which is the fruit of that working there is a definite turning unto God.

But, on the other hand, the homeward journey of the exiles was not a going without weeping. There may be an amendment of life in which there is no real contrition, but the true penitent weeps as he goes. Not necessarily literal tears; weeping of that kind is often largely a matter of natural temperament. There are people in whose constitution the fountain of tears lies near the surface; there are others whose deeper grief does not readily "gather to the eyes." In any case, as was pointed out in an earlier chapter, in the soul's return to God there is some measure of sorrow for sin. With the awakening of conscience there comes a remembrance of past iniquities. The sinner is confronted with his life in the far country—the wasted years, the lost opportunities, the wrong done to his neighbour, the hurt to his own soul, the dishonour to his God. And even

in which the vision of Zion sometimes breaks through the screen of our sensuous life and conveys its appeal to the hidden man of the heart. The gifted writer represents herself as

> musing all alone
> The sick diversity of mortal things.

And in the midst of her reflections there arises within her heart, in some strange way, " the vision of a world unlike our own," a world to which she gives the name of Zion. It seems like a mirage in the desert, mocking the thirst of the weary traveller, this glimpse of a fairer land—an illusion, begotten of need and desire, which haunts " a soul that hath no wings " ; a dream of stability and perfection and immortality set over against the waking realities of change and failure and death. Nevertheless it *does* haunt the soul, and, further, it provides a certain satisfaction, because it conveys a message and creates a hope.

> Yet as a passing mirror in the street
> Flashes a glimpse of gardens out of range,
> Through some poor window open to the heat,
> So in our world of doubt and death and change
> The vision of Eternity is sweet,
> The vision of Eternity is strange.

It is a finely conceived figure. The limits of a sonnet entail, of course, a severe economy of words, but it is not difficult for us to fill in some details of the picture. In a room overlooking a city street we see a solitary figure whose mind is occupied with thoughts of those darker experiences of life—its sorrows and disappointments and partings—which tend to make the heart sick with a sense of the emptiness of mundane things. Through an open window there fall on her senses, perhaps without leaving any conscious impression, the sights and sounds of a busy thoroughfare—the din of unceasing traffic, the constant tramp of hurrying feet, the endless procession of human faces. And all this represents one aspect of life, the aspect to which we generally give the name of Reality. Suddenly, however, the attention of the preoccupied spectator is arrested, and her eye is focussed on a definite object. Past the window beside which she sits there is being carried a mirror, which, for one brief moment, reflects—we cannot, perhaps, exactly tell *how*; but let the poets have liberty to make full use of their licence—a scene which lies far off beyond the city walls—gardens where, as Bunyan would say, "the sun shineth night and day"; where flowers delight the eye with their beauty, and fill the air with their fragrance; where there are trees that yield their pleasant fruits, and afford a restful shade at noon; where, too, there is "heard continually the singing of birds"; a land of Beulah such as Christian and Hopeful saw on their way to the Celestial City. And shall we not believe that this glimpse of gardens out of range causes the heart of the surprised beholder to break into a new song in the midst of all the distractions of the noisy street? The poet's conviction at any rate is that the vision of Eternity belongs as certainly to the world of Reality as those hard facts of this work-a-day life of which we are undeniably aware through the medium of our sense perceptions.

And that surely is a sound argument, the experience of countless thousands of Christian men and women being witness. The vision reflected in the mirror is no mere poetic fancy. I am not thinking of those emotional reactions—whether they tend in the direction of hopes or of fears—which are produced by "a fancy from a flower-bell," or "a chorus-ending from Euripides." It may be doubted whether impressions such as these, even if it is admitted that the æsthetic side of our nature makes a distinctive contribution to the theistic argument, have any religious value whatever: how many of the saints of God have ever heard of a chorus-ending from Euripides anyway? I have in view rather those moments of spiritual vision in which, in the depths of his being, a man becomes vividly conscious of the fact of God. In the glass of the Divine Word, for example, he beholds the glory of the Lord, with effects which attest the reality of the experience. Or through a sudden flash of intuition, begotten, we may be sure, of the silent working of the Spirit of God rather than of any inner light of nature, his heart leaps across every material barrier and arrives at a perception of the truth which enables him to affirm amid every subsequent fluctuation of experience, " I have seen, I have felt, and *I know*."

There are other ways also through which Christ—" by what secret stair " we often cannot tell—enters a human heart and makes His dwelling there. Sometimes the mirror of a godly life gives men a reflection of the King in His beauty which causes them ever after to be strangers and sojourners in the earth. Sorrow, too, through the Divine blessing, " makes the chastened heart a seer," and eyes that are dim with weeping often look on things that are unseen and eternal.

The seeking of which Jeremiah speaks bore the mark of sincerity ; the fact that the pilgrims' faces were turned toward Zion afforded sufficient proof of that. If a man says he is a follower of Christ, we want to know whether, in the habit of his life, he is " looking unto Jesus." For there are many who profess to be on the way to Zion whose back, rather than their face, is turned toward the City. They claim to be stepping heavenward, but their eyes are fixed on the things of earth with an intentness which belies their profession. Others again belong to the family of Bunyan's Mr Facing-both-ways, for they hope to enjoy the benefits of religion when they die, but are eager to secure the advantages of the world while they live. And there is a further company who expect to arrive in Heaven at last, but have never turned their back on anything ; they are still in the place of bondage ; the appeal of Zion has never touched their heart.

The return of the soul to God, however, must be authenticated by practical evidences. Aspiration must be accompanied by renunciation. Emotion must be translated into action. The face of the seeker must be turned toward the place which he desires to reach. Of this kind is the seeking of every sinner who really desires to find the Saviour. He feels drawn to the House of God, for example, for it is Christ's promised trysting-place with needy souls. He desires the fellowship of the Christian Church, because it is his dearest wish that God's people should be his people. Like John Bunyan, he is " often in the Bible," and often also on his knees before the blood-sprinkled mercy-seat. To be a seeker in this sense, wrote Oliver Cromwell once, " is to be of the best sect next to a finder." " Such an one," he added, " shall every faithful humble seeker be at the end."

III. A Pilgrimage in which there is Mutual Encouragement.—The people of the Return were of one heart and one mind. Judah and Israel—as many of them as entered on the journey—were united in their purpose to reach " the Holy City beyond the rim of the sky." And that was no small wonder, for they had long been alienated from one another. But a common need and a common desire had broken down the wall of separation, and caused them to seek the way " together." Which reminds us incidentally that there is nothing that more effectively heals broken fellowships than a genuine revival of religion. But the reunited tribes were not only fellow-travellers on the way home: they were mutual encouragers. Each exhorted the other to patient continuance in the common quest. " Come," they said one to another, " and let us join ourselves to the Lord in a perpetual covenant that shall not be forgotten." It was an exhortation that revealed sound wisdom. For in every enterprise in which men engage, it is a great gain for them to define their purpose and to proclaim their hope. That will provide them both with direction and with inspiration in their efforts to reach their goal. And what these men had in view was this: in returning to Zion they were coming back to God, in order that they might enter anew into that Covenant relationship with Him which had been broken through their own disloyalty. It was a lofty aim, but it offered a hopeful prospect. For the words with which they encouraged one another were an echo of God's own call to them. "Come unto me," He says, ". . . and I will make an everlasting Covenant with you."

Blessed are they who, having first heard for themselves that "Come unto Me," enlist in this gracious Fellowship of Encouragement. It is a Fellowship of which Christ Himself is the Head, for He is the Prince of all encouragers. John Lydgate, more than five and a half centuries ago, represents Him as urging a lagging pilgrim to haste on his way toward his heritage, and to "be of right good chere," remembering that his place is "bigg'd above the sterres clere."

When Philip Henry, the father of the famous commentator, became engaged to the young lady who afterwards became his wife, the parents of the bride-to-be were opposed to the union, and urged in particular one objection against her suitor. "He may have many good qualities," they said, "but we do not know where he has come from." Their daughter, however, had a mind of her own, and gave a spirited answer. "You may not know where he has come from," she replied, "but I know where he is going to, and I want to go along with him."

Well for us if those who see us on the pilgrimage of life will have to say, with no less conviction, that they know where we are going to.

XXII

REMEMBERING JERUSALEM

In view of the future overthrow of Babylon, Jeremiah, with his eye still fixed on that coming day of judgment, exhorts his exiled countrymen to flee the land as soon as the way should be opened for them, lest they should be involved in the doom of their oppressors. "My people," he cries, "go ye out of the midst of her, and deliver ye every man his soul from the fierce anger of the Lord." "Go away," he adds; "stand not still: remember the Lord afar off, and let Jerusalem come into your mind." It is to the latter part of this exhortation that I wish to draw attention in this closing chapter: "*Let Jerusalem come into your mind.*" [1]

In its bearing on the circumstances to which the oracle particularly refers, namely, the end of the Chaldean supremacy and the consequent release of the captive Jews, it may be regarded as a summons to the exiles to turn their thoughts in the direction of home. While the prophet's intimation of approaching disaster might well constrain them to "fly the Babylonian woe," his reference to Jerusalem might be expected to give direction as well as impetus to their flight. It was designed, indeed, to quicken within their souls that attitude of religious devotion and patriotic loyalty which they might be tempted to abandon under the influences of an alien environment. The call of their native land, with all its lofty incentives and inspirations, should make itself felt in their hearts when the decree of Cyrus set before them an open door, and should give them courage to face the difficulties of the Return. As a matter of fact, there were some of them who needed to be reminded of Jerusalem.

[1] li. 50.

They had settled down in Babylon, and were adapting themselves with no great difficulty to its modes of life. For them the thought of Jerusalem had faded into a dim and unalluring memory, and the desire to return was gone.

But not all the exiles had lapsed into this degenerate condition. There were many of them whose hearts were knit to Jerusalem with a passionate devotion, and their loyalty finds unique expression in one of the most stirring of all their Psalms. The opening part of the 137th Psalm, indeed, is one of the most moving utterances in the whole range of sacred song. In accents of plaintive sweetness it lays bare for ever the heart of the Exile, in all its loneliness and yearning, as well as in the loyalty which it often manifests to " the kindred points of heaven and home." The Psalm represents the Jewish captives in Babylon as sitting beside one of the rivers of that alien land, and thinking sadly of the holy city which used to be the gathering place of all their tribes, but was now a tragic desolation. Perhaps it was of deliberate choice that they assembled to muse and lament amid such surroundings ; in any case the quiet flow of the waters would no doubt have seemed to them a fitting accompaniment to the flow of their tears, and the droop of the willows which lined the river's banks would have appeared a fitting symbol of the dejection of their spirit. It was in such circumstances that one day their captors approached them with the request that they should sing for them one of the songs of Sion. Perhaps it was mere curiosity which prompted this invitation, but a more likely view is that the exiles were expected to make an interesting contribution to some national festival. This, at least, appears to be suggested by the passionate energy with which they declined to acquiesce in the proposal. Compliance, they felt, would involve religious disloyalty. So, first of all, they answered, with simple pathos, " How shall we sing the Lord's song in a strange land ? " But this quiet objection is immediately followed by a more vigorous refusal. As with the voice of one man—mark how the "we" of the common sorrow becomes the "I" of individual determination—they give utterance to this noble resolve, "*If I forget thee, O Jerusalem, let my right hand forget her cunning.*" The words have all the binding force of a solemn oath. "Let my right hand," they said, "fall to my side—the hand that is the symbol of my strength, and, in particular, that is wont to touch the strings of the harp as I sing the songs of Sion—let it become a dead, shrivelled thing, before I degrade my art to make a Babylonian holiday."

I

It would be well for all of us to manifest a similar loyalty amid all the changing circumstances of our life. It is not always easy to remember Jerusalem, and it is especially difficult when the claims of Jerusalem are challenged by the appeal of Babylon. This is the thought that is most obviously suggested by the exiles' words. We forget Jerusalem when we lower our moral and religious ideals through the influence of a new environment. Many a man begins life with lofty ideals, and with a firm resolve to translate them into practice. But in course of time it may happen that he finds himself in a strange land where the helpful associations of his early life are lacking. He is cut off from the Jerusalem of his youth, and has to pass his days of work and rest amid the influences of some kind of Babylon. Jerusalem, let us say, stands for all that is good and holy in human life—the favour of God, the fellowship of the Church, the call of conscience, the sanctions of religion. Babylon represents the world, with its sordid ambitions, its selfish maxims, its hurtful fellowships, and its insidious appeals. And too often the exile forgets his past, and accommodates himself to his new surroundings. Perhaps he is caught in the snare of earthly ambition, or swept away on the current of pleasure; in any case he ceases to remember the standards of his former life, and sinks to the level of his new environment. How often does it happen that a young man, who has been brought up in a religious home and by and by comes to live in a great city, renounces his early training, forgets his father's counsel and his mother's prayers, and falls into evil ways. There are people who, even when they are on holiday, often fall below their ordinary level, and seem to take a rest from religion as well as from work. They neglect the house of God, profane the Lord's Day, and exercise a hurtful influence on the community in which they are sojourning. In such cases, unhappily, Babylon wins the day against Jerusalem. But it is not always with this side that the victory rests. Many a man retains the simplicity of his early faith amid all the complexities and unsettling influences of our modern life. On the world's battlefield, with all its dust and grime, he keeps his shield untarnished, for, with steadfast loyalty, he lets the Jerusalem of his youth come into his mind.

II

On a wider application the words we are considering may be used with reference to THE SOURCE OF OUR CHRISTIAN FAITH. For us Jerusalem stands for the Lord Jesus Christ. In the most literal sense, the very mention of Jerusalem recalls the thought of Him. In the midst of Jerusalem stood the temple which He called His Father's House. On its streets He spoke some of His most memorable words and performed some of His mightiest works. Through one of its gates He entered in triumph as a King ; through another He was led forth, in humiliation, to die as an impostor on the Cross. In one of its gardens He slept for a little while in the tomb. From one of its hills He ascended unto His Father after He rose from the dead. No true Christian can long forget Jerusalem. But we forget it practically when we fail in gratitude and loyalty to Jesus Christ.

There is, of course, the forgetfulness of those who are living in utter unbelief. Even in our own Christian land there are multitudes who spend their days as if Christ had never lived or died in this world to redeem men from death. His Cross makes no appeal to their heart. His teaching has no influence on their life. They have never rejoiced in the good news of His salvation. Jerusalem has no place in their thoughts or in their hopes. But the believer, too, has his seasons of forgetfulness. The love of Christ does not lay its constraints on his heart as it should; the will of Christ does not always make its demands felt in his conscience; nor does the spirit of Christ fully control his life. And because of this there is the forgetfulness which reveals itself in a lack of diligence in the Lord's service. It is easy, indeed, to give Jerusalem a secondary place in the activities and aspirations of our everyday life. Not without reason did the Psalmist call upon his soul to bless the Lord for His benefits, "and forget not," and equally necessary did it appear to the Lord Jesus to ordain that His followers should continually observe the Sacrament of the Supper "in remembrance" of what He did for them. But where the passion of the Christian soul is kept fresh, the thought of Christ will not be long absent from the mind, and there will always be a fervent reiteration of the old words, "If I forget thee, O Jerusalem, let my right hand forget her cunning."

III

Once more the words of the prophet may be applied to THE BEGINNINGS OF OUR SPIRITUAL EXPERIENCE. In most Christian lives there is a more or less definite experience of the power of God which marks a turning-point in their history. Jerusalem, in this sense, stands for the tender grace of a day when all things become new for us. It represents the high moments of the spiritual life—the moment of vital decision and of conscious deliverance, the moment of profound emotion when the soul begins its new song, and of clear vision when the darkness passes away and the true light shines. That is an experience which should imprint itself in indelible characters on the heart, and should therefore prove an abiding source of encouragement. But here, again, the believer often forgets his Jerusalem. He has his seasons of despondency, in which he is tempted to conclude that his past experience was a delusion. Hours of darkness come upon him in which he fears that his way is hid from the Lord and his judgment is passed over from his God. Now it is not suggested here that the Christian soul is always to live on its past. That would scarcely be nutritious fare. But it is affirmed that in hours of weakness and temptation it may derive fresh courage and inspiration in recalling the morning of its spiritual life. We find that Paul, for example, in his own seasons of conflict, used to go back again and again to that experience on the Damascus road when first the vision of Christ's face flamed on his soul and the sound of Christ's voice thrilled his heart. That was for him a Jerusalem which never failed to fortify his courage and stimulate his zeal.

One likes to recall the scene which was witnessed in that old house in the Netherbow of Edinburgh on the day when the fiery spirit of John Knox passed into the light of the presence of God. "Go, read where I cast my first anchor," the dying man said to his wife, and she, with a sureness of direction which indicated that the matter had been a familiar subject of conversation between them, turned to the seventeenth chapter of John's Gospel. That was *his* Jerusalem, the place where, in the morning of his spiritual experience, his soul found rest and security amid "the tossings of an inward sea." The anchor had proved both sure and steadfast throughout all the storms of the intervening years. Another great preacher of the Gospel, George Whitefield, used to find inspiration in revisiting the very spot of earth where he first found peace in believing. "I may perhaps be superstitious," he writes in his Diary, "but whenever I go to Oxford, I cannot help running to the spot where Jesus Christ first revealed Himself to me and gave me a new birth."

The Psalmist, too, when his soul was cast down in him, sought relief in remembering his God "from the land of

Jordan and of the Hermonites, from the hill Mizar"—scenes, beyond doubt, which were associated with experiences of the loving-kindness of the Lord to his soul. And John Bunyan's comment on the Psalmist's words is particularly relevant in the same connection. "It is profitable," he says, "for Christians to be often calling to mind the very beginnings of grace with their souls. Call to mind the former days and years of ancient times . . . look diligently, and leave no corner therein unsearched, for there is treasure hid, even the treasure of your first and second experience of the Grace of God toward you. . . . Have you never a hill Mizar to remember? Have you forgot the close, the milk-house, the stable, the barn, and the like, where God did visit your souls? Remember also the Word, the Word, I say, upon which the Lord caused you to hope." Bunyan's counsel is a call, expressed in other words, to let Jerusalem come into the mind.

IV

Finally, the passage may be said to have a special application to THE HERITAGE OF OUR NATIONAL HISTORY. Jerusalem, on this view, stands for our native land with all that is best in its traditions. So far as our own land is concerned, there has come down to us from the past a noble heritage of civil and religious privileges, won for us by the courage and devotion of our fathers. When we think of the long succession of confessors and martyrs who lived and died in Scotland for their religious faith, we may well exclaim, "If I forget thee, O Jerusalem, let my right hand forget her cunning." Patriotism, indeed, as Edith Cavell reminded us, is not enough. But in its own place it is a healthy human instinct, and in the case of a country like our own it is a specially laudable sentiment. But there are different kinds of patriotism. There is the kind which consists in a lip homage to the past, with no kind of practical loyalty to the ideals for which admiration is professed. There are many who are willing enough to build the sepulchres of the prophets, while at the same time they are busily engaged in undoing the prophets' work. It is easy enough to praise the witnesses of a former age, but it is a different matter to walk in the steps of those witnesses in our own time. But that is what true love of country implies. We forget Jerusalem when we despise our national birthright and are false to the best traditions of our race, when we make light of the privileges which we have inherited at so great a price, and are ready to let them slip through indifference, or to barter them for our own pleasure or gain.

There are features of our national life to-day which should lead us to give earnest heed to Jeremiah's counsel, and at the same time to renew for ourselves the ancient vow of the Jewish exiles, "If I forget thee, O Jerusalem, let my right hand forget her cunning."

Made and Printed in Great Britain
by Turnbull & Spears, Edinburgh